Some Bears Kill

Some Bears Kill

True Life Tales of Terror

by

Larry Kaniut

Safari Press Inc.

P.O. Box 3095, Long Beach, CA 90803-0095, USA

OTHER BOOKS BY THE AUTHOR

Alaska Bear Tales
More Alaska Bear Tales
Cheating Death

The trademark Safari Press ® is registered with the U.S. Patent and Trademark Office and in other countries.

Kaniut, Larry

Third edition

Safari Press

1997, Long Beach, California

ISBN 1-57157-293-7

Library of Congress Catalog Card Number: 96-071771

10 9 8 7 6 5 4 3 2 1

Printed in USA

Readers wishing to receive the Safari Press catalog, featuring many fine books on big-game hunting, wingshooting, and sporting firearms, should write to Safari Press Inc., P.O. Box 3095, Long Beach, CA 90803, USA. Tel: (714) 894-9080 or visit our Web site at www.safaripress.com.

Table of Contents

Stories

Acknowledgments

With great enthusiasm I'd like to thank Ludo Wurfbain for asking me to "do another bear book" for him. With his suggestion and Jacqueline Neufeld's diligence in editing and producing the work, Ludo's publishing house has brought to fruition another outstanding collection of bear stories from the Great Land.

I'd like to thank my wife, Pam, for her loyalty and hard work, for without her effort this book would not be what it is.

And I'd like to thank all the story contributors for their kind consideration and continued work.

Last, I'd like to thank all the family members, friends, acquaintances, and even strangers who steered me to yet another bear tale.

Foreword

Three of the best-known writers about Alaska are Rex Beach, Jack London, and Robert Service. Beach wrote such Alaskan classics as *The Iron Trail, The Spoilers,* and *The Silver Hoard,* all works of fiction. London also wrote fiction, his best-known Alaskan works being *White Fang* and *The Call of the Wild.* The poems by Service—*The Spell of the Yukon, The Cremation of Sam Magee,* and *The Shooting of Dan Magrew*—are well known, even to folks who have never been north or west of Cleveland.

All of those authors are from a period, early in this century, when Alaska was a vast, unknown territory. Their stories and poetry helped in formulating a vision, often inaccurate, of Alaska that continues to this day in the minds of armchair adventurers.

Larry Kaniut is destined to join Beach, London, and Service as one of the best of Alaskan writers. But unlike the writings of these authors, Larry Kaniut's *Alaska Bear Tales, More Alaska Bear Tales, Cheating Death,* and now his latest, *Some Bears Kill,* are fact, not fiction. Kaniut's true stories of bears are to Alaska what Capstick's lion stories are to Africa.

Larry Kaniut and I love bears. We believe there is something missing from a woods that has no bears. A woods without bears is little different to us than a city park, and strolling through such places is usually a pretty tame experience.

The person who chooses to venture into the wild places of Alaska, on the other hand, knows that sooner or later a bear might appear. The Alaskan hiker also knows, or should, that bears are unpredictable. As a result, a stroll through the Alaskan wilderness is an exciting experience, because whether or not a bear is seen, the hiker knows the bear could be there, in the bushes, watching, waiting, and perhaps in a bad mood.

The bears in Larry Kaniut's latest book did more than watch and wait. And therein lies the fascination of Larry's stories. Larry has interviewed hundreds of people while gathering tales of what happens when man and bear came into contact, and the bear was hungry, or cornered, or angry, or just being a bear. These are stories of people like you and me who simply found themselves in the wrong place at the wrong time.

This book is not recommended for reading around a campfire on a dark night in bear country.

In about 1973, I faced a charging brown bear near Cordova. I killed the bear when he was only eleven steps away. To this day, I still don't know what the bear's intentions were. He might have been attacking, he might have just been curious, or he might have just been the local version of the "welcome wagon," coming to welcome me to the neighborhood.

I still wonder whether I had to shoot that bear. I suppose the only way I could have been sure of that bear's intentions would have been to see if he bit me. I chose, however, not to let the bear get close enough to do that. That incident left a lasting impression on me about bears, and was, to say the least, a most interesting experience.

Larry interviewed me shortly after that had happened. Since my bear story was published in Berthold Kohr's *Reisen Der Wildnis - Abenteuer mit Grizzlies* (1991), Larry Kaniut didn't publish it himself. At the time he was collecting many other exciting bear stories to write about. Some of these stories are in this, Larry's third bear book, *Some Bears Kill.* I know you will find this book as fascinating as I have.

Larry Kaniut's fervent patriotism, his love of adventure, and his knowledge of the outdoors are well known and respected here on the Last Frontier. But Larry is most known for his bear stories. Larry Kaniut's bear tales are the stories of Alaska, the true stories that continue to contribute to the mystique of our great state . . .

AND THEY ARE ALL TRUE!

Wayne Anthony Ross
Past Vice President,
National Rifle Association of America
Anchorage, Alaska
16 June 1997

Introduction

Anatomy of a Bear Attack

Red blueberry bushes carpeted the area above timberline. Downhill the frosted berry bushes abutted golden yellow willows studded with dark green spruce trees. Farther down the mountainside, alder patches dissolved into thick black spruce forest.

Two moose hunters crested a knoll above the berry patch only fifty yards from the willow thicket. Both shouldered backpacks and rifles. Then it happened.

Without warning a brown-beige grizzly erupted from the willow patch. Its ground-eating gallop was accompanied by an ear-shattering roar of defiance as it barreled toward the hunters from behind.

The beast swatted the rear hunter, knocking him ten feet to where he landed unconscious. Without slowing, the bear grabbed the lead hunter's right shoulder in its jaws and yanked him off his feet and onto the ground. Savagely the beast punctured his head, then legs, with bites.

The hunter screamed. Meanwhile his partner had regained consciousness and groggily struggled to stand up. The bear lunged at him.

In its biting frenzy the brute failed to notice the lead hunter point his rifle and fire. His bullet hit the bear just aft of its powerful forelegs and expanded into its spine, partially paralyzing it and dropping the beast beside his companion. A second shot to the head took the bear's life.

The men assisted each other stanching the flow of blood and rendering the maximum medical assistance their first aid kit afforded. Their task now was to reach their vehicle and proper medical help.

These veteran outdoorsmen did not know that the boar grizzly was defending his moose kill, buried behind the wall of willow branches. Most large grizzly boars will defend their kill during a surprise encounter by downing the intruder with a blow from its right paw, then mangling him with his teeth or claws for good measure.

This grizzly attack was not uncommon. Nearly all North American black or grizzly bear attacks are defensive and take place when the human is within sixty yards of the animal. The attack usually involves one or two people and ends within thirty seconds.

In general there are two kinds of bears: people bears and wild bears. People bears have had at least some contact with humans. Wild bears run the gamut from the meek and passive to the malevolent marauder.

Most attacks are nonfatal, though grievous injury results from powerful paws and jaws. One-third of maulings in Alaska occurred while people were hunting, and 36 percent of the hunters were rescued when their partners shot the attacking animal off them.

This Book

This book is one more effort to educate people on how to avoid bear attacks, in the hopes of saving both bears and people. *Some Bears Kill* contains stories of close calls and maulings by all three North American bears: black, grizzly, and polar.

While compiling two other bear books, I interviewed hundreds of people and researched hundreds of maulings, primarily in Alaska. My research over forty years has exhausted dozens of books and hundreds of articles, resulting in the submission of 1,500 pages to publishers.

There are a few other bear books on the market that give detailed information about specific encounters. The suggestions they offer for safety in bear country require so much effort that I wonder if it wouldn't be easier to forgo the outing.

I have listed information on bear behavior, its probable meaning, and man's best action. I have not touched upon every situation, but I hope I've covered enough to keep you safe in bear country. My hope is that you will glean safety tips from the stories and the follow-up section, Bear Attack Prevention, found in the Appendix.

May you enjoy many hours of informative reading as you delve into *Some Bears Kill.* And may all your hours in the outdoors be safe and rewarding.

Mountain Monarch
by Larry Kaniut

From Alaska's interior tundra—high benches, blueberries and such—

to the Great Land's southeastern Panhandle—devil's
club, alders and brush—

from a six-inch-long, kitten-sized bear cub, stone blind
and near hairless at birth,

to a Mountain Monarch of thirty springs, the grizzly's
the king of the earth.

❖   ❖   ❖

He is born the first month of the season, with his
twin their mother gave birth.

Together they live in their winter's den, in the deep,
dark bowels of the earth.

And in April or May at their den site, on a slope
facing to the north,

they emerge, guaranteeing their debut. At thirty
pounds, each cub comes forth.

The cub's nourishment comes from his mother, though
she feeds on grass and some roots,

skunk cabbage, blueberries and carrion, small
rodents, slick salmon she loots.

His mother's warm love is protective, and all of his
needs she supplies.

For two seasons long she's directive; her stern Code
of Law she applies.

As the young cub matures to adulthood, he learns from the Law of the Zone.

Soon he wanders away from his mother, to search for a life of his own.

❖ ❖ ❖

He meets her above a big river, on the slopes where the winter winds boom;

they spend several long weeks together, from May to the middle of June.

Their courting begins rather lightly and lengthens, as summer days see

down countless streambeds interwoven, on spruce-covered hillsides and scree.

Summer ends and their mating is finished. She'll not mate again for three years.

But during mom's time without callers, her cubs will learn all about fear.

❖ ❖ ❖

There's no beast upon earth that's more awesome. Old Ursus is greatest by far

in spite of the places one finds him, whether mountains or river bars.

He lumbers along in the morning mist, upon a gray, gravel shore;

he wades to the center of boiling froth, unfazed by its maddening roar.

His eyes are glued to its silvery host, that he's watched in the years gone past.

The ear-splitting *nyeee* of chain saws, tells him loggers are at their task.

Regardless of all, he is master here. He proudly surveys everything—

from tundra to thicket in the Great Land, from his birth to death he's the king.

❖ ❖ ❖

But then comes the day he faces his foe, and the doings of man are heard.

Ursus is wakened from slumber below, by the drone of a distant bird.

He cocks an ear and looks into the sky as a Super Cub passes low;

from within its gut four eyes peer out and their great bear they see below.

This aged veteran of many a brawl, has never a battle lost—should any opponent get in his way, he'll fight to the death at all costs.

He strolls across the green, grassy slope; Mother Nature has turned her back.

Two men hunker near a far alder patch, awaiting with rifles and pack.

A softpoint bullet mushrooms through his frame, and he feels the stabbing of pain.

The wind shifts then, springs up at his back— Monarch catches man's scent once again.

Rage bursts within his hammering chest; he charges to the echoing *boom.*

Undaunted by lead expanding in him, he presses the charge to his doom—

as one shot is more than he can withstand, it shatters his massive bear spine.

A final explosion bursts in his face; his reign upon earth he resigns.

Yet part of the tale has already spread, how he grew from an infant small

to the Mountain Monarch . . . His Majesty. His reign's just begun after all.

Larry Kaniut
22 February 1976

Dedication

This book is dedicated to:

All bear-mauling victims—those who survived and the memory of those less fortunate—in hopes that from their misfortune we can learn to save more human and bear lives and . . .

All those who responded to the needs of the maulees in rescue and in providing medical assistance and rehabilitive support.

He Never Quit

by Don Coverston

"I thought about the ravens coming down and
picking at my skull while I was still alive."

*When I first read about Don Coverston 8 August 1989,
I was finishing a second collection of Alaskan bear stories.
Don had encountered a grizzly four days after an Eskimo
family had had a similar experience with another grizzly.*

*I called Don at Fairbanks Memorial Hospital and
explained my project. Although sedated and recovering, Don
was friendly and cooperative. He said, "We've got to educate the public about bears. They are very strong animals.
I don't know how long I'm going to be in the hospital. There's
so much more that happened than what was in the newspaper. I don't know where to start."*

*I later visited him in Wasilla where we finalized his
story. I've since lost track of Don, but his story is still powerful. I hope you enjoy it.*

In December 1983 the state of Alaska opened up a
remote parcel program, where individuals could stake up
to forty acres of land. My younger brother John; James
West, my longtime friend and hunting and fishing buddy;
and I decided to stake land together. Although some
parcels were very remote, we chose to stake one at the
Middle Fork of the Chulitna River, within a mile of
the Parks Highway near Broad Pass.

It was an opportunity to pick up some nice property, so we hit the woods. With chain saws and flagging tape, we carved our own Oklahoma Land Rush and spent two weeks working it. I was amazed at all the wildlife we saw—every day we shared our plot with wild animals—which was a wonderful experience. We registered with the state and paid our lease fee.

Afterward, then whenever I visited the continental United States, my desire to get back to the Middle Fork intensified. When I returned to Alaska, I wanted to build a cabin.

Because bears were in the area, I asked my friends if they would go with me. None had the time, so I waited for good weather and went alone. Although it's not smart to go into the woods in Alaska by yourself, I headed my car up the Parks Highway with my camping gear the first nice Saturday, 5 August 1989.

I picked up a young hitchhiker from Germany who told me about things he'd seen throughout Alaska. I told him about the wildlife on my property, inviting him to accompany me for photographs. He agreed.

Along with my backpack I carried my .357 Ruger Magnum handgun. It's an old single action, and not the safest thing to carry because it has a tendency to go off by itself.

We struggled like the dickens working our way through the alder brush, stopping to rest every hundred yards. We saw a couple of old bear tracks, spruce hens, lots of fresh moose signs, and a beaver. I finally managed to find a survey mark, which was my principal goal.

The German stopped and watched a moose looking at some ducks. He said, "What would happen if a bear attacked hikers in the woods?"

I gave him that Alaskan look and my little speech. "Nothing to worry about. I see bear tracks back here all the time. When you see big tracks and little tracks you can worry, because that's the sign of a mama bear and cubs."

I smiled and looked at my .357 magnum slung over my shoulder. I grew up around bears in Kodiak. All Alaskans going into the woods are bound to see bear tracks, or Alaska wouldn't be Alaska.

After tromping through the heavy alder brush, we were worn out. We headed back toward the road. We struggled through the alders until we crossed the Alaska Railroad track, which connects Fairbanks to the north with Seward to the south, a span of over five hundred miles. I blazed a trail with my camp ax until we reached the highway, and I gave the German a ride to the little trading post in Cantwell. We got soda and chips, then split paths.

I headed back to my property at six o'clock in the evening. It was early to set up camp, so I decided to return to that survey mark and follow it to the next one. It was beautiful T-shirt weather, so I thought I would go to the river and back, brushing out the trail to work up an appetite. *I won't need my backpack.* I grabbed the ax from my pack, picked up the pistol, and looked at it. *I won't need this—it's clear to the riverbank.* I set it back in the car, loaded and ready.

I reached the train tracks, clearing branches along the way. I made enough noise to warn any animals of my approach. I found the survey mark and without any prob- lems crossed the river on the tree that spans the water. Once I got on the far side of the river, I started seeing bear signs. I didn't feel alarmed enough to run back to the car and grab my pistol. I was only going a little farther before heading back to cook dinner.

I walked down the open trail, and lo and behold, there was the marker with our names on it—the one I had driven in six years earlier. It was my trapping partner's marker. Since my land was just to the west of his and I had walked the property line of his land, I wanted to see one of my markers.

Before I knew it, I was on my property. I looked at likely places to build a cabin. The equipment I'd stored

in a tree was still there and unmolested; no critters had
shredded my gear. I moved up the ridge a little and sat
down to look out over the valley. A short time later I
started along the property line and got into some heavy
birch trees. Then I hit some spruce trees and alder
brush. I grunted my way through the alders and ended
up near the riverbank and a bear trail that bore signs
of heavy use.

I noticed what appeared to be the same bear tracks
we'd seen earlier that day. I moved rapidly and found a
way off the riverbank to distance myself from the bear
trail. It was gentle terrain about fifty yards from the river.
I reached another game trail; it showed no sign of bears.
It was approaching 7:00 P.M., and I was getting hungry.
The property marker where I'd cut up the ridge was a
short distance ahead. From there the trail would take me
back to the car in a jiffy.

Clearing a patch of alders and approaching a
forty-by-fifty-foot clearing, I heard rustling in the
brush behind me. Hoping it was a moose, I turned
but saw nothing. Forty feet across the clearing I saw
the brush move and watched a brown animal move
into the clearing. *What is it?*

A brown bear stood up.

I froze. Her big black eyes stared straight at me. I
thought about my pistol. *Oh, God, this is the first time I've
been back here without my gun.* I looked down at the ax.
At the same time the bear stood up. She stretched her
neck and perked her ears. I froze. *Lie down. Play dead.*
My only option was to be quiet, crouch down in the grass,
and be still.

I started to move and the bear stood up more, riveting her eyes on me. I stared back. Man and bear were
locked eye to eye. *I can't run. Can't move. God, just
help me. I could die. I better make some noise and scare
her. Maybe she'll run.* I gave her the old, "What the hell
do you think you're doing? Get outta here!"

The echo thundered through the silence.

4

The bear dropped to all fours. She stepped forward, hesitated, then charged. *Oh, no. This is it. She's coming after me.* I took four or five running steps to the side, then turned around and planted my feet.

The bear's just a blur. She's coming straight at me. Her nose is down. She's looking at me. She's only a few feet away. Time stopped dead. I was 32 years old, 5-feet-10-inches tall, and weighed 165—no match for this bear. It seemed like an hour passed.

I raised the ax in my right hand. Just before the bear got to me, I swung down toward her head as hard as I could. The sharp edge hit her head and glanced off to the side. The ax fell.

The next thing I knew I was down. Many people mauled by bears were protected to some degree by their backpacks. But I had no pack, so I tried to cover my neck and head with my hands. The bear bit into my neck, picked me up, and shook me. She pinned me to the ground with her front paws and grabbed my head with her teeth, trying to pull my head off. I yelled, "*AAAhhhh!*"

The bear lifted me again and moved full speed backward, shaking her head back and forth like a dog shaking a rope. My arms and legs were flying in the air. Abruptly she let go, dropping me to the ground. *She must be gone.*

I pulled myself up with my elbows onto my hands. *Oh, God my arms hurt. Blood is all around me.* I got on my hands and knees. *What's that rustling in the brush? Oh no, she's coming back!* Her eyes were piercing. She roared "*Aaaaarrrrrggghhh!*" and came full speed.

She hit me again. *She's got my right foot. She's dragging me. She's trying to pull my foot off.* I started pushing myself toward the bear to relieve pressure on my foot. *Oh, my foot hurts.*

While I was pushing with my hands, I felt the ax. I picked it up in my right hand and looked straight into the bear's eyes. Our eyes locked, and the bear let go of my foot and lunged toward my head. I dropped the ax. Curling my arms over my face and head, I cupped my hands over my neck and forced my body into a fetal position. I put my hands on my face and blood ran over them and onto the ground. *Oh my God. My face and forehead are shredded. There's a huge cut through my cheek, my nose, my face.*

As blood poured from my wounds, she returned and bit my arm. She shook me, then clawed in my side in an attempt to roll me over. She pawed my head and her claws ripped through my flesh.

This is it. My life's over. This is the way that I'm going to die. I'm dead.

I yelled, as loud as I could, "Help!" I went limp. She bit me a few more times. The biting sounded like a rock dragging across my skull. Then the bear left, probably to check on her cub. I had seen only one smaller brown clump of fur behind the bear at the beginning of the attack. I turned in her direction and saw her bolting through the brush in the direction I'd come from. *I can't believe it's over. I gotta get outta here.*

But she was back. She pounced on me again and picked me up. I had no sense of direction. Again she let go. I huddled on the ground. She didn't stop. She was all business, no play. She opened her jaws around the back of my head, crushing the bones. *It hurts so bad. This is it. She's going to eat my brain out and leave me.*

Suddenly the bear was gone.

I struggled to my hands and knees again. I couldn't see the sow. There was so much blood pouring out of me that I thought I wouldn't survive. *God, I'm so bad off I'm not gonna make it. I know I'm not gonna make it. So bad. Oh God.*

I could stand up. I had no vision at all out of my right eye. A big chunk of skin hung down over it. I rubbed enough blood out of my left eye with my T-shirt so I could see, but it was blurry. All the grass around me was mashed flat and covered with blood. The sun shone through the alders in patches. It was still a beautiful day. My legs bled very little. She had bitten through my boots and

6

punctured my foot. The major injuries were to my hands, shoulders, neck, and head.

Knowing my only chance of survival was to reach the road, I carefully listened for the sound of the river, then picked up my ax and hat and tottered toward it. I had to will myself through the alders, planning every step. Branches poked into my loose scalp. I stopped to wipe the blood from my eye and face. As I stumbled on, my vision was a red blur, the top bright, the bottom dark.

I would stop to rest for a minute, plan my next step, then take it. *I hear the river getting louder. That's encouraging.* I was getting closer. I fell two or three times. It seemed like an eternity. I forced thoughts of the road from my mind and focused on reaching the river.

My strength is waning. Along with the blood running from my head into my eyes, I feel warm blood running down my back and chest.

Near the river I made out a beaver pond. The beavers had built a seventy-foot dam across a tributary. I worked my way toward it. *It will be easier crossing the beaver pond than fighting the brush.* I reached the pond and eased into the water. *Feels so good.* I gingerly stepped through the chest-deep water. I moved as fast as I could, through the soft muck on the bottom, telling myself not to stop until I was across.

The pond ended and the dam dropped sharply into the river. I needed to be cautious because I was on the deep and swift side of the river. Making it to the river encouraged me—*Maybe I'll live after all.* I slipped over the dam and into the waist-deep river. It was glacial water. *So many things to consider. The water will get rid of my scent should the bear decide to follow me. I can't go too far downstream because the river leaves the road. I have to end up by the old railroad refuge yard. Got to be careful not to lose my balance and go down—I don't want to drown.* I slowly moved against the powerful current, planting each foot carefully. The current tugged at me. *Glad the river's only thirty feet wide at this point.*

The current carried me farther downstream than I'd wanted, but I reached the far side safely and collapsed on the gravel. Because my arms and shoulders were so chewed up, it was hard to get back on my feet. I splashed some water on my left eye and wiped it with my T-shirt to get my vision back. *Got to get my bearings so I can keep headed toward the road.* A thick patch of willows and alders met me on the bank. I knew that Fourth of July Creek entered the river just a little south of me.

My next objective was the train tracks. I was back to forging through the alders, planning each step: a very slow process. I tried to keep the limbs from hitting my head and the blood out of my eyes. *I'm getting there. Don't have much time. Gotta keep going. I'll make it. Getting so tired. Probably taking a minute a step in the alders. So hard to see where I'm putting my feet. Trying to keep my balance.* The cooling nighttime temperature coupled with the cold water chilled me, but it probably helped stop the blood flow.

Next I found easygoing in ankle-deep swampy muskeg. I picked my path from high spot to high spot and was soon across it. A twenty-foot hill stood between the railroad tracks and me. I kept thinking that the bear would wander back and finish me off. Whenever I stopped, I thought about the ravens coming down and picking at my skull while I was still alive. My hunting and trapping experience reminded me of this reality. *I've gotta go. If I don't get up, this is my final resting spot. No one will find me.*

I crawled to the tracks, where I could see a three-wheeler trail. I knew the road was just over the hill from there. *Got to make it to the road . . . just a little bit farther. Please, God, help me.* Fifty yards of thick, willow-brush bog stood between me and the highway. I plunged into the thicket. I got stuck. I cried. I prayed. I cursed. More than anything else I hurt, and I was so tired.

At last I emerged from the infernal thicket and collapsed onto the ground. *I'll rest. I need a break. I deserve it. Everything hurts. My foot hurts. My right ear. I can't even feel it. Nothing there but a big bloody trench where my ear used to be.* I could hear the cars on the highway. I knew I had only a little farther to go. I crawled up the final hill. There was a ridge of gravel left from the road's construction. The ground was leveling out. I walked uphill on the gravel. Just as I reached the top, I heard a car go by. The occupants didn't see me, and I didn't see the car.

I was twenty feet from the road when I saw a vehicle coming. I waved my hands and yelled, "Please, God, stop! Please, God, stop! Please, God, stop!" The vehicle passed me. I stumbled to the edge of the road, got down on my knees and continued yelling, "Please, God!"

Another vehicle pulled off the road. It parked a few feet in front of me. The occupants sat in their vehicle looking at me in disbelief. I was yelling at the top of my lungs, "A grizzly got me! Please, God, help me! A grizzly got me!"

Then another car stopped. Someone asked me if there was anyone else with me. I said, "No." They asked if I had a gun. "No," I replied, "I left it in the trunk of my car. It probably wouldn't have helped me anyway."

The man's name was Steven Ballek. He and his wife were traveling from the North Pole to the Kenai River on a fishing excursion. They made a U-turn and another car (northbound) stopped.

I asked if my ears were still on. He greatly reassured me. I don't remember what he said, but it was pleasant. While he spoke to me, they organized a place for me in the back of one of the cars and put a sheet of plastic down on the seat. They helped me to my feet, and I stumbled over and into the car. They got me on my side and put a pillow underneath my head. They took me to Leon's Igloo City, twenty-two miles south of Cantwell.

Once we got to the igloo, they went in. Gordon Waterman was the attendant. They returned and told me that a helicopter had already left from Anchorage and should be there any second. Evidently someone had seen me earlier and called rescue people.

I lay there beside the Jeep. I asked the owner of the igloo to get my vehicle and move it to his place. I was trying to think of the things that I had to do. The state trooper arrived and asked me questions, most of which I don't remember.

I told them how to treat me for shock: unbutton my pants, take off my boots, get my feet up. I was extremely thirsty. Although I knew that fluids could have sent me into shock, I asked for water. They wet gauze and let me suck on it—very soothing.

One man must have knelt beside my head. I don't know who he was, but he talked in the nicest, calmest voice. He kept the same soothing tone. I don't know how long he talked—probably until the ambulance got there. His voice was like a voice from Heaven.

By this time, State Trooper Roger Ellis had arrived. Within twenty minutes an ambulance rolled up. Marge Nord of Cantwell Volunteer Ambulance reassured me. Calls for an air ambulance had been made. They called Medical Air Support Transport (MAST) helicopter out of Ft. Greely. Providence Hospital's Lifeguard helicopter in Anchorage would be faster, but it was down for repairs. They called Humana Hospital-Alaska in Anchorage; they had no chopper available but offered a fixed-wing aircraft.

There was talk of blocking off the road and landing an aircraft on the highway, but the FAA nixed that idea. Trooper Ellis recalled MAST, whose crew needed forty-five minutes to assemble and warm up, plus an hour and fifteen minutes of flying time to reach me. Trooper Ellis was frustrated that the helicopter wasn't coming from Anchorage. The people in the ambulance were disgusted because the airlift was out.

At length the ambulance people said, "That's it. We're going north now. Have them meet us anywhere along the line if they can." An hour and a half after they spotted me on the roadside, we were finally on our way to Fairbanks. I couldn't have been happier.

It seemed like we had driven a long way when I heard a Huey, a UH-1 Army helicopter. Sure enough, a chopper from Fort Greeley landed at Mile 193. The ambulance stopped, and I was put on a stretcher and placed inside the helicopter. It was a rough ride, especially with the solid neck brace. My neck injury was so severe that I felt great pain with every vibration of the helicopter.

At Fairbanks Memorial Hospital I thought the emergency people were going to fix me. But they smiled and told me, "No, you've just made it to step two." Step one was getting me there. Step two was to evaluate my injuries, writing down where they were.

They took me to the X-ray room, which took quite a while. Because I couldn't move my neck, others had to help. Two staff braced my feet and two others pulled my shoulders apart. They could barely get me into position to get the necessary pictures.

Next I spoke with the doctor. By then I was actually smiling. I was so happy to be alive. They were putting me together. They told me about the anesthetic, and I was thrilled to death. I asked the doctor how good he was at sewing. The next thing I knew I was out. I was in surgery over nine hours. They put in an average of three and a half stitches per minute, which amounts to nearly two thousand stitches.

Later I was told that the scalp above my left eye had opened and was torn around the back of my head. I had puncture wounds about one inch long and a quarter of an inch wide. My jugular vein was exposed. Some bite marks were so deep that the doctors had cleaned dirt away near my vertebrae. The back of my neck was sliced to the bone from ear to ear. I had no broken bones. A claw or fang had pierced the corner of my right eye two inches, but left my eye intact. I had suffered significant blood loss. They said my injuries could easily have caused death had the bites been a little deeper or a little off to one side.

My rescuers and medical staff were the most wonderful people I've run into.

EPILOGUE

Taping my story helped me rid myself of nightmares; it was good therapy. I have no idea what this experience is going to cost me. I've just been a little over eight months in training for Alaska Army National Guard, and that only pays six hundred dollars a month.

If I had had my .357, I would have had a fifty-fifty chance: if I had only wounded the bear, it would not have stopped until it had torn me to shreds, but if I had hit a vital spot, I would have come out without a scratch.

I did three things that significantly contributed to my accident and injuries: 1) I left my old trusty Ruger .357 in the car; 2) I crossed the river, even though I had planned to stop there; and 3) I yelled at the bear. If I had it to do over again, I wouldn't have yelled.

It's hard to say what enabled me to survive. I didn't want to come back to town and be a mangled face, an ugly freak holed up somewhere forever. I can't say that I really wanted to make it back. I would just as soon have had it be over right then and there. But God gave me a chance to move my feet in the right direction. And I've always lived by one rule: winners never quit, and quitters never win.

God gave me the chance to win, and I did.

[Although Don's injuries necessitated great care in cleaning and required hundreds of sutures, he healed quickly and recovered completely.]

Don Coverston struggled alone to safety. Having a partner would have helped, as it did in the case of Diane Nelson and her two surveying companions.

It's a Bear Attack!

by Diane Nelson

"She shook me as though I were a rag doll."

At the end of their work day, three land surveyors hiked toward a meadow. Kyle Scholl was in the lead, followed by Diane Nelson; their coworker, John Pex, trailed behind. They eagerly anticipated the helicopter flight out of their work area and the return to their camp for the night.

Kyle was working his first summer for the Bureau of Land Management in Alaska. He was a twenty-two-year-old cooperative education student from the University of Southern Colorado in Pueblo. Diane was thirty-one years old and had begun her employment with BLM in Alaska in May 1985 in a field position. John was twenty-four years old, the crew chief, and a full-time employee.

They had been working hard all day, cutting trees and performing their land-surveying duties. Even though they had seen signs of bears in the area earlier, they made enough noise with their chain saws and general work hubbub that any self-respecting bear would have left long before.

As they walked toward their designated pickup point, their good-natured banter was meant as talk among friends, as well as to alert any wildlife that people were present.

They never would have guessed that they were minutes from a full-blown brown bear attack.

Diane Nelson graciously shared their experience with me on 11 September 1989.

At the time of the interview I was employed with the BLM in the Federal Building in Anchorage, Alaska. However, on 24 July 1985, I was surveying a 160-acre native allotment near Lake Iliamna with John Pex and Kyle Scholl.

About 4:00 P.M., Bob Campbell flew overhead in the helicopter until he spotted us. Because we were working on a steep hillside, there was no place near us to land, so Bob radioed and told us that he would pick us up at a meadow a few hundred yards away. He pointed out a nearby drainage we could follow to the meadow.

The draw was so distinct that we figured we'd have no problem finding the meadow. It was extremely brushy with lots of alders, spruce trees, moss-covered boulders, and neck-high grass. Knowing we'd return the next day, we left the chain saws near our survey cutline, took our personal things, and started hiking down the draw. Kyle was ahead of me; I was in the middle; John brought up the rear. We've always hiked together like that.

It was a nice day. The sun was out so we didn't have cumbersome rain gear with us. Moving toward the meadow, Kyle and I talked about the day's events. Usually, if we didn't want to converse, we sang to ourselves or made continuous noise, warning wildlife of our whereabouts. Considering all the noise we'd made running chain saws, coupled with the clatter of the helicopter overhead, talking among ourselves seemed the only extra noise necessary for the hike out to the meadow.

Bear signs indicated their presence; we'd seen fresh bear tracks on the beach where we'd landed that morning. Earlier I had noticed flattened grass, obviously a bear bed only minutes before. My chain-saw noise probably moved that bear out of our path.

We always carried one rifle. Sometimes each person carried a gun, but not today. My experience with bears demonstrated that noise normally eliminated any surprise situations: You let them know you're there; you go your way; they go theirs.

We'd been hiking about fifteen minutes when we encountered a lot of devil's club (a large-leafed, thorny plant that grows from waist to head high). I'd been hit several times in the face with devil's club thorns while running the chain saw and felt I'd reached my quota of devil's club for the day, so I skirted them on the right side of the draw. Although little patches of brush dotted the area, we could see each other.

Carrying the tripod and hiking up the ridge, I spotted the meadow. I yelled to Kyle, "I can see the meadow. Come back over this way."

I anticipated the reply, "Okay, I'm coming." But was I in for a surprise when he responded, "Bear!"

I looked in his direction and saw the head of the bear. She was standing and she woofed, then dropped down and charged Kyle. Her two cubs scattered. They were three-year-old cubs and nearly as large as their mother. They were of age and spending their last summer with her before she would kick them out on their own. Although I could no longer see her, I heard Kyle.

He had perhaps thirty seconds to respond. He ran a bit, then crouched into a ball and hoped she would whiz on by. Since he wore a backpack, it would provide some protection should she choose to attack. She didn't run by! Rather, she ran up, straddled him, and tore into the backpack. It took no time for her to demolish the eight-thousand-dollar surveying instrument in the backpack.

The sow chewed on the back of Kyle's head, tearing away a large portion of his scalp. Then she tried to roll Kyle over with her paws, leaving deep claw lacerations in his shoulders and arms, and threw in a few random bites to his right leg.

When I realized that she was mauling Kyle, I dropped the tripod, wondering what I could do to help him. Even though there were plenty of foot-wide, climbable trees close-by (large for that part of Alaska), I never considered climbing one. I was fully into helping Kyle.

Since John had the rifle, I had to alert him so he could come to Kyle's assistance. Amidst the pandemonium I was thinking that John wasn't far behind me, as we're usually right on top of each other when we hike out of the woods. Unfortunately, of all days John had taken a fall on some moss-covered rocks, banged his knee, and had sat down to massage it. This put distance between us.

Since I knew where Kyle was, I figured the best plan was to yell so John could come toward my voice and rescue Kyle. I walked a ways from where I'd dropped the tripod and yelled, "John, bring the gun. There's a bear on Kyle! Bring the gun! John, over here." When not yelling for John, I listened. I still couldn't hear John, so I yelled louder and moved a short distance in his direction, not wanting to get too far away from Kyle.

During the mauling Kyle put his hand up, which probably saved his ear because the bear bit into his thumb area. The bear briefly stopped mauling Kyle, and he thought that she was going to leave. He moved a little to check, and she lunged again and bit into his thigh. Then she left him.

I finally heard a shot, which sounded close. John hadn't heard what I'd said, but he knew something was unusual, and he tried to scare the bear by shooting into the air. I yelled, "John, John, bring the gun!"

While John charged toward my voice, he saw one of the cubs run by so closely that he could have touched it. He thought, *Hah, that's the bear that's bothering them.* So he stopped.

I didn't hear John's next shot, probably because I was making so much noise. Then he heard me continuing to yell and ran toward me all the harder. There was so much commotion between Kyle and the bear that I never dreamed the bear would come after me. As I yelled for John, I had one of those sensations people have when they feel somebody staring at them from across a room. When I turned my head, the bear was right in front of my face!

She slammed into me like a wrecking ball against a building wall. She bowled me over, then bit me under my left eyebrow, where she caught her tooth. Another canine tooth went into my skull as she gripped my head. She shook me as though I were a rag doll. I felt my left eye pop out of the eye socket. She continued chewing on my head, tearing my scalp into shreds. I put my hand out to push the bear away as one would an annoying dog, but it was futile. The bear was too strong. I thought, *This is it. I didn't think I was going to die from a bear mauling.*

By that time John was forty feet away and had spotted the bear and me. His first thought was, I'll try and shoot wide and not hit Diane, but maybe Diane would be better in the long run if I do hit her. His first shot from fifteen feet hit the sow in the shoulder. She stopped chewing on my head. She took one more bite into my left arm and then charged John. His next shot was at ten feet, and he got her in the eye, momentarily stopping her. She continued her charge. His third shot hit her in the neck and dropped her. She rolled downhill and lodged against a tree.

If anybody from our group should have had the gun that day, it was John because he'd been hunting ever since he was a kid. Another plus was that he had his own gun. (BLM field workers are allowed to carry their own weapons after completing a required gun handling exam. See Appendix 8.) Even with his adrenaline going and seeing that the bear had me, he was able to do the right thing. John approached the bear and kicked at her. Unsure that she was dead, he fired one more shot into her skull. Then he came over to me.

While the bear was attacking me, Kyle had been able to use a hand-held radio to call Bob in the helicopter. "Bob, I've been attacked by a bear." (Kyle did not know that I was being mauled.) Amused, the pilot said, "You're kidding me."

Kyle yelled into the microphone, "Get the medics!" The call screamed volumes of alarm and Bob went into emergency action, activating communication with the FAA and the retrieval of two other surveyors from the other side of the lake. The FAA at Iliamna called Providence Hospital in Anchorage, requesting a med-evac Lear jet to pick us up at Iliamna. Arrangements were made and two Cessnas came to Pedro Bay—by Cessna it's about twenty-five minutes, quicker than by helicopter.

I lay on the ground reminding myself to stay conscious. It was important for me to hear myself talk because I thought I should be dead. John helped me assess my injuries. Communicating with John and listening to the radio chatter helped me understand what was going on.

I told John to check Kyle because he wasn't aware that Kyle had been mauled. I was about seventy-five feet from Kyle with heavy brush between us. John knew that there were other bears in the area, and he had used up all his bullets.

I'd been hiking with a sweatshirt tied around my neck. I removed it and wrapped up my head as best I could using my one good arm. My head felt sloshy with mingled hair, flaps of scalp, and oozing blood.

John went back and forth between Kyle and me, helping us until the helicopter returned with surveyors Brent Jones and Kent Foster. They had a handgun.

Kyle was eager to get out of the woods, and he leaned on others and hopped the 100 to 150 yards to the meadow. Within half-an-hour of the mauling, Kyle was at the helicopter. It had just enough fuel to complete two trips with us. Another helicopter was en route from Igiugig to bring more fuel for the helicopter.

I had tried getting up on my elbows, but this made me dizzy. Lying down and being still was better. (Actually, when the seven-hundred-pound bear hit me, it threw a disc out in my neck. This injury was not fully diagnosed until two and a half years later. It was necessary to fuse the fifth and sixth vertebrae. It's a good thing that I stayed flat and didn't move around a lot.)

John, Brent, and Kent took another half-an-hour to prepare me, since I was unable to hike out. They made a stretcher by pulling some small spruce trees out of the ground for poles and utilizing our four belts and a raincoat that one of the other surveyors had. The raincoat was laid between the two limbs for my head, and the belts supported my torso.

I had all their shirts wrapped around my head for pressure and to protect my eyes. Once in a while I'd hold open an eyelid; but because it was intensely bright, it felt better to keep my eyes shut. While carrying me, the men's effort was compounded by the thick brush and soft tundra. They stopped often, put me down, checked that I was okay, then continued. The distance to the meadow was not great, but it seemed like a long way because of my discomfort and concern that other bears might come.

After reaching the meadow, John and I got into the helicopter and left immediately for Pedro Bay. The two other surveyors had to wait for another helicopter to come from the other end of Lake Iliamna, eighty miles away. They stood back to back in the meadow with one handgun, reassuring each other that they saw no bears. The mosquitoes were atrocious and Brent and Kent were shirtless. They said it was the longest twenty minutes in their lives.

In short order I got to the Iliamna airport near the villages of Iliamna and Newhalen. A Lear jet from Anchorage was circling and landed right after us. The med-evac doctor and nurse administered painkiller and pushed my eye back in the socket, even though the bone was cracked. That was neat. The doctor had to hold open my eyelid but asked, "How many fingers do you see?"

I said, "I see two fingers." Everybody gathered outside of the plane cheered, "Yeah! She can see!" I had signed off the use of my left eye.

We got to the hospital in Anchorage in an ambulance shuttle at almost 8:30 P.M., four hours after the bear mauling. They took me into surgery. During the eight-hour surgery, the doctors saw a portion of one of the bear's teeth embedded in my skull above the left temple. They removed the whole tooth: a rotten tooth from an old bear. (The other surveyors kept claws to give to Kyle and me.)

I do have sight in my left eye. Having twenty-twenty vision to start with was a plus. Although the doctor pushed my eyeball back into its socket, there was extensive damage to the muscles within the eye orbit and the nerve that controls the levator muscle used for eye control. I had several surgeries to improve the eyelid, but I can't retract it. I can only move it down.

I do have permanent partial double vision. Two of the six muscles around the eye are gone. The left eye can't fully move up or down. If I need to look extreme upward or downward, I see double, so I move my head around. The double vision is the pits, but I'm lucky considering the whole ordeal.

I had over two thousand stitches, mostly in my scalp. It reminds me of a patchwork quilt. The stitches were numerous because the scalp tears were deep, requiring intricate layers of stitches. I also have some muscle damage and scars on my left arm from the bite near my elbow.

Kyle had more problems with the initial surgeries and was in the hospital for thirty days because of infection to the skin grafts on the back of his head. The bear had chewed off a big patch of scalp from the back of his head, but the backpack had shielded his back and his neck from further injury. In fact, they found the scalp when they went back to the site of the mauling to look at the bear and check the area. Kyle's instinct to curl up underneath the pack saved his vitals and reduced injuries to the face.

Kyle's injuries included head lacerations and deep lacerations on his shoulders from the bear's claws when the bear tried to roll him over. After a year, doctors used tissue expanders by which they balloon and cut out the extra scar area and tighten the scalp back together. Now he only has a scar the width of a pencil on the back of his head.

AFTERWARD

My medical costs for the six-hour surgery by Dr. Kralik and Dr. Nathansen, including my stay at Providence Hospital, was $10,000. The next surgery (including MRI scan) a year and a half later in March 1988, plus a week's recovery in Anchorage's Providence Hospital, was $8,000. Three follow-up eye and eyelid surgeries, including outpatient tests with eye specialist Dr. Wobig in Portland, Oregon, were around $3,000 each. There were numerous follow-up visits and yearly checkups with specialists in neurosurgery, neurology, and ophthalmology.

Several factors led to our immediate rescue and evacuation. Having John's rifle and his expertise saved our lives. If the gun hadn't been available or used with such marksmanship, the bear would have gotten into my skull and killed me. We were in a working situation in which we carried hand-held radios. Aircraft was immediately available. Timely arrangements with extra hands helped meet our emergency needs. Providence Hospital in Anchorage, the closest city with the necessary medical facilities, was equipped to meet unplanned medical needs in the remote parts of Alaska. Without the timing, the radio communication, the other surveyors' help, the Cessnas and the Lear jet transportation from Anchorage, and the logistics that afternoon, we would both have bled to death from our severe wounds.

I wish I didn't have the double vision. On the other hand, if I hadn't turned my head to look right at the bear when I did, she would have lunged at my neck. That one chop would have ended my life. Her weight hitting me and the fierceness of her shaking caused most of my injuries.

The Alaska Department of Fish and Game went to the site to assess the situation. They removed the skull. John returned to the site the next year. He examined the spot where the bear died and found the bear's shoulder blades and spinal column. He also found the bullet that killed the bear next to its shattered vertebra.

Problems between bears and people can be reduced by understanding the possible causes and effects of their interactions. BLM conducts a course prior to every field season. They show videos, slides, and presentations by people who have been in bear situations. BLM made a video with the three of us in it. For more than the fifty years that BLM has surveyed land in Alaska, there have been many close encounters with bears, but Kyle Scholl and I were the first people to be mauled while on a remote job.

It's easy to feel comfortable by the middle of the summer when you've been working a six-day week and nothing extraordinary has happened after two months. Maybe one day you'll forget to carry the gun, or forget that you're supposed to be talking to each other. The course objective is to help each other remember you're still in bear country. Everybody needs to help each other practice safe habits. Somebody at camp or at home should know where you are, including times that you expect to arrive at camp or at the trailhead. If you're not back at a reasonable time, others should be concerned and follow-up.

The actual bear mauling took only minutes. It took rescuers, doctors, and others hours for the rescue and to repair the immediate damage. A bear mauling happens very fast. It's something you never want to experience. It is certainly something you will never forget.

POSTNOTE
15 June 1996 (an update from Diane)

Both Kyle and I continued land surveying with the BLM in remote sections of Alaska. Kyle went back to work during the summer of 1986, moving back to his home state of Colorado after that field season. He is presently employed out of a BLM project office nestled in the Rocky Mountains. He is married and has two daughters.

I went back to the field in Alaska on a land-surveying crew during the 1987 season. I can remember to this day the exact place I was when I regained my confidence in remote Alaska. Numerous times that summer a bird swooshed out of a bush near our work area, startling me. Near the village of Takotna at the end of the summer, we were packing out equipment after a long day at the cutting line, just as we had been on that disruptive day in July 1985. It was then I realized that I had met the unnerving challenge, and I knew I would be making it back to camp for dinner with the crew.

I continued to work in Alaska until 1993, when I accepted a new position with the BLM and transferred to the National Training Center in Phoenix, Arizona. As I write this, it is 109 degrees (the desert has its challenges, too).

Over the past eleven years, many people (including family, friends, and acquaintances) have heard of my "encounter of the close kind" with a grizzly bear in Alaska and have asked me how such a traumatic experience changed my life. I'm not sure that I have a single answer, other than I landed an office job sooner than I had expected. Perhaps I have more respect for the unpredictability and wildness of nature. I know I am sincerely glad that I'm still around to enjoy all of the natural wonders of the world. Perhaps I now know more about human vulnerabilities, at least my own. There are things I am just unable to do after sustaining the eye and neck injuries. On the other hand, I'm constantly amazed at how the body recovers and adapts.

I often ask myself if there is anything I could have done differently "that day" to change or prevent the bear attack. I don't think so. It was the wrong bear, at the wrong time, and we were in her place. At best, the suddenness of the bear attack lets me believe that things can change, and will continue to change, even with the best plans. The answer may be "added value," or just that I have a thick skull.

Whereas Diane Nelson's encounter with a mother and cubs brought excruciating pain and near death, William West's encounter brought an adrenaline rush and great relief when danger passed.

Two Mamas Too Close

by William West

"I expected to feel claws digging into my
shoulders at any second."

*William O. West from the Kenai Peninsula has had
numerous outdoor adventures and sent me a couple of tales
that demonstrate the need to know the environment, to be
prepared with a "bear-stopper" firearm, and to practice
preventative actions (in this case, quick thinking).*

One evening in early June after work, I decided to go
muskrat hunting near my home in Soldotna, Alaska. I
took my kayak and cruised along the shoreline of
Bottenintnin Lake, just off Skilak Lake Loop Road. I got
out of the boat in a small cove to observe two sandhill
cranes perform a mating dance in a nearby swamp.

After several minutes, I heard brush crackling and
assumed it to be the cow moose with calves that I had
seen earlier. I returned to my kayak, and while attempting to enter it I heard a low "woof" from behind. I looked
back and saw a huge blond-brown bear with a blocky head
running toward me from a small hill. She had two small
cubs with her. I yelled "Oh God!" and pitched myself into
the lake, grabbing the rope loop on the end of the kayak,
as I frantically waded out up to my neck in the cold water.
I expected to feel claws digging into my shoulders at any

second. I reached into the kayak, grabbing my rifle, then dropped it realizing how worthless the .22 caliber would be.

By now the sow was standing on the lakeshore, staring in my direction. She looked around at her cubs behind her, not threatened by me. She slowly turned and disappeared into the trees, leaving me shaken and hanging onto the kayak in the lake. After she left, I towed the boat to shore, quickly hopped in, and pulled out of the area.

My second incident occurred less than two months later while hiking with a friend up Moose Creek Trail, east of Tustamena Lake. We were about a mile above the lake when I noticed a partially eaten salmon on the ground and some kinky brown hair hanging on the rough bark of a spruce tree nearby. We stopped and briefly discussed turning around, but decided to proceed for a short distance.

I pushed out into an opening and halted when I sighted a dark brown bear and two large cubs across the clearing. I started backing quietly the way I had come, when the sow apparently noticed and came to full attention. Without warning she came on all fours in a dead run directly at me.

I raised my .270 caliber rifle, planning on firing a warning shot, but noticed that in a second she'd be on top of me. Instinctively I found her head in the scope and fired. Not having time for a second shot, I was expecting to have to use the gunstock to shield myself when the bear tumbled end over end and lay still some fifteen steps away. The semi-grown cubs stuck around for a while, then disappeared into the brush. With nightfall near we feared the return of the cubs and hiked back to the beach.

Returning the next day to skin the bear, we found that the bullet had hit the bear's brain, entering through the nose. State Fish and Wildlife Protection Officer Al Thompson remarked that if the bullet had struck two inches in any other direction, the bear would likely have only been maddened by the shot. He also assured me that cubs of their size should have no trouble fending for themselves.

Mother bears are nothing to take lightly.

Sometimes man escapes bruin's wrath; sometimes he doesn't. William West got a scare, but Forrest Roberts and Ed McCracken weren't so fortunate.

Following the Blood Spoor

Larry Kaniut

"Like a bouncing ball, the animal popped up."

In the late 1970s, I sought information for a book that I hoped would enable people to avoid bear attacks. I visited the Lake Hood headquarters of the Alaska State Troopers, where Sgt. Rod Mills permitted me to review their bear attack files. While sifting through those files, I stumbled onto one of the saddest accounts I'd ever read. I did not use the story but always wanted to. In it, two men made a fatal decision; a man tried to carry his mauled hunting partner from the woods to medical help.

In 1995 I tried to locate the same files. I came up empty at the Alaska State Troopers and the Alaska Department of Fish and Game. They said "You might contact Larry Kaniut who has compiled a thorough list of encounters. He may be able to help you."

I thanked them and called Dr. John Middaugh, the State Epidemiologist who had compiled a list of bear attacks. I spoke to him about my dilemma, and he agreed to help. Before long I received a package in the mail from Dr. Middaugh, it included a query letter to Jackie Allen, coroner for the Matanuska-Susitna Borough, and the documents I sought. I am beholden to these fine people.

The fall of the year begins a tradition that's as old as history, when normally sane men get a glazed and distant look in their eyes. They round up the old smoke pole, check on their hunting gear, and blather about getting back into the woods. They make a last-minute run on the gun shop, the donut shop, and the flower shop (to bribe the bride). They don red and blaze orange, skedaddle into the buck brush, return to the cabin or fire ring in the evening, and regale each other into the night with "nothing but the truth."

In the continental United States, hunting fever ignites over deer and elk, whereas in Alaska the fever is over moose. When the nighttime temperatures dip below thirty-two degrees, the fever intensifies. Summer's over, kids trudge back to school, and the hunters resemble rut-weary bulls. Three and four-wheelers, tracked off-road vehicles, airplanes, and watercraft are fired up. Hunters fantasize about bagging Old Buster, bringing home winter's meat, and sharing around the campfire before returning to civilization and that four-letter word: work.

When the fever hits, the hunter wants to be in the woods. That's the way it was for Forrest Roberts and Ed McCracken. Forrest was a retired U.S. Air Force supply sergeant, 42 years old, 5-feet-11-inches tall, and 165 pounds. Ed was younger by eleven years, weighed 180 pounds, and was 5-feet-9-inches tall.

They headed out Saturday, 6 September 1975, at 11:15 A.M. The two-hour drive north out of Anchorage, Alaska, sped by as they shared their enthusiasm for the hunt. Forrest had hunted the Big Lake area two years earlier, but Ed had never hunted the locale.

Forrest felt confident that they could locate a moose. Other wildlife in the area included beaver, coyote, wolf, and bear. Although their quarry was America's largest deer, they decided to take a black bear if the opportunity presented itself.

Forrest's memory of the area was rusty, and he over-shot the turnoff from Big Lake over the Little Susitna River.

They drove seven miles east of the Little Su and back-tracked two roads. Before long they found his chosen camp spot with fresh water nearby. They were fifteen miles south of Big Lake off Burma Road near the Little Su.

Cloudy gray skies and rainy weather greeted the men as they set up camp at 4:30 P.M. They unloaded their Amphicat, a hunting machine they used to traverse muskeg or similar terrain. They drove to a nearby lake to glass for bull moose. A few hours later, having found nothing to shoot, the men returned to camp where they fixed a meal and went to bed just after the curtain of darkness fell.

At 7:30 Sunday morning the men roused themselves. It was later than they'd expected to rise (they didn't have a clock), so they chose to road-hunt all day. They covered several miles, stopping occasionally to glass for moose. Ed and Robby shared hunting stories, recalled experiences afield, and soaked up the joy of the great outdoors. The hunters saw nary an animal and disappointedly chose to hunt around camp in the late afternoon.

Discouraged from the lack of game and tired of the ever-pesky mosquitoes, Forrest and Ed considered returning to Anchorage. But they decided to stay the night and give it one more try the next morning.

Monday they arose, prepared for the day, ate breakfast, and left camp, hunting eastward on foot at 7:30 A.M. They would hunt some of the many cuts in the tall spruce and birch. Forrest chose one clear swath while Ed took another that paralleled it. Though brush blocked their views periodically, they were in sight of each other most of the time. They hunted 150 yards apart as the morning wore on.

After a while McCracken spotted a bear through the timber on a crossroads. Before Ed could decide what to do, the animal walked into the brush and disappeared. Within a minute the beast reappeared on the road walking toward the hunter. Ed decided to shoot the bear and dropped to a knee for a more steady shot. About 150 yards distant the animal stood on its hind legs, gazing in Ed's direction. Wondering if the bear saw or heard him or Forrest, Ed shouldered his Browning 7mm Magnum scoped with a Leupold 2X7, and squeezed off a shot. At the rifle's report the bear dropped to the ground. Like a bouncing ball it popped up and Ed fired a second shot. Showing no sign of being hit, the bear ran northward into the timber.

Having heard his partner's shots, Forrest moved in Ed's direction. They met about fifty yards from where the bear had dropped, and they walked to the spot. Forrest told Ed he'd heard the animal crashing through the woods. He asked Ed if he'd hit the bear. Ed replied that he had, and they looked for blood on the ground and the surrounding bushes. A few minutes later Forrest found blood, indicating the bear was well hit.

Because the overcast threatened rain and the men feared it would wash away the blood sign before they could find the bruin, they immediately took up the trail. Together they followed the sign, navigating downed timber that looked like pick-up-sticks. After moving through two clearings, they stopped. Robby knew it would be safer if they separated and told Ed, "We both don't want to be up here. I want you to stay off to the side." Ed agreed and followed Robby about twenty-five yards to one side.

They followed the blood trail another 200 to 300 yards, then stopped. After waiting ten minutes, they resumed their tracking. Moments later Ed heard Robby scream. Ed saw the bear charging Robby and raised his rifle. But before Ed got the rifle to his shoulder, the bear was on Robby.

Things happened so fast that Rob didn't have time to get a shot off either. He didn't even have time to reach his holstered Smith and Wesson .357 Magnum revolver on the cartridge belt around his waist. The animal knocked him to the ground and pinned him with a skillet-sized paw. The bear stood on all fours atop the hunter. Forrest's

Levi's, shirt, jacket, and hip boots offered virtually no protection as the animal tore into him with one-and-a-half-inch canines and razor-sharp claws.

Hoping to hit the brute or scare it off, Ed fired two rounds at the bear's shoulder-back area. It left Rob and walked several feet from the downed hunter. Ed shot the bear again and dropped it, then fired a fourth shot. He quickly reloaded his rifle with 180-grain bullets.

Approaching the downed bear, Ed unholstered his .41 pistol and shot the animal two times. Within a minute of the bear's attack it lay dead. Ed left his rifle on the ground with Robby's .300 Winchester Magnum. The Winchester's bolt was open with no round in the chamber.

Ed rushed to his partner who lay on the ground with his hands on his face. Ed asked Robby how he was. Robby said of his face, "It's gone."

Ed turned Robby over. He was shocked to see the damage the bear had wreaked upon Forrest: His left hand was nearly severed at the wrist; he had a four-by-three-inch laceration on his left bicep; his third finger on his right hand was missing; his left eye protruded from its socket; his head was deeply lacerated with the skull punctured above the right eye; and his bottom lip was torn in the middle to the top of the chin. Confused about the best way to get Forrest to medical aid, Ed stood there wondering what to do.

Robby told Ed that he couldn't see. When Ed asked Robby if he thought he could walk, Robby said no. Then Robby told Ed that he wanted him to go for help, stating, "You'll never get me out by yourself; we're too far in."

Wanting in the worst way to help his injured friend, Ed replied, "Well, I could," then added, "I'm going to try to take you out."

At that point Ed placed Robby's arms over his shoulders, clasped Robby's arms and dragged him away from the bear toward the road.

McCracken managed to drag his pal a quarter of a mile. Both men were exhausted and they stopped to rest. By now Robby's left hand was bothering him a great deal. After resting Roberts wanted to walk with McCracken. They made virtually no progress and stopped a second time.

McCracken placed a tourniquet around Robby's left arm, then helped him sit with his back against a tree. He wasn't sure of the road's location, and he wanted to find it to save them from going in the wrong direction and from expending extra energy.

Seeking a familiar landmark, McCracken walked for twenty minutes. He came upon a logged area and spotted a bulldozed clearing. Ed realized he was not near the road and that it would be extremely difficult to get Forrest to this point. In frustration and thinking it the best thing to do, Ed walked on. In a short time he reached his vehicle and sped over the dirt road toward Big Lake, hoping to find someone to help him. Eight to ten miles later he encountered two men in a green Chevy Blazer.

Ed stopped and told Sgt. Thomas D. Eddins and Bill Smith about the mauling and the need to get Forrest to medical help. The men had a citizens' band radio and contacted a Big Lake REACT monitor, requesting help. The monitor relayed the message to the Alaska State Troopers, who in turn contacted the Rescue Coordination Center at Elmendorf Air Force base in Anchorage, forty air miles away. RCC dispatched a helicopter from the base.

Pilot Paul M. Weathers, copilot Thomas R. Hill, and Dr. William Brant, Major U.S. Air Force, lifted off and sped to the Elmendorf Hospital helipad where they picked up John A. Taylor, an Alaska Department of Fish and Game protection officer. They departed for the Burma Road area.

Meanwhile, Eddins and Smith offered to drive back behind McCracken. After driving a mile Ed noticed the headlights behind him flashing. Ed stopped and the men, who had been monitoring their CB, told him that the Alaska

State Troopers wanted them to return to the blacktop and be picked up in a helicopter. They discussed the situation, then drove to a higher, flatter location where the helicopter could spot them and land. Three or four hundred yards farther they spotted a flat place with a landing sock nearby. They stopped and built a fire, calling the chopper on the radio to give their location.

The man on the other end of the radio said he would bring the troopers in his Jeep. Ed wondered if the Jeep driver could find them. Fifteen minutes later the helicopter appeared and landed at the wind sock. Ed got into the chopper to search for camp from the air and to direct Eddins and Smith, who had agreed to drive Ed's vehicle to camp.

They landed near camp where Doctor Brant, Hill, Taylor, and McCracken set off on foot in search of Roberts. Although Ed thought he knew where Rob was, he couldn't locate him. Forty-five minutes of fruitless searching passed, and it seemed they were going in circles. They decided to return to the chopper so copilot Hill could rejoin Weathers and go airborne to assist the search.

Hill said they would wait fifteen minutes to lift off, giving the ground searchers time to find the bear. The chopper would then fly above as the ground searchers backtracked the bear's blood spoor to Roberts. Minutes later McCracken and the searchers reached the bear, just before the chopper lifted off. Near the bear, two rifles leaned against a tree. That's when Ed remembered where he'd left Rob, and pointed it out to the others.

The helicopter searched the area near the bear, located Roberts, then directed the searchers to him. The ground searchers started for Rob. When they approached within two hundred yards of the place where McCracken had left Robby, the group observed the hovering helicopter nearby. Doctor Brant examined Roberts and found no sign of life. Pulse and respiration were absent and Roberts' body was cooling, though *rigor mortis* had not set in. The major wound was to the right side of his face;

Dr. Brant had to give the others the tragic news that Roberts was dead. A body bag was lowered from the helicopter. The rescuers placed Roberts in the bag and carried him to a hoist position. The helicopter crew then hoisted Roberts into the chopper.

A man on the ground with a radio called the pilot for directions to the road. Somehow they miscommunicated and the ground crew turned the wrong way. They floundered in the timber for an hour before deciding to set off a smoke signal to alert the helicopter crew to their dilemma. The helicopter crew located the men on the ground, lifted them up through a hole in the trees, and flew McCracken to Elmendorf with his deceased partner.

EPILOGUE

Fish and Wildlife Protection officers and a search party including McCracken returned to the scene of the attack on 12 September. Contrary to McCracken's report and the newspaper account of a wounded black bear, the searchers found a dead seven-and-a-half-foot brown-grizzly bear. They also found a hat, two empty .41 caliber casings, one live .41 Magnum shell, and a human finger.

They noted that the bear had been hit at least four times: in the left front neck, shoulder area, head, and abdomen. Upon opening the bear's body cavity, they discovered violent disruption and damage to the internal organs. They took photographs at the scene and removed the head and paws for identification and sealing purposes. These bear parts were taken to Alaska Department of Fish and Game in Anchorage, where Lee Glenn verified the bear was a brown-grizzly.

When man ventures into the outdoors where dangers abound, the possibility of injury or death always exists. What began for Ed and Forrest as a wonderful experience in the woods turned into a tragic event. Two hunters became the hunted. Sometimes the hunted escapes; sometimes he doesn't.

Moose hunters aren't the only hunters who encounter grizzlies. Sheep hunters Ralph Borders and Bill Gonce experienced an attack high on a mountain.

Three Bears Right There!

by Ralph Borders and Bill Gonce

"We were eyeball-to-eyeball with three bears."

Ralph Borders and Bill Gonce left their respective homes in pursuit of Dall rams in the fall of 1992. Their anticipated sojourn into sheep country turned into a fight for life.

I called Ralph Borders in January 1995 to learn about his bear encounter. He willingly shared his tale.

Although we departed on our hunting trip Saturday, 5 September 1992, our hunt began years before. Ours is a hunting heritage. We've shared many hunting adventures, but we'd never hunted sheep. The thrill of the outdoors and sharing a campfire fueled our enthusiasm. The opportunity to pursue Dall sheep produced an added dimension.

My brother-in-law, Bill Gonce, came from Juneau to my home in Haines, Alaska, where we completed our plans and preparation. We enjoyed discussing old times and anticipated the next two weeks, hunting sheep for the first week, followed by a moose hunt. We were eager to see Alaska's interior, knowing that it offered country far different from southeast Alaska's heavily timbered and lush rain forest.

We had taken great effort to select the lightest food-stuffs for the sheep hunt to reduce the weight of our packs. Our meals would consist of things that could be eaten dry (pilot bread, cheese, smoked salmon, hard sausage, candy) or mixed with hot water (instant oatmeal, Top Ramen soup, MRE-meals ready to eat, hot cider mix, tea bags, and Kool-Aid).

We are both experienced hunters, in good shape for hiking but not used to packing. We didn't anticipate much packing on the sheep trip because we would be dropped off in the mountains by a bush pilot. We were filling a fly-in trip that other hunters had been unable to complete.

Bill is a carpenter-contractor who came to Alaska in 1971. He is 41 years old with graying red hair, 6-feet-1-inch tall, and weighs 180 pounds. He has hunted an abundance of deer.

Bill got me a meat-cutting job in the Haines grocery store in 1973. For the past five years I've helped maintain roads, water and sewer lines, and vehicles for the Haines Department of Public Works. I'm 43 years old and have graying brown hair. I'm 5-feet-10-inches tall, weigh 160 pounds, and am blind without my glasses. I enjoy photography and have shot a lot of bears with my camera.

On Saturday we left Haines at 6:30 A.M. It was a beautiful, clear forty-degree day. We talked sheep hunting as we enjoyed the journey north. Stopping at the beautiful turquoise Kluane Lake in the Yukon and watching one hundred Dall lambs and ewes heightened our excitement. When we reached Tok, I purchased a bear tag, in the event we ran into a bear worth collecting. Our trip went without a hitch, and we arrived in Fairbanks at 6:30 P.M., where we spent the night in a motel.

Sunday and a beautiful, clear day beckoned. That afternoon we began the last leg of our journey. As we drove toward the airstrip at Salcha forty miles to the south, we encountered local hunters with three and four-wheelers, as well as tracked off-road vehicles. The annual excitement of moose fever prevailed.

We finally reached the dirt airstrip between the river and the highway. A half-dozen variously colored, single-engine airplanes dotted the strip near the bush pilot's home. We noticed two Super Cubs fitted with special tundra tires. This Piper aircraft is the bush pilot's plane of choice for getting into and out of tight strips, such as high-mountain gravel stream bars. The twenty-nine-inch-tall balloon tires add to the plane's performance and its look of strength and superiority. The pilot, Bill Sewell, stowed our gear in his plane, and before we knew it, we were airborne, flying into an area where neither Bill nor I had previously been. On our way in we saw a few caribou and one black bear.

Forty minutes later we landed on a gravel strip in the middle of the river. For the uninitiated, an Alaskan bush "strip" is not an asphalt runway a mile in length. A bush strip is a level stretch of ground one hundred yards long or longer, which could be rocky or mushy firmament. We noticed an old wrecked plane off to one side, the result of an inexperienced pilot, a sudden wind shift, or too much weight aboard to maintain flying status. This did not dampen our hunting desire.

This strip was not the object of our hunt but would have to do until the weather permitted our pilot to move us. We were fifteen miles from our planned drop-off point at a miner's cabin at 4,000 feet. If the wind died down in two days, Bill would return to ferry us away from this 1,500-foot elevation, deeper into the mountains and closer to ram country. Before the pilot left, he flew Bill around the area for twenty-five minutes, looking for rams and pointing out various drainages.

Along the river was a packer's hunting camp with four moose hunters. The packer had mules and horses for hire, should a hunter want a moose packed to camp. He had a spare wall tent, eight-by-ten-feet that he let us use. It was much nicer than our two-man tent. We went to bed anticipating hunting in the vicinity until Bill returned.

On Monday (Labor Day) we loaded our packs and hiked from the packer's camp carrying our spike camp: tent, single-burner Coleman stove, sleeping bags, and a two-day food supply. We crossed the river, skirted some muskeg, climbed a hill, and set out for the mountains three to four miles away.

We set up camp around 5:00 P.M. at the base of a mountain. Packing our gear had taken its toll, but a plus was my Danner boots: they kept my feet dry and comfortable. There was no water in the area, and were we glad the packer had told us to take along canteens!

While resting we saw a ewe and a lamb above camp. Later we watched a wolf cross a ridge in front of us. I decided to shoot it but overestimated the range and missed with the only shot I fired. The wolf was still running two miles away.

On Tuesday we climbed the mountain behind camp and noticed two more ewes. We spotted one hundred caribou, but the season was closed that year. We also saw a wolf and three Dall ewes by afternoon, when we heard wolves howling. We ran into another sheep hunter who said he'd seen no legal rams.

Deciding to return to base camp, we trudged down the mountain to camp, packed our gear, and headed for base camp by 5:00 P.M. We retired for the night hoping the pilot would show up in the morning.

Wednesday surprised us with a snowstorm and wind. There would be no hunting or flying. We spent the time with the other hunters around the stove in the packer's tent waiting for the weather to change. Thursday the tenth dawned clear and cold with a low of twenty degrees during the night.

The packer told us about the hunting possibilities and two cabins where we could spend the night, nine miles away and deeper into ram country. Two miles beyond the cabins at timberline was another spot to set up camp. He said if we'd flag a spot at timberline to drop our gear, he'd bring it up the next day.

With that in mind we took sleeping bags and a little food to last until supper Friday. Upon reaching the cabins and discovering other hunters, we were surprised. The packer had not known they were there. They had come in by three-wheeler part of the way, having left the machine two miles away because they couldn't descend the steep sidehill.

They occupied the newer cabin, so we took the old cabin, which was a twelve-by-fourteen-foot log structure. It was built over a spring and had a rotten wood floor, two stories, and no windows on the first floor. The rusty woodstove had no damper, making it nearly impossible to boil water, much less heat the room. Nevertheless, we prepared hot water, mixed instant oatmeal chased down with hot chocolate, and hit the sack. The temperature dropped to ten degrees that night.

On Friday we prepared for rams. My wool pants and Pendleton shirt were comfortable. Before leaving the cabin we split our gear, which included a spotting scope and tripod, knife-steel, ammo, extra sweater, gloves, lunch, and survival gear (space blanket, candles, matches, nylon cord, emergency flares).

Two miles up the valley from the cabin we reached timberline, where we flagged the drop-off spot for our gear. We dropped our sleeping bags off amidst six-inch-wide trees fifteen to twenty feet high along the riverbank. We headed up the mile-and-a-half-wide valley. Mountains rose from the valley floor. High tundra and rocks led the way toward the head of the valley ten miles beyond. We saw caribou again. After three miles we spotted twenty lambs and ewes across the valley. Realizing our best chance for rams was ahead, we pushed on.

Our objective was a 6,500-foot peak. Stopping for lunch, we glassed for rams. I observed what appeared to be old bear tracks in the snow—that of a sow and two cubs. We crossed a 5,500-foot pass around 3:00 P.M., stopped, and glassed for an hour. With darkness only four hours away, we decided to make a hurried search of a bench about one hundred feet above us. We thought the hike would eliminate another place to look later and warm us up before returning to set up spike camp.

It had just begun snowing and we had a mile-and-a-half visibility. With an eye peeled for rams we climbed the ten to twenty-degree slope. As we neared the bench, we noticed wolf tracks. Then we saw a single set of bear tracks going downhill that was fresher than the wolf's. The vegetation consisted of berry bushes. We scanned the valley through the falling snow but saw nothing. While I looked downhill, Bill looked uphill. Suddenly, Bill said, "There they are . . . RIGHT THERE!"

I followed his gaze and saw three bears. The sow, which had been lying down and looking over her shoulder, exploded into action. The cubs followed suit and all three bears came for us. Bill and I stood side by side. There was no growl, no noise. The bears came quickly and silently through the fresh snow. We were eyeball to eyeball with three bears.

I watched the sow looking from Bill to me, sizing up the situation and deciding which one to go for. She came for me. One cub was just behind her off her right flank, and the other was the same distance off its twin's flank.

My brother-in-law said later, "It was like three large dogs and they were rushing up to play. It was like, 'Well, fancy meeting you here.' It seemed so innocent."

Bill carried a bullet in the chamber of his .06 and he was shooting, handloaded 180-grain Nosler seconds. I was trying to get my gloves off so I could chamber a round. (My .338 Ruger has always had a problem getting a shell from the clip to the chamber.)

Within four seconds of sighting us, the bears were on us. The sow ran past Bill and grabbed me above my left bicep, pulling me off my feet and carrying me thirty to sixty feet downhill. She slipped or rolled onto her back, dropping me. Just as the sow grabbed me, Bill fired from his hip at the closer cub. His shot spun the cub around, rolled him onto the other cub, and spooked them. Both cubs turned and took off.

The bear and I rolled over and over down the slope. I kept thinking that I should play dead; I made no attempt to fight back. The sow bit my face rapidly. It wasn't a tearing, just bite, bite, bite. I yelled to Bill, "Get her off of me!" Suddenly, she bounced up and grabbed me by the left foot and chewed on it. I didn't hear it, but Bill had shot her. I hadn't heard his first shot when he hit the cub, either.

While she was chewing my left foot, Bill fired again, hitting her and knocking her off me. Bill timed his shots to shoot the bear when she rose above me. I had told him enough over the years that he knew to break the bear down in order to disable it (shoot it in the shoulder, spine, or hip). She came down the next time and grabbed my right foot and chewed on it. I wasn't concerned as long as she chewed on my leg and Bill kept shooting. I didn't think her bites were life-threatening. She bit into my foot at the same time I heard Bill's final shot. The pain was so intense that I knew he had shot my foot. The bear went limp, and I realized he had hit her in the spine, killing her instantly.

Thinking I wouldn't be able to walk on a shot foot, I stood up. I could walk. I hadn't been shot after all. Bill reloaded immediately, fearing the return of the cubs. I yelled, "Find my glasses! We gotta go!" Then I crawled around on all fours feeling through the snow for my glasses. Halfway between where the bear grabbed me and where she died, I found my glasses.

Bill thought I was done for. He didn't tell me that he could look beyond my lipless mouth and see raw flesh and teeth and the back of my throat. He also saw holes in my temples and head. He was concerned that I might have other injuries hidden by my clothes, but I figured as long as I could walk I was okay. I didn't bleed much. I pulled my cap over my head to slow the bleeding. I knew I was okay and refused to let him look for other injuries.

The only major injury was to my lips. I lost about two-thirds of my upper lip and a third of my lower lip. We found part of my upper lip frozen to my coat (they tried to sew it on, but it didn't take). There were a number of puncture wounds to my face and feet. It was hard to believe that the entire attack took thirty seconds.

Bill saw blood on the snow from the cub. The bears were the least of our concerns, and we started out. Bill followed me down the mountain. Convinced I was going to bleed to death, he kept looking for spurting blood.

Although hiking out was difficult, I was buoyed by adrenaline and an eagerness to receive medical help. I stopped periodically and cleaned the blood off my glasses. Within an hour we'd covered four miles to the drop-off site we had marked for the packer and where the packer happened to be. It was 5:05 P.M. We'd covered four miles in fifty-five minutes.

The packer boosted me aboard a horse and led me out, while Bill jogged behind with the day pack. We reached the hunters' cabin, and the packer yelled, "Bear attack!" We could never have known when we met these men that they would play a huge part in my rescue.

The pilot's brother, Leroy Sewell, volunteered to make the trip out for help. His plan was to retrieve his three-wheeler and drive to a mining camp to radio for help. Concerned that I could bleed to death, he grabbed his Mauser rifle and took off. Leroy crossed and recrossed the creek many times, climbing uphill for two miles from 3,000 to 4,000 feet before he reached his machine. (Ralph and Bill never got to speak to Leroy again.)

At the mine camp, Pat Peedle called 911 on a cellular phone. Although low on fuel, a helicopter was dispatched from Fort Greely. Some confusion followed, as the pilot could not locate the cabins and mules nearby. Peedle finally made it clear via radio contact that the helicopter was going in the wrong direction, and the bird landed for specific directions from Sewell. Once he got his bearings, the pilot flew to pick me up. During our wait Bill attended me, mostly dabbing at the blood on my face to keep it from going down my throat.

The mauling took place at 4:10; the helicopter came in at 8:30. The medic cut my clothes off and they loaded me into the chopper. Thinking I would die before he saw me again, Bill talked them into letting him ride in the upper rack. The crew wore night-vision goggles. They flew me to Fairbanks. Just before arriving at Fort Greely, the chopper encountered a snow squall, reducing visibility to zero. The pilot was redirected. However, since he was on bingo fuel (nearly depleted), he blasted through the squall and landed safely.

My medical treatment and care in Fairbanks was superb. I was there a week, then went to southern California where my folks live. Both my wife and I were enrolled with Blue Cross, and they covered $40,000 in medical expenses. The psychological effect of the bear attack is negligible to both Bill and me.

The week following the attack it snowed three feet, covering the sow, and we never went back to retrieve her. We don't know what happened to the cubs. The fish and game officer wanted us to retrieve and give up the bear, but Bill refused, since he had a bear tag. I wanted the beautiful hide but the snow depth negated the retrieval. The officer finally relented since the bears were all the same size, it was self-defense, and the snow was so deep.

Most people knowledgeable of bears think the attack is the result of the bears' staking out a game trail in hopes of ambushing a caribou or sheep.

Bill Sewell volunteered to take us back in the spring to look for the bear and Ralph's lost rifle. We're not eager to run into another bear family, but we would like to get back into sheep country to bag a ram.

From Dall sheep mountain meadows to Kodiak Island's deer pastures, hunters experience bruin. Chuck Lewis was deer hunting when he met his bear.

Leave Well Enough Alone

by Chuck Lewis

"I heard '*woof, woof, woof.*'"

Chuck Lewis, Jr., is the skipper of a commercial fishing tender who has had numerous bear encounters. While visiting with him and his family at Larsen Bay, we talked bears. Chuck told me about a time he was hunting on Kodiak Island.

I was deer hunting in 1974 on Uganik Island with Bob Gaines and two other men. Bob was an assistant guide for Leon Francisco and one of my best friends. We hunted together all the time. I was walking up the side of a hill on a clear morning. I was hunting deer and am strictly a meat hunter. I had no desire to shoot a bear then and I have no desire to shoot a bear now. I saw a sow and two cubs below me a mile away. They were running away from me. You see bears all the time when you're hunting. I usually don't pay them much mind. I'm not afraid of them.

I had shot a nice three-point buck. I dressed it out and was dragging it down a steep hill in a thick alder patch when I heard a "*woof, woof, woof.*" I knew what it was, so I dropped the deer and walked to a clearing. The dead fall grass was tall, but I could see the bear below. It would disappear; then I'd see it again. It was coming straight up a trail. I could see the grass moving. I was ready.

The bear stood up. I hollered, which I found out later wasn't a good idea (Dick Rohrer, a Kodiak bear guide, said sometimes they take that as a threat). It came down on all fours and pawed at the ground, then came at me like a freight train.

I looked in the scope, and all I saw was brown. I shot and hit it in the back. It came up and I shot it again with my Remington Gamemaster pump .30-06. I've had that gun since I was twelve and I can really make it smoke. I was shooting 150-grain bullets. I shot it as fast as I could in the chest, and that killed it. I wasn't scared at that point. Later that night I thought about it and then I got scared. Bob was in the next valley when he heard the report of my rifle. He said he couldn't believe it was a pump, that he'd never heard an automatic shoot that fast.

They were the same sow and cubs I had seen earlier. We skinned the sow out and took the skull. The little cubs sat watching me, whimpering and crying. It was a big job and a big mess. I left the carcass thinking, "Maybe I could eat some of this. I'll try it." I was going to cut out the backstrap and try to salvage some of it, but I think the cub thought that I was bothering her and came back.

When I got to town, I called Ben Ballinger, who was the head of the game division and has since retired—a good fellow. I explained to him what had happened and showed him the hide full of holes and the skull. He contacted a man in Anchorage who was trying to get cubs for a zoo.

When we returned to the carcass to catch the cubs, there were no cubs in sight. It had snowed by then and big bear tracks surrounded the carcass. Another bear had buried it under two inches of dirt, sticks, and leaves. We saw the cubs the next day. I suspect the cubs had been eating on the mother's carcass. We were unable to catch the cubs, and we speculate that the big bear, probably a boar, ate the cubs.

The day before I had shot at some deer and missed. My gun jammed. It had never jammed. A dime in my pocket had gotten in the clip and went into the magazine. It fit perfectly and wedged in the barrel. I went to the boat and took the dime out with a pair of needle-nosed pliers. If that dime had jammed the gun the day I ran into the sow, I'd have been in big trouble.

Chuck recounted another bear story while out fishing.

We were over in Kukak. The skipper and another man were clam digging, and I was on the boat. They had dug holes along the beach. They were about one hundred yards away from me, and the wind was blowing.

A bear was walking down the beach. Every time he'd come to one of the holes, he'd dig in it. He'd go to each hole and inspect it. He got closer to the men, so I waved and hollered. But they couldn't figure out what I was saying.

The skipper got in the skiff and ran it toward the boat, leaving the other man there. I still waved and hollered, but he couldn't understand me through the wind. When he got close to me, he saw the bear, which was only thirty yards from the man on the beach by now. The skipper went back and rescued his partner.

Although Chuck Lewis escaped serious consequences while deer hunting on Kodiak Island, Greg Brown's foray into the forest nearly cost him his life.

One Tough Alaskan

by Hank Taylor

"It was awful the way my guts wiggled in my fingers."

Within a year of Alaska Bear Tales' *appearance on the newsstands, I received a phone call from a generous gentleman who complimented me on a job well done. He said, "It's about time someone told the truth about bears in Alaska. You did in your book." Then he told me, "If you do another book on Alaskan bears, include some of these," and Hank Taylor told me bear stories for nearly an hour.*

After deciding to do another bear book, I went back to my notes from our conversation, determined to contact Hank. In the fall of 1987 I tried to locate him. I checked the phone book, called the Anchorage Telephone Utility, and phoned a former student and paralegal, Leonard Hackett. I told Leonard I was working on another book, and he said, "If there's ever anything I can do to help, let me know."

"As a matter of fact," I said, "I'm trying to locate a guy who told me bear stories a few years ago and I'm not having any success."

Leonard responded, "What's his name?"

I replied, "Hank Taylor."

Leonard said, "Oh, Hank works right down the hall from me."

I couldn't believe it. We made arrangements to meet Hank. Two unusual bear stories involved Hank's friend George Brown. Hank called him Greg. Before Hank told me the tales, he shared Greg's bear-hunting philosophy.

Greg Brown used to say he was part Aleut, part Siberian Eskimo, part Scottish sea captain, and part brown bear. He was an interesting man whom I first met in 1958. Greg always used to say the Aleut prayer before he shot a bear. It started with the Aleut word for *ursus.* "Old Man in the fur coat. My wife needs your hide for our house. My children need your meat for their bellies. I must kill you; please forgive me." *Bam.*

God help you if you shot before you apologized because it was believed if you took the life of the bear without respect, that bear would come back to get you. The Aleut's apology states the reason for taking a bear's life. To his dying day, Greg wouldn't shoot a bear without saying that.

The Aleuts considered brown bears a form of people in prehistory.

During his lifetime, Greg's grandfather was *the* bear hunter in a village on Kodiak Island. His grandfather told him what it was like to hunt bear before guns came, and he passed on much of his knowledge to Greg. I call Greg's first serious encounter with a bear "The Mirror Bear."

Greg was hunting with his family up the Kenai River as a twelve-year-old. It was fall; the sky was blue, the trees were yellow and pretty. He was thirsty. They came to a beautiful spring and Greg laid his rifle down and kneeled to get a drink of water. He was using the water as a mirror as boys will do, looking at his reflection and how pretty he was, and letting the water get still from the ripples after the drink.

From behind him something big and brown and dark loomed in front of the sky. He saw that it was a huge bear standing upright over him. As he turned hoping to get to his gun, the bear hit him and knocked him through the air. He came to twenty feet away, hanging in the alders with his shoulder dislocated. They put his shoulder back in again, but it hurt all of his life. The bear just gave him a swat. That was all he remembered.

That bear injured Greg, but it was another bear that nearly killed him.

The next time Greg had a run-in with a bear it was late summer or fall of 1932 or 1933. He and his brother were fishing and getting ready for the winter's trapping in Chulitna Bay, where glaciers abound. He walked up Middle Glacier, prospecting a trapping area. He looked up the hill and saw a monster bear, a great big bear. Greg was raised on Kodiak Island, and when he says big, you can bet your boot on it.

He said, "My gosh." Times were hard in the Depression, and he thought he could get a lot of money if he could sell the hide. He had a little .25-20 and figured he could kill the bear with it. He climbed up a deep gully to the bear which was feeding on grass. He got in a good position and drilled the bear right through the engine room. The bear let out a spine-tingling roar, jumped in the gully, and started downhill.

Greg thought the bear would go downhill, so he ran to his right down the hill to intercept the bear and to pump a few rounds into him. He stood with his rifle on his shoulder waiting for the bear to come out at the bottom of the hill. The bear didn't show up.

Enough time had transpired for the bear to come before it dawned on Greg that the bear had circled and that he had been had. *He's behind me.* Subconsciously maybe Greg smelled him or heard him (he was a great believer in the subconscious). But somehow Greg knew that the bear had reversed his course, gone up the gully, climbed out, and was coming right behind him on the ledge Greg had just come down. He spun around as fast as he could, bringing the gun up to fire. The bear was in midair. The bear hit him and broke the stock of the lever-action Winchester in half. The gun went flying, and Greg went tumbling. The bear caught up with Greg and climbed on top of him.

Greg had listened to men talk about playing dead. He felt that if you play dead the bear might oblige you. His grandfather told him, "Fight. He might leave you alone. Don't play dead. A man's supposed to fight. Let the woman play dead."

Greg continued, "Since I was pretty good with my dukes when I was young, I fought the bear. I hit him in the nose as hard as I could with a one-two punch in the chops. The bear shook his head. In my mind I can still remember the smell of that bear's breath."

As the bear opened his mouth wide, he came down on Greg's head, ripping the scalp off. Greg pulled his head out of its mouth. The bear was tryin' to crush his head, and he would get mad and bat Greg in the shoulder. Greg said, "I'm fightin' all the time. The bear got pissed and stepped back and hit me. I went flyin' down the hill. I was still conscious.

"I lit in the top of some alders. I'm hangin' up there, thinking Thank God, I'm away from that son of a gun.' He knocked me a long way off the side of that steep hill. Then he came again.

"He pulled me down on the ground and we went at it again. He hit me and rolled me in the leaves. He straddled me face-to-face. I grasped the chest hair under his fore-legs in an effort to pull myself under him and away from his jaws. I slid under and he backed up. I kept trying to hold onto the fur, and he got mad and clawed me. As his head came down between his front legs to get me, I slid downhill under him.

"I had on some heavy, stiff boots. I kicked him in the belly as hard as I could. I believe I kicked him in the balls, because after a good kick he let out a *Ruuurrrrhhhh*! The brute turned me loose and ran over me and down the hill like a freight train, *Ruurrrhhh*! I passed out.

"When I came to, my arm was dislocated again. Here I am bleedin', my scalp's lyin' over, blood in my eyes, I'm bitten all over, and I can't move my left arm. And I look down and my guts are hangin' out. I spoke to the missing bear, 'You son of a bitch, you knocked me down the hill.'

"There's nothin' runnin' out of the guts, it's just blood with the guts pokin' out and wigglin'. I figured that I was gonna die. I figured the bullet injury was awfully hot, and he was goin' to water to cool off. At the foot of the hill was a beaver pond with a beaver house in the middle. I knew that son of a gun was goin' down there to get in that water to cool off. I'm gonna die, but before I die, I'm gonna kill that bear."

It was eight miles or so back to the cabin. He had no hopes of getting back; his brother had gone in a different direction to prospect for another trapline. He crawled back up the hill to retrieve the rifle. The stock was off, but the action still worked. He took the rifle and then crawled slowly, because his guts were hanging out, and his arm was in tremendous pain. He couldn't use it because he kept bleeding and fainting.

He crawled down to the foot of the hill. Sure enough, there was the bear, lying on the beaver house. He was spread front legs akimbo, grasping the beaver house. His head was lying on top of it like a big bushel basket, and his body was under water below his forelegs. The bear sounded like a man saying, "*Oooooo, oooooooooo.*"

Greg said, "I couldn't raise the rifle up with just my right hand, hold it with no stock, and get a good aim. I knew I needed to shoot him in the head and kill him or he'd finish me off.

"I crawled to a mossy log. I lay down and flopped that gun up on that log, just like putting it on a bench-rest—it was perfect. I put the sights right in his left ear and I fired. He collapsed on the house, dead as could be. That's the last thing I remembered."

Greg's brother came home that night. At first light he went looking for Greg and found him in the trail. Greg had crawled a long distance down the hill trying to get back, but he was delirious. He didn't remember having crawled. His brother picked him up and packed him back to the cabin. Greg came to and told his brother, "Build a fire and sterilize your knife in the flame. Go out and cut willow bushes to make probes and bring them back. Then sterilize your knife again and don't touch the blade."

His brother did and brought in a bundle of green willow limbs. Greg instructed his brother to "trim them down to probes, to open up my wounds that are full of brush, grass, dirt, and bear slobber. Lay them out so they don't touch anything."

Greg was a smart man. I've talked to doctors about this, and they said you couldn't get a more sterile instrument to probe. Back then gangrene, not the jaws, caused death in most bear attacks. He knew that he had to clean the wounds that had closed up—in his shoulders, back, neck and arms—get them bleeding, and wash them out with soap and water, which was a good antiseptic.

His brother probed, then washed and scrubbed Greg with yellow laundry soap and hot water. He cleaned all the wounds and the skin flap. His brother got all the dirt and leaves washed out of his gut. Greg said, "It was awful, the way my guts wiggled in my fingers."

After the wounds were cleaned, Greg told his brother to rinse his wounds with kerosene. It was the only thing they had except whiskey, and he'd given up all drinking. Greg said, "It hurt like the devil because I had so many injuries."

Next Greg told his brother to get some braided nylon fish line (this was before monofilament) and a sail needle. Even in those years they still had sail and they had to sew canvas. Greg told his brother to sterilize the needle and line in the kerosene and "sew my stomach up."

His brother started, then stopped and said, "I can't do this."

Angrily Greg retorted, "It's just like sewing up a sail. Sew it up."

Greg goes on, "So he'd stick that needle in and pull a notch up and I'd faint." He'd come to and his brother was doing it again, and his hands were trembling. Greg would say, "For goodness sake, you're gonna punch my guts and kill me. Be careful." But his brother told Greg he just couldn't do it, and collapsed in tears.

Greg exploded in anger and said, "Give me the needle." He said, "I sat there and tried to push my guts in. I'd get a hold of them and sometimes I'd sorta faint, but I just kept going. I concentrated on sewing like sewing a sail. I worked all the way around my belly. That's the last thing I remember."

Incidentally, after his brother took care of him, he went back and skinned the bear, then got one hundred dollars for it, a twelve-foot hide. It was the biggest bear he'd ever killed.

For two weeks he was unconscious. His brother would bring him around and pour soup and water down his throat until he came to again. He didn't get gangrene. He said, "It was another week or so before I could get around. I looked out the window and saw another brown bear. I got a bigger rifle and went over there and shot him dead. I walked up and kicked him and turned around and walked back to the cabin. For a long time after that I was hell on bears. But I don't hate 'em anymore."

He would tear his shirt off and show his scars. "See that." Greg got to town and showed old Dr. Howard Romig, who looked him over and said, "By gosh, George (what Dr. Romig called Greg), I couldn't have done a better job myself." Greg was proud of that. He didn't have to pay the doctor for it either.

Later I asked him, "Greg, how in the world could a 165-pound runt like you—stocky Aleut, bowlegged, strong-shouldered, good packer—take all that and live through it?"

He said, "Simple. I didn't want to die."

Later I talked to Bill Poland and asked him if he knew George Brown. Bill said, "I met George Brown up at the headwaters of Caribou Lake. He and I hunted together on Caribou Lake, in the Caribou Hills on the Kenai. He could really tell stories. He had one hell of a lot of experience. It wouldn't surprise me if he had been mauled and sewn himself up. He couldn't have made up all that stuff."

See Appendix 8, Medical Aspects (this appendix applies directly to a number of these mauling victims and indirectly to all).

Greg Brown had no problem shooting at the brownie he met; however, Marti Miller did not want to shoot the black bear that stalked her.

To Shoot or Not to Shoot

by Marti Miller

I finally told myself, "Get a grip here. You're in control. Do something."

Over the years it has been my good fortune to know a number of people who worked for the U.S. Geologic Survey. Two years ago I met another. Our family friend, Barbara Dean, steered me to her friend Marti Miller, who had a close call with a black bear. I contacted Marti and discovered that she and Cynthia Dusel-Bacon, another family friend of ours, were friends. Each woman had been stalked by a black bear. The difference between Marti's and Cynthia's experiences was that Marti had a weapon.

Marti was willing to share her experience. On 25 January 1995 we met in her office. On her wall was a picture of a dead black bear on an open hillside. She led me to a conference room where we spent an hour talking about the incident and looking at pictures of the area where it occurred.

This diminutive 5-feet-3-inch tall, 120-pound, 40-year-old woman sat across from me. Long brown hair framed her blue-gray eyes. She wore a white turtleneck under a winter wool sweater, brown-green corduroy pants, and hiking boots. She was eager to tell her story.

Shooting the bear was not something I wanted to do. Thoughts flashed through my head. I raised the rifle. *If I shoot in the air to scare it, it could charge. If it runs, I'll still be alone for several hours, and it will probably come back. If I don't shoot, it looks like it's going to walk right up on me. It didn't scare when I yelled at it. I think it's stalking me.*

I felt exceedingly vulnerable, extremely alone. There were no outcroppings or trees to offer protection. If I did succeed in scaring the bear off, I was certain it would return. I preferred to confront the bear head on instead of waiting for it to stalk me from behind. Being an animal's prey was foreign to me and I found it quite unnerving. The bear was acting instinctively and my human reasoning was useless. You can't stop and say to an animal, "Hey, you're making a mistake."

At the time of the encounter, I was engaged in geologic field mapping for the U.S. Geological Survey. I began working for the USGS full time in 1981 (after completing my bachelor's and master's degrees at Stanford). I had connections to both Alaska and the USGS prior to moving up here. My father had worked for the Branch of Alaskan Geology from about 1941 until his death in 1961 while performing field work in southern Alaska; I was six years old at the time. No one is sure what happened, but my father and his field assistant drowned when their raft burst. I went on to study geology as he had, and found that I shared his love of the remote spaces in Alaska.

It is the love of field work that gets most geologists hooked. I always look forward to going to the field, even though it means time away from my husband, Kelly, and our little girl, Caitlin. This was the first day of the season for me. I was the lead geologist on a new project to assess the mineral resource potential of the Sleetmute quadrangle.

To assess the mineral resource potential of an area, field data is collected by a team of geologists and geochemists. The geologists usually walk ridges collecting bedrock data, and the geochemists work primarily in the creek bottoms collecting sediment samples. In

Alaska, the work is often helicopter-supported. The pilot hops back and forth from ridge to creek, moving workers to different parts of the study area, which in this case was the Buckstock Mountains (part of the Kuskokwim Mountains), about thirty miles southeast of Aniak. We had contracted four weeks of helicopter this season to be split fifty-fifty between the geochemical crew and the geologic crew. Although I was scheduled for the second half of the four weeks, the lead geochemist invited me to join him earlier to get a few days more ridge coverage.

We were all eager to get to work that day. We boarded the helicopter and left Aniak in relatively clear weather, but the mountains were cloudy and foggy—enough so that the 800-foot knob I got off on was barely visible. I had planned a traverse on the top of the ridge above the knob, but the clouds negated our reaching that site. We had expected the ceiling to lift by mid-morning. Because I was actually bumming rides from the geochem crew and felt like I was taking up their helicopter time, I said, "Just let me off there and I'll walk up the ridge."

It is not USGS policy to work alone, but we occasionally do so. I have always enjoyed wilderness solitude, and I had no qualms about being alone that foggy morning. In fact, I felt great! We were just beginning this study and I was well equipped for the day out, wearing warm clothes, leather boots, and my eye-catching bright orange field vest, which has numerous pockets for tools and instruments. I carried a map and geologic hammer in my hands; everything else that I might need during the day was in my pack, including extra sample bags, extra clothing, and lunch. I carry a rifle, butt-up in the left ski slot of my pack. My radio, a hand-held walkie-talkie, resides in the right outside pocket. Following standard procedure, when the helicopter pilot took off, we spoke by radio to make sure contact was good.

I looked at my watch. It was about 8:30 A.M. I said, "Give me a call at noon."

The pilot and geochemists would be working only about five miles away, so I felt confident that I could reach them by radio. I started my work. It was rather quiet. When I work alone, I keep my ears open and am mindful of wildlife, even though my focus is on the rocks.

The surrounding country was rolling hills, 1,000 to 1,500 feet in elevation. Open tundra with scattered patches of birch and alder brush covered a third to half of the lower slopes; the ridges were open. There were no outcrops but enough broken rock pieces so that I could occupy myself for a while.

This was my first time in this particular part of the study area, and I was baffled by the rocks that I saw. I didn't understand what unit they belonged to. They weren't the familiar Kuskokwim Group that I was used to, so I spent a good hour poking around the initial drop site.

I wasn't making much noise other than knocking rocks with my hammer. I lined the rocks up to label and describe. I spent an hour on the rocky knob. It was still and quiet, and I didn't hear or see anything during that time. After finishing my station notes, I packed up my rocks and prepared to move on. Before leaving, I peed.

I angled toward the ridge, which I could not yet see through the fog, but I had the map. The map clearly showed a draw between my knob and the ridge I planned to traverse (about a quarter of a mile apart). Although it would have been quicker to go straight up the side of the ridge from the draw, I would potentially miss some bedrock exposure. I decided to angle west to hit the ridge crest at a lower elevation.

I started down the draw to determine where to cross to the main ridge. I zigzagged because it was easier to pick up rock samples and see more exposure. There were some interesting pieces of felsic dike that I was tracing out. I got to the bottom of the draw and encountered a large blueberry patch. The berries were extraordinarily large and sweet. Not only was it a good year for berries, but they were also at the absolute perfect ripeness. I paused for five minutes picking and eating berries. It was still very foggy but starting to clear. *Golly, this is a perfect place for a black bear. I wonder where they are?*

After that I looked up and discovered a game trail along the hillside. But because I was trying to get onto the ridge crest, I crossed through brush bypassing the game trail, and I hit the main ridge. I climbed up the moderately steep ridge, and about one hundred feet above the last of the brush, I paused to catch my breath. I put my hands on my hips, inhaled and exhaled vigorously, and turned around to survey the scene.

As I looked down on the knob about 9:30, I saw a black bear where the helicopter had dropped me. I thought, *Hmmm . . . I didn't hear anything and I was just there a short while ago.*

My immediate notion anytime I see a bear is to radio the pilot. I tried to reach the pilot, but didn't get a response. However, I felt no threat at that point because I have seen many bears a quarter of a mile away. Being very cautious, I stood and watched him for a few minutes. After pausing momentarily, the bear started moving down into the draw where I had crossed. It was zigzagging a bit. *Wait a minute. I zigzagged as I was pounding rocks; it looks like he's tracing my steps. What's going on?* I took it as a red flag.

I tried the radio again, but I couldn't reach anyone. *It should be working because we tested it.* I tried getting the repeater channel. That failed also. *That's odd.*

I continued watching the bear. It reached the draw. *Good. The bear's going to find those blueberries and head off down the other way.* But the bear stopped at the same place where I had picked berries, and it stood up and looked around, sniffing in my direction. Then it dropped down and headed along the path that I had taken. *Uh, oh. Something's up.*

I tried the radio again, but I still couldn't get anyone. The bear was getting close enough that I felt threatened and concerned. I tried to think about what I should do.

It was as if I were trying to draw lines in the sand. I figured I'd leave my thirty-pound pack and climb farther up the ridge; that way if the bear was following me, he'd be distracted by my pack and I'd have some space. I'd made and packed a salmon sandwich wrapped in wax paper that morning. It was zippered inside the pack right on top. I turned the pack sandwich side-up. Since bears can smell through plastic, the wax paper offered even less barrier.

Leaving the hammer and map, I took the radio and extra ammunition. I normally never leave my map, but frankly I was frightened. My plan was to climb another two hundred feet up the ridge and watch what happens. *That way I'll have a good view, but lots of space.*

The bear was out of sight now. I knew that the game trail went up the side hill. *If the bear chooses the game trail, I won't be so concerned, but if the bear comes out where I came out, I'll really be concerned because then I'll know it's following me and my scent.* It was still foggy though clearing where I waited on the ridge. I had not chambered a round. I had the radio in my hand as I watched. Sure enough, the bear came out exactly where I had.

My pack was about one hundred feet above the brush, and I was another two hundred feet up. The bear walked very purposefully, not fast, up to about five feet from the pack. It stopped. It did not touch the pack; it did not go near it. The bear looked right at me. Then it quickly moved to my right. I lost sight of it.

This bear must be trying to circle behind me. My good friend Cynthia Dusel-Bacon had lost her arms to a bear just like this one. She and I shared identical experiences, except I had a weapon. She had told me the bear that attacked her had run around to ambush her from behind. And the previous summer another black bear used this technique to stalk four of us simultaneously. I thought, *If that's what this bear is doing, I'm going to climb as fast as I can and try to keep above it.* I felt that being higher than it was a statement of control. It made me feel better.

I still had the radio in one hand and the rifle in the other hand. At that point I chambered a round. I climbed the ridge very fast. It was a significant slope, but the adrenaline was pumping, and I progressed more quickly than normal. A flood of feelings and thoughts filled me. I said out loud, "Oh, God. Oh, God. Oh, God . . . "the verbalized part of my otherwise silent prayer. At the same time my wisecracking side said, "How much hospital time is this going to be?"

I'm here. I'm alone. I have to deal with this. There's nobody around to help. You've got to get yourself out of this situation, and nobody else is going to come to your rescue.

I became more aware of what was going on around me. My senses tuned up. Instinct told me, *Turn here. Turn now.* And I yielded to it. Normally I'm a cerebral scientist, and am reluctant to recognize those feelings, but now I followed my instincts. I walked across the ridge from west to east. I tried another call on the radio and got nothing. I stopped, and that's when I saw the bear. I literally flung the radio aside because I wanted to have my hands free for the gun—and there was no time to put the radio in my back vest pocket. I walked farther across the ridge until I was directly above the bear. It was an aggressive posture on my part.

We looked at one another one hundred feet apart. I have dogs and horses and am used to speaking in commanding tones. I yelled in my deepest, gruffest voice, "Get outta here!"

The bear looked at me and shook its head laterally. It didn't clack its teeth together. It didn't slather. After shaking its head, it continued its purposeful walk toward me.

I aimed at the bear's nose. At the moment before pulling the trigger—perhaps what made me shoot—I thought of my daughter Caitlin, and I thought of my friend Cynthia who had been attacked by a black bear. I knew that the bear could be on me at any moment. I had control of the situation and I didn't want to lose control by letting the bear charge. I pulled the trigger, but I did not hear the shot. As soon as I pulled the trigger, the bear went down, "*fwump.*" And then I heard the echo. It took me by surprise that the bear dropped. I remember pausing, taking the gun away from my shoulder, and thinking in a surprised way, *This thing worked.* Then I shot again.

When the bear was first hit, it was facing me and then it fell sideways and diagonally with its legs pointing downhill and its head up. On the second shot I aimed at the top of the neck, which was closest to me. The bear was still twitching. I walked forward a few feet and shot twice more. By that time I was shaking so badly that the last two shots kicked up tundra, missing the bear completely.

I was so adrenaline-charged and frightened at that point that I didn't want to go over to the bear. I envisioned the bear getting up, the way the robot in the *Terminator* movie keeps getting up. This was an odd sensation. I kept looking at the bear and expecting it to get up.

It was 10:00 A.M., maybe thirty minutes since I'd first seen the bear. I still had one round in the magazine, none in the chamber. I carry a .30-06 loaded with five rounds. I had hit the bear with two rounds and two went into the tundra. I was shaking badly. I looked for my radio. I regretted having flung it in the heat of the situation because it took me a while to find it. The black case was hard to spot in the tundra, but I finally stumbled across it. I tried calling repeatedly and couldn't get anyone. I finally told myself, "Get a grip here. You're in control. Do something." So I went downslope to get my pack.

Having to retrieve my pack took me out of view of the bear. I started for my pack but retraced my steps several times to reassure myself that the bear was still there (*Terminator* again). I got my pack and immediately walked to a point where I could again check on the bear. He was still there, which somehow surprised me.

I called several more times on the radio without success. At length I climbed higher to get a straighter transmission. I spotted an outcrop and was relieved because it gave me something to do, to take my mind off the incident.

If there had been any place to hide, I would have because I felt so vulnerable. I was plagued with the thought that bears were all around me. I kept wondering, *Do I have enough ammunition?* I did have extra ammunition in my pack, but I had the overwhelming fear of being pursued by more bears and that I would run out. I didn't see any other wildlife, but that didn't reduce my fear.

I went over and measured the strike and dip of a sandstone bed, knocked open a piece, and took a sample. It calmed me to be doing something familiar and comfortable. (I kept wondering what caused the bear to act the way it had. It followed me, and even after I vocally made my presence known to it, it kept coming. I was not menstruating. I believe the animal sought me as food.)

I moved another twenty feet up the ridge and finally reached the pilot. Even though we have our own USGS frequency, we've been trained to be careful about what we transmit, not wanting any messages to be misconstrued. Transmissions, particularly about killing animals, are sensitive.

I proceeded with, "Jim, Jim. I need you."

"Oh," he responded, "you need a move."

"No, I had to deal with a bear."

"You had to deal with a bear?" He was obviously confused.

Forgetting protocol, I said, "I . . . shot . . . a . . . bear."

"I'll be right there."

He didn't know if I'd been hurt, so he beelined it. When he landed, he got out with the blades still turning. He could see me standing. He had seen the bear, and he was looking for blood on me. I broke down in tears.

After turning the engines off, he kindly, patiently let me talk and cry and talk. Then he said, "Let's go look at the bear." He was thinking straight and threw a rock at the animal. I hadn't even thought to do that. The bear was definitely dead, so we went down to see it.

I stroked the bear's head. I cried. It was the only animal that I had ever killed. It hurt me deeply, but I was so darn scared when the bear was stalking me that I had no other choice.

The pilot was very gentle, allowing me to blather on, and go over the whole scenario twice. I wanted to take a picture, but I'd left my camera with my pack at the helicopter. We walked back to the ship, retrieved it, and photographed the bear.

We needed help to get the bear to the helicopter, so we flew down to the geochemists to tell them what had happened. John Gray and Peter Theodorakos flew back up to the ridge with us. We estimated the sow's live weight at 175 pounds. She had a nice coat and wasn't thin. We gutted and dragged her to the helicopter and strapped her on the skid.

We were about thirty minutes from Aniak by helicopter. We dropped the others to continue work while the pilot and I took the bear to Aniak. I had the notion that I would go back out to work that afternoon. Pointing out how badly I was shaking, the pilot asked, "Are you crazy?"

From the Aniak airport I phoned the local protection officer to report what had happened. I always purchase a hunting license before going into the field because you never know what will happen. The officer asked me if I had a license, to which I replied affirmatively. He said, "You could just take the bear on your license."

I pointed out that I had flown in a helicopter, which is in violation of fair chase regulations. He told me that I needed to skin it and file a report that he would drop by later that day. Next I called the Benders, who run the bed and breakfast where we were staying. They helped me get the bear back to their place, where we removed the hide and skull. A local family who depend on game gladly accepted the bear carcass. I've always felt good that the meat wasn't wasted.

As I was recovering my nerve, I thought a lot about my friend Cynthia. I met her in 1975 when I cooked for Helen Foster's camp where Cynthia Dusel was serving as field assistant. I was a sophomore undergraduate interested in veterinary medicine. Watching people going out every day hiking, I realized that geologic work was something that I might like to do. Cynthia and I developed a close relationship that summer. I was in "camp" most of the day while she was out in the field, but we'd often run together in the evening. We'd discuss the events of the day, especially the frustrations.

During the summer of 1977, I was cooking for another camp in the Brooks Range when we heard of Cynthia's accident over the radio. As soon as the field season was over, I returned to California and visited Cynthia at the hospital. Good ol' Cynthia. As I walked into the hospital room wondering what on earth to say, she took charge. "How was your summer?" It relaxed the situation. Even though Cynthia and I are separated by a good distance, we maintain a close friendship.

I came away with two things from this incident that have affected my life: 1) I have learned to rely on my instincts. We all have these instincts, but I have not necessarily been listening to them. I do now. 2) There are things we can change; and there are things that we cannot change. Appreciate what is good; deal with what is bad; but don't expect to have control over events in your life.

AFTERWARD

Prior to Cynthia's attack there was a less formal policy on weapons: you could carry one if your project chief requested it, but you didn't necessarily receive training in its use. Now any Alaskan field worker who wants to carry a gun receives training and is provided a weapon and plenty of ammunition for practice.

By the time I came on full time with the Geological Survey, it was standard procedure to take a gun-training course before going out into the field. In our Anchorage office Steve Nelson teaches the class. He has experience as a hunter and woodsman. He brings to the course the technical aspects of shooting, but also he talks about bear behavior.

The course that he has been teaching for a number of years emphasizes bear scenarios. One of the training techniques he developed is to use three bear targets placed at successively closer intervals. This exercise simulates a charge situation and the adrenaline involved. Your gun is left on the shooting table pointing down range with nothing in the chamber. You run up to the weapon, pick it up, chamber a round, and shoot at the three targets, starting with the farthest and ending with the closest.

Because I had been trained using bear targets, aiming at the bear's nose came naturally to me. The shot went in just shy of the nose, entering the bear's neck. The bullet exited through the spine, breaking the animal's neck (using a 180-grain Nosler partition bullet, which Steve had recommended).

It's important to have a zone of comfort in training. If the bear is within twenty-five yards, it can be on you within seconds. That's the distance we've worked with in practice, so it was natural for me to draw the line and decide to shoot from about seventy feet. After my incident Steve altered one aspect of training. In practice I was used to seeing the bear keep coming. However, when I shot the bear, dropping it with one shot, I was somewhat confused about what to do next. Steve incorporated that response and taught students to keep shooting after the animal drops.

Cynthia Dusel-Bacon's story is chronicled in her own words in *Alaska Bear Tales* by the author.

See Appendix 7

Marti Miller killed a black bear with a single bullet, but Will Atkinson was not armed when he met a black bear at a resort.

Swim for Life

by Will Atkinson

*"Because I was a little taller than the bear, I stood on the
bottom with my head above the water. "*

I read about Will Atkinson in the newspaper in August
1994, in an unusual story of how he punched out a black
bear. He invited me to his place to hear the story. When I
saw him, I could see how he could take on a black bear:
This blue-eyed husky was 6-feet-4-inches tall and tipped
the scales at 260 pounds.

He showed me a video aired by an Edmonton, Alberta,
television station. The focus of the TV footage was to
provide information on avoiding a bear mauling. It was
interesting that one of the tips given by the experts was to
"play dead if a black bear attacks." Contrary to all I've
learned about black bears, playing dead is the worst
advice you can give someone.

Will had a close encounter in which he chose activity
rather than passivity. His story has good information about
bears habituating themselves to man and advice on avoiding bear maulings.

Every summer for the last four or five years I've driven
the Alaska Highway. I have relatives along the highway
stretching from British Columbia to Utah, and I visit them.

I nearly always stop at Liard Hot Springs on the way down and on the way back.

On 6 August 1994 in the late afternoon, I stopped at Liard on my way south. My twenty-three-year-old nephew, Kevin Kovach, and I were going to Boise, Idaho, where my folks live. From there Kevin planned to fly to Oklahoma to visit his family. We were looking forward to enjoying the hot pools at Liard. It's a popular spot along the Alaska Highway and boasts two hot spring pools. The Alpha pool reaches temperatures of 116 degrees. The Beta pool is hotter with temperatures of 124 degrees.

Liard Hot Springs campground encompasses several heavily wooded acres and can accommodate 1,500 patrons. The campsites range from primitive fire rings to modern sites that have electricity. A circular road exits the parking lot and snakes several hundred yards into the woods, with individual camp spots dotting the way. Four or five year-round rangers are employed, and student rangers conduct research projects in the summer. No firearms are allowed in the park. Near the entrance is a large parking lot, camp buildings, and a gift shop. A boardwalk leading to the pools beckons from the edge of the parking lot.

Campground garbage cans are not the bear-proof ones, which many state parks have, but rather regular garbage cans. We were amazed by the huge amount of garbage at the camp, which becomes quite an attractant for a large number of local bears.

A few days before our arrival a woman had had an encounter with a bear. She had been warned about approaching too closely; nevertheless she took a picture of the animal as it fed on highbush cranberries. The bear reacted by standing on its hind legs, placing its front paws on the woman's shoulders, and staring her in the eye.

The woman froze. The bear dropped to all fours, and ambled off into the bushes. In the process it cut her upper shoulders and her breast and tore off her clothes.

The woman was startled, but she was all right. The woman's encounter seemed unusual, but we harbored no presentiment of having problems with bears. I've seen lots of bears over the years.

Kevin and I arrived at the hot springs anticipating a leisurely time. We grabbed our towels and walked toward the springs in our trunks and bare feet. We reached the elevated boardwalk that crosses a swamp prior to reaching the first hot springs. There were about fifteen of us, your basic tourist group carrying camcorders and cameras. Near our group was a turn-out for resting or eating.

As we reached the eating area, we saw a bear eating from a garbage can. Several people took pictures. Within minutes the bear started chasing people down the boardwalk toward the parking place. We thought it wise to retreat. Somebody returned to the campground to get a ranger. Shortly thereafter a young college girl dressed in a ranger uniform appeared. She didn't know much about bears and announced that they were going to close the park.

People didn't want to leave the park and got upset. Meanwhile, others appeared from the upper hot springs and waited to get past the bear. Under normal conditions a bear leaves the boardwalk, goes into the berry bushes and eats berries, and gives the campers peace of mind. A year-round park ranger arrived and announced, "We're not going to close the park. Everybody back off and we'll shoo the bear into the bushes," which they did.

We went on to the lower hot springs and spent an hour and a half there. Although we did hear some thrashing in the bushes, there was no problem. We then went to the waterfall, which was halfway to the upper hot springs. The waterfall comes out of the side of the mountain and runs through a garden. We enjoyed the view, then walked to the upper hot springs. As we approached, we heard people making noise. We reached the upper pool and discovered about eighteen people and a few children. Eight people were getting out to go to the parking lot.

The boardwalk is U-shaped around the pool, with a set of stairs descending into the water on either end. It was about this time that same bear we'd seen earlier came out of the woods and got onto the boardwalk. He was a large black bear, about three hundred pounds, but he had a round face and a brown crown all the way down his back, which are unusual features for a black bear.

We tried to keep the bear busy so someone could get the kids out of the pool and started toward the parking lot. Steve, one of the Canadians, yelled, "Try to keep the bear there so he won't go after the kids." That lasted a minute, and then we were in trouble. The bear wouldn't stop. Everybody hollered for the kids to go down the trail, and they did.

We brought up the tail end of the group headed for the parking lot. An Alaska State Trooper and his wife were behind Kevin and me, with two men from Alberta in front of us. Suddenly the bear turned toward one of the Albertans and, like a sheep dog, cut off our group of six from the others. The Albertan grabbed a switch to try to fend off the bear (we didn't know until later that the bear swiped him in the arm and drew a little blood, mostly scratches). The bear was upset and aggressive. He came closer, forcing us off the boardwalk. The Albertans tried to stop the bear from coming for all of us.

It was too fast, and we didn't have any weapons. Kevin threw a pop can at the bear to divert him. Thinking I could dive into the pool and get out of there, I got up on the railing. Kevin, the state patrolman, and his wife tried to get by the bear. Although concerned, they continued videotaping the event.

I stepped down into the water, and the Albertans jumped up and over the railing and into the water with me. The bear jumped into the water behind us. Kevin had jumped onto the railing and was going to jump onto the bear if it attacked me. We swam across the pool with the bear behind us. Reaching the far side, we got out of the water.

I went around behind and started walking through the woods. Evidently the crunching noises in the brush alerted the bear, because it came after me. I ran all the way around the trees. Thinking I could make the changing shed, I ran as fast as I could. With the bear gaining on me, I could see it was fruitless and jumped back into the water. I hoped that the pool's heat would keep the bear out. But it didn't.

He was a little behind me. Everybody was yelling at me. I got to the steps just as the bear got there. As I grabbed onto the right railing, he grabbed the left one. Because I was a little taller than the bear, I stood on the bottom with my head above the water. The bear reached its left paw out for a railing, balancing itself and looking at me. Luckily he was off balance or he would have swiped me with one of his big paws.

He came at me with his teeth clacking together. He wanted to bite me.

I yelled and growled at him. Then I hit him in the nose with my right fist. It was a moderate blow to the front of the nose. He backed off a bit. I have bailed out of KC-135s in the Air Force, but that didn't scare me half as badly as this. I waded through the water for the steps, and he shot through under the railing onto the stairs and cut me off from the boardwalk.

He came for me again. I stuck my fingers in his nose and twisted it. He yipped a couple of big yips and yipped to the top of the steps. Exhausted, I yelled, "Come on you guys. Do something!" I'd swum the length of the pool in that hot water twice, and my heart was beating so hard I thought I'd have a heart attack.

Kevin and an Albertan picked up a wooden park bench and launched it at the bear. It was about ten feet long, made of two-by-sixes, and weighed around eighty pounds. The bench hit the bear in the side of the head. He yipped, tucked his little tail down, and scooted off into the woods behind the changing shed and sat down. I staggered out of the water. The Alaska State Trooper came around the side; his wife stayed way over on the other side and continued filming. Unable to get my breath, I sat down on the bench. I was exhausted.

After a minute and a half the bear started toward us through the woods. I stood up and walked slowly with the state patrolman's wife around the horseshoe walkway. We stopped at the waterfall stream for cold water, then went to the parking lot.

Kevin and the two Albertans picked up the bench and walked behind us. Every time they picked up the bench, the bear sat down. When they put the bench down, the bear got up and followed. They did this two or three times. They were finally able to get enough distance between them and the bear so they could walk to the lower pool.

We could hear the bear thrashing in the bushes by the upper pool.

It was a dangerous situation. We were worried because there were a lot of kids in the big lower pool. There were no adults around and the bear could have come out of the woods and eaten a couple of kids. Twenty minutes later the rangers showed up with rifles. They walked to the upper pool and within the hour shot the bear.

Three hours later we were sharing our experience in the parking lot with the crowd of people who had witnessed it, letting the air out. The rangers brought the bear out in a wheelbarrow, covered with a yellow rubberized tarp. All we could see were big bear paws hanging out the side.

Kevin took a picture of the bear in the wheelbarrow. The bear was in good shape. He didn't look dangerous; he looked like a teddy bear.

Even though that was the climax of the story, it had a funny ending. Kevin and I continued on to Muir Park fifty miles down the road for dinner. Everybody was talking about the big bear attack. We told them it was us, and they were interested in our story.

We drove south and visited my folks in Boise. Kevin flew on to Oklahoma, where we rendezvoused later and drove back up. Stopping at a little restaurant just north of Prince George, British Columbia, we overheard four elderly people who had driven the Alcan. They were talking about the big bear attack at Liard Hot Springs, and about a nineteen-year-old kid who had warded off bears and saved a bunch of kids.

Twenty minutes went by before we realized they were talking about our bear attack. There was no nineteen-year-old kid and no bunch of kids involved. As we traveled north, we heard other stories that had been greatly exaggerated or misstated.

When Kevin and I stopped at Liard Hot Springs for a day and a half, I had another bear encounter. I was looking at the sign describing the park and payment when a woman shouted, "Hey, mister, who's your partner?"

I turned around and a huge black bear was standing right behind me. I scooted over to the campground, and the bear moseyed right on by me on the boardwalk. He wasn't bothering anybody, just looking for berry bushes.

An Edmonton television station aired video footage taken by a Michigan tourist during my attack. The announcer told of the attack at Liard Hot Springs Provincial Park, close to the B.C.-Yukon border. An expert at John Jansen Nature Center had seen it and said that the three-hundred-pound black bear could easily drown a man. Then the station offered advice on how NOT to handle a wild bear:

1. Back off slowly.

2. Find shelter.

3. If the bear is closing in and you have no other option, make noise and act aggressively toward it.

4. If the bear pursues you, drop to the ground, cover your neck, and play dead.

Will concluded, "All I have to say is if I had played dead with that bear, I'd be dead."

Will Atkinson did not have a weapon, but John Coogle did. And the weapon saved his life.

Cool-headed Coogle

by Larry Kaniut

*He immediately took several steps backward
while shouting a warning to the bears.*

John Coogle navigated Ship Creek alone. His is one
of the most incredible stories I have ever heard regarding a close call between man and bear. The tale came
my way in early fall in the 1980s. The Anchorage Daily
News carried a story by Howard Weaver about
Anchoragite John Coogle and some bears he had trouble
with near Arctic Valley. The saga climaxed moments after
John's initial shot.

A blast reverberated up the canyon, thundering off
the timber-sided walls. Adrenaline pulsed through the
lone hunter's veins, riveting his attention to the business
at hand. Momentarily shaken by the gun's roar breaking
the morning's solitude, his energy focused on his survival. Before the echo of his shot died away, he realized
he was in trouble. He had just dropped one of two brown-
grizzly bears. The other fled. Even as the canyon sounds
returned to normal, another pair of brown-grizzlies rose
to face him.

A thousand thoughts flashed through his mind. How
could he have known that these four bears only moments
before had been feeding on a moose carcass? He had
surprised them, and they chose to fight for their cache.

Even though the hunter, John Coogle, wasn't looking for a fight, he was confident in his shooting ability. He had spent countless hours afield in Florida hunting white-tailed deer with dogs, which provided fast action as the rocketing deer crashed through the timber.

Now here he was on an Alaska moose-hunt-turned-survival-outing. Earlier that morning he'd left the lights of Anchorage behind and driven in the predawn darkness the few odd miles to the Arctic Valley ski area. John had eagerly anticipated a successful moose hunt. He had left his rig and hit the trail toward Ship Creek.

It was 20 August, the first day of moose season. In a few short weeks a kaleidoscopic landscape, Disney-fied in living color, would capture the grandeur of Alaska in the fall. Jack Frost's autograph would grace the countryside. A yellow patchwork, from streamside cottonwoods on the valley floor and aspen groves higher on the crimson-fired hillside, would polka dot this dale. Green-black tongues of evergreen would lick their way up the alder-pocketed slopes. Alder leaves would shrivel in the cold and meta-morphose from sticky green to crinkled brown. A blend of highbush cranberries and dying cottonwood vanes would fragrance the valley. Willow-bordered beaver ponds would be layered with a skim of thin ice, and Old Man Winter's white head and silver beard would be but a whisper away.

But at the moment John Coogle's mind was occupied with thoughts of moose meat on winter's table. He hastily thumped along the trail, his goal the public hunting ground that lay beyond the military reservation he was crossing. Early on, the ghostly dawn shrouded the woods and pre-vented him from discerning details, but as he neared his hunting area and the light became better and the details became clearer, he had a sharper eye for moose, know-ing they inhabited the environs. Rounding a corner, Coogle came face-to-face with two brown-grizzlies. He im-mediately took several steps backward while shouting a warning to the bears and thinking, *This is it* !

His hunting experience tempered his action; he responded in a heartbeat. He shouldered his scoped Ruger model 77. It was chambered in .338 Winchester Magnum. His bolt-action rifle held four rounds, one in the chamber and three in the magazine. The 250-grain Nosler bullets were designed to mushroom on impact for greatest effect.

When he'd initially encountered the two bears, his first shot had dispatched one while the other bear had run away. He had instinctively chambered a second round. But now he was faced with two additional bears. One stood up.

With two bears in his face and three bullets in his weapon, John fired. His second bullet ripped into the standing animal's chest. The other bear charged. John bolted a third shell home and hammered his shot into the beast's shoulder, turning it. But its mate was still coming. John found its head in his rifle scope and launched his final bullet. The bear was four steps distant when the Nosler took him through the skull and jellied its brain, dropping the final curtain on the party. John reloaded and dispatched the shoulder-shot animal.

Four bears . . . five bullets . . . three dead animals . . . one missing in action. Total time elapsed: twelve seconds. John's knees turned to jelly. How many men have faced four alarmed brown-grizzlies (three of which charged), cradling a weapon with four bullets, and survived the episode?

Quick thinking coupled with instant action (based on extensive experience) prevented serious consequences to John Coogle. And one must wonder about God's part in providing protection in this drama.

Hunters have the advantage of being armed in the field; recreational hikers like Larry and Lois Bond are usually unarmed.

Saved by Prayer

by Larry K. Bond

*"Out of the corner of my eye I could see the bear's
open jaws a few inches from my face."*

*I first learned of Larry and Lois Bond while reading an
article in the* Anchorage Times *20 August 1991. They were
only a few miles from our family's home in Anchorage when
they had an unpleasant run-in with three bears, and they
weren't mama, papa, and baby. Along with his account of
a beary scary encounter with a mama grizzly, Larry sent a
letter of explanation.*

*In the letter he wrote, "We had spent a week vacation-
ing in Alaska: Matanuska Valley, Denali Park, all the way
to Wonder Lake, then on the Kenai. Stayed with friends,
Jerry and Carolyn Purser of Wasilla. . . . This was our last
full day in Alaska before heading back to Logan, Utah."*

Here is Larry's story from his journal.

Whenever I travel, I carry a spiral notebook to keep
journal notes. Because my hands were bandaged in the
hospital, I had Lois do most of the writing. When I got
home, I wrote my journal on the computer; I had a
removable cast on my left hand.

A number of friends have expressed a desire to read
the portion of my journal dealing with our encounter with
a grizzly bear. They were interested in the spiritual aspects of the incident. I have extracted entries from my

journal: the first two days in their entirety with minor modifications later as I was able to write and think better.

This account, along with my thoughts and feelings, represents the facts as I remember them. I give my Heavenly Father credit for saving my life and do not write this as entertainment reading. I sincerely pray that those who read this will do so with reverence for God, and be strengthened in their belief that we are His children, and that He does watch over us and answers our humble petitions.

Monday 19 August 1991

We spent the night sleeping in our rented station wagon in the parking area just a few miles east of Beluga Point. It was clear and beautiful when we got up this morning. We looked for whales but didn't spot any so we drove west to Beluga Point, about ten to fifteen miles southeast of Anchorage, Alaska. We stopped two or three miles closer to Anchorage at McHugh Creek picnic area. Since the sky was clear, we decided to hike up Potter Trail to see if we could get a good view of Mt. McKinley, North America's highest landmark located 125 miles north of Anchorage. The well-maintained trail included wooden bridges over wet areas.

A mile and a half up the trail we rounded a corner and saw a grizzly sow and her cubs, fifty to sixty feet away and walking downtrail in our direction. There was an incline in the trail, and I saw them through the branches. One of the cubs was in front of its mother and the other was alongside. I think they might have been yearlings.

Everything happened so fast. I said, "Bear!" to Lois, who was walking behind me. We turned, and because there were branches blocking the view, we thought we could get into the brush and away without their noticing us. We started to run. The next thing I knew, I was on my knees. I have knelt in prayer by my bed daily since I first learned to talk. Without even thinking, I said, "Heavenly Father, please help me." Out of the corner of my eye I could see the bear's open jaws a few inches from my face. I knew I was in trouble.

I think I remember a growl. All of this happened in a split second. I felt impelled to get down on my stomach and lie still. Almost simultaneously I felt her bite me on the right side of my head. Whether she had slapped me with her paws or bitten me before that, I don't know. I remember that I didn't want my face scarred and chose to lie on my stomach with my face in the grass and brush. I guess this is how the bottom third of my front tooth got broken off. I put my hands on the back of my neck and head.

Because of the direction of the claw marks on the top and back of my head, I think that I actually pulled my head out of her mouth as I went facedown on the ground. Otherwise, there would probably have been more damage to the right side of my head than the ripping of the cheek, ear, and surrounding area. Next, it seemed as if she shook me like a dog does when it has a rag in its mouth. I felt pain in my right hand and then felt her bite my left hand. That bite shattered my ring finger. It was painful, but I never moved or yelled. Lois said later that I made a sound, but it wasn't loud.

I offered another silent prayer: *Heavenly Father, please send the bear away.* It was as if I had been told what to pray. I repeated it in the same breath and the bear stopped biting me immediately. She never bit or clawed me after that. Knowing to lie down on my stomach and cover my neck with my hands was undoubtedly a direct answer to the first prayer. I don't remember ever being told to lie down and play dead during a bear attack, but that's what I did.

During the attack there was never any time that I felt my life would be lost or that I would be crippled or disfigured. Everything seemed to happen at natural speed and my life did not flash before me. After the bear stopped biting me, I could hear Lois calling my name, but I remained perfectly still—for all I knew, the bear could have been saying grace over her food. I wanted the bear to get far enough away that any noise or motion would not attract her attention again.

After about a minute I stood up and walked ten to fifteen feet to where Lois was standing on the trail. Even with blood in my eyes I could see a big hole on the back of my right hand. My left hand was in bad shape, with a big hole on the back. The back of the hand near the knuckles must have swollen an inch high, and the ring finger was broken and bent in an S shape and pointed to the left. I asked Lois to wipe the blood out of my eyes with my handkerchief, then we started walking back to the car.

I carried my camera in my ripped and bloody right hand. After walking a ways I asked Lois, "Could you carry my camera for me?" Since she was walking on my left, she had not noticed me carrying it. She was calm and handled the situation admirably.

We met a Japanese couple about halfway down the trail. When Lois told them a bear had attacked me, their eyes got big and they followed us. The trail didn't seem any longer going down than going up. I could have walked a lot farther had it been necessary, but I was glad to get to the car.

We drove about fifteen minutes to the first highway exit and stopped at a restaurant to get directions to the hospital. David Hansen was coming out of the restaurant when Lois told him about our need for medical attention. He works for IBM and happened to have the day off. He volunteered to take us to the hospital.

He suggested that I ride with him and that Lois follow. Despite my pain, my thinking was clear and I got a large plastic bag out of our car to put on the seat of his van to keep it from getting bloody, although I was not dripping blood. He kept Lois in his sight while we drove three miles to Providence Hospital. We arrived about 10:00 A.M.

I walked into the emergency room, where they had me lie down on a table. A nurse named Tricia Fyfe was assigned to me. They gave me a tetanus shot and something to ease the pain. They asked if we had reported this to any authorities and we said no. A short while later three rangers arrived to take our report (we learned later that a ranger had gone back a day or so after the incident and found my glasses and cap at the attack scene a mile and a half from the parking lot).

One of them, Brian Larsen, remained behind and asked if we were LDS (Latter-Day Saints, commonly referred to as Mormons). We said yes. He contacted members of our church here in Anchorage, some of whom spent time with us the rest of the day.

We believe in blessings as taught in James 5:14 of the *Holy Bible*. We were asked if we wanted a blessing. We did, and I asked that Lois be given the first blessing. Among other things, my blessing included a promise that the doctor's hands would be guided as he worked on me. Then I relaxed and must have fallen asleep.

A short while later Dixie Lucas from the Thirteenth Ward (*ward* is a congregation in our church) arrived to see what she could do to help. She stayed most of the day. Although Dr. George Siegfried, a plastic surgeon, was in the hospital, he was busy. They wanted to wait for him because of my face.

I waited in the emergency room for nearly five hours before Dr. Hummer, the anesthesiologist, prepared me for surgery. I was in surgery for four hours, and it was 9:00 P.M. before I woke up. I was told it took about two hundred stitches to patch up my head and my finger. Most were to fix my face and head. My right ear canal was broken where it enters the skull. There was a long rip in front of my right ear, and two rips in the ear itself. The long rip behind the ear ran from the ear lobe upward nearly to the curve of my head and was stapled with wire staples, as was a shorter rip in the back of my head. There were several long scratches across the back and top of my head. However, most were not deep enough to require stitches.

The bear had bitten all the way through my ring finger, next to the big knuckle, shattering it and making it difficult to set. Siegfried had to make an incision about 1½ inches long to set the finger, then put in two 0.028-gauge pins to stabilize it; one pin was 2½ inches long and the other 1½. He left all the broken pieces there held together by the flesh. For some reason I had left my ring at home, which was probably a good thing. If the ring had been smashed, it could have cut off circulation, and I would have likely lost the finger.

My left arm is in a protective cast to the elbow, to protect my finger. The doctor did not sew up the holes in the backs of my hands where the tooth went through the underside of my finger, the flabby portion on the outside under my right armpit, nor the hole in my back. The medical staff packed these with gauze soaked in Betadine solution but left them open so they could drain and not become infected.

My Pendleton shirt was ripped to shreds in the back and arms, but miraculously there was little more than abrasions on my back, except for one deep puncture. The upper portion of my right arm is black and blue. I have a 1½-inch slit in the outside flabby portion underneath my arm, and the upper right arm of my jacket and shirt are ripped. In the center of the arm slit is a deep puncture that the doctor will treat for several days before stitching. There are a couple of long, wide scratches made by a tooth in my right shoulder.

I learned two weeks after getting home that I have three claw marks about two inches apart on my upper back. Since my underclothes were not torn, these scratches did not draw blood. They were abrasions (they were visible for several months).

When I was recovering from surgery, Pete Glenn, my niece's husband, called from Ogden about 9:30 P.M. My mother and LeAnn, one of our daughters, were in Odgen, Utah, helping Shannon Glenn, who had recently had surgery. They had heard the report about us on television before I was even out of recovery. Lois had wanted to wait to call home and inform the family of our misadventure until I came from surgery so she'd know how I was doing. It was unfortunate that the family had to first hear about our accident over the television.

Lois stayed behind the hospital in Providence House, a sort of dormitory with common kitchen facilities for people who need to stay close to the hospital. She said it was scary walking back there after dark, especially after the first morning when one of the workers said that a bear had been seen that morning roaming around the house.

Tuesday 20 August

There were lots of phone calls from friends and strangers. People offered their homes, cars, money—whatever we needed. The switchboard was jammed with calls. Lois handled most of the calls from people we didn't know. I talked to family and friends.

The public relations officer for the hospital said they were plagued with calls from the media and wondered what to do. They hadn't remembered getting that many calls for a single patient before. They didn't think I was up to answering a lot of questions. I glanced at Lois, then said, "It might help save lives if people hear about us, so we should talk to them." They suggested bringing the media in for a press conference rather than putting me through the ordeal several times.

Three TV stations, including NBC and ABC, and two or three newspapers had representatives (about ten people in all) there for about forty minutes. One of the last questions they asked was, "What made the bear go away?"

When they asked me that, it seemed that the Holy Spirit whispered to me, "Now is the time. This is why you are here. Don't be ashamed of Me now. Tell them the truth."

So I said, "I prayed, asking our Heavenly Father to please send the bear away. She never touched me after that."

After the media released the story, many more calls came with offers to help. Preschool kids drew and sent get-well cards. Parents called and said, "Our little boy offered a special prayer for you today."

I've thought a lot about my prayer at the time of the mauling. Not all prayers are answered in the way we want them to be, but even as I said that simple prayer while the bear mauled me, I knew that it would be answered and that I would be all right. I'm not one to pray only when I need a favor. Daily I thank Heavenly Father in a prayer.

I always try to look for the positive in everything. Some of the greatest spiritual growth comes by experiences that we would never choose willingly. I hope and pray that my faith in the power of prayer will strengthen the faith of others in our Heavenly Father.

There are reasons we sometimes must go through traumatic experiences. Perhaps I needed to learn what it's like to be in a hospital. I can better understand how people feel who have to spend time in the hospital, and how important it is to call sick people and tell them you're praying for them and want to help them. It is so important to do more than just say, "If there is anything I can do, let me know."

Don and Dixie Lucas from the Thirteenth Ward came over. They had previously offered to let Lois stay at their house and loan her a car. They were going to the Lower Forty-Eight and said we'd actually be doing them a favor if she stayed at their house. I suspect that was just a way to make us feel good about accepting their offer. We still didn't know how long I'd be in the hospital, so we didn't give an answer. I felt it would be better for Lois to stay in Providence House; to be alone at night in an unfamiliar place and possibly relive the experience would not be good.

Brian Larsen's wife came by with a box for Lois to pack things in so we could check everything but one bag when we flew home. We had traveled standby so only had carry-on luggage, complete with tent and sleeping bags.

Saturday 24 August

At 9:30 A.M. I went to the burn center where they spent three hours working on me. Stitches and staples were removed from my face, ears, and head. They sutured the injuries that had been left to drain: my hands, finger, and under the arm. Those fifty stitches ran my total up to 250.

Sunday 25 August

The long scar in front of my ear is hardly noticeable, even though they removed the stitches only yesterday. Others have commented on how quickly my face healed, and without noticeable scars. The body has a marvelous capacity to heal itself, but I think it significant, even miraculous, that one of the few plastic surgeons in Alaska "happened" to be in the hospital when I needed him. My body has certainly been "renewed."

They released me about 12:30 P.M. Even though I don't feel well, it's Sunday and I want to go to church. I almost never miss a church meeting. Lovita Givens, of the Thirteenth Ward, came by to take us to church. We went to all three meetings, then she took us back to Providence House.

Nola Hogge, wife of one of the bishops, came by about 4:30 and took us to her house, five minutes from Anchorage International Airport. I went upstairs and tried to sleep, but was quite uncomfortable. I got up and went downstairs for a while before going back upstairs to lie down. I was

91

quite miserable. About 12:45 A.M. Nola took us to the airport. We arrived at Salt Lake City Airport and were home in Logan by mid-morning, two and a half hours later.

Wednesday 11 September

It's been nearly a month since my encounter with the bear, and I've never once dreamed about it. I sleep well, although my head is still too sore to sleep on my right side. The back of my head is tender, but I can lie on it if I have a soft pillow. I sleep in a sitting position with several pillows behind my back to keep the pressure off the back of my head.

I was most thankful that the bear did not attack Lois. The only time I get an unpleasant feeling is when I think what would have happened if the bear had attacked her instead of me. I quickly put that out of my mind. My heart goes out to her. She watched it all from a tree just ten to fifteen feet away. That must have been a very traumatic experience to watch and to feel so helpless.

The attack probably lasted thirty seconds, but I know it lasted long enough for Lois to hide and become perfectly still. She said her first impulse was to try and scare the bear away from me, but realized the danger and probable futility.

I think she was inspired to do exactly what she did. She told me later that when we ran, she fell. She saw the bear chasing me and started to follow, but came to a tree and felt she should climb it—that there was nothing she could do to help me anyway. She was only a few feet up the tree and could see the bear on top of me, but couldn't see much of me because of the brush.

She has never had a nightmare with bears chasing her. But almost every night for the first two weeks she had a rerun of the episode. She is about over it now. She told me the other day that while she watched from the tree, the bear stopped mauling me and looked up at her, then turned and went away.

It would be interesting to know what was in the bear's mind and whether there was a guardian angel that neither of us saw, one that was responsible for sending the bear away when I prayed. This I do know: divine help was there. How thankful I am, that when I called on our Heavenly Father for help, the communication lines were open and He responded immediately.

EPILOGUE

I wore a removable cast on my left hand for two to three months until the pins were removed from my finger. It has been nearly four years since the encounter with the bear. I have yet to have a bad dream or thoughts about the incident. Even though my ear canal was reattached without sutures, it healed perfectly and my hearing has not been affected. There are no noticeable scars on my hands or face. It took three months of therapy to get my hands in shape, and I can play the guitar almost as well as before.

No one can tell from looking at me that I've been mauled be a bear. And although I have no problem with my hand or anything, I've given up dancing with bears.

Is it possible the bear that attacked the Bonds is the same animal that attacked a mother-son-grandson hiking group four years later?

Running into Death

by Larry Kaniut

*Perhaps she'd been charged by a moose . . . wondering if
she was okay, he yelled back to his grandmother.*

Stunned surprise was my reaction when someone at church asked me if I'd read about the two
deaths resulting from a bear mauling. I replied, "No,
I haven't read this morning's paper."

When I returned home and saw the front page,
I couldn't believe it. Not the Marcie Trent I knew.
How could this be?

And the story was even more bizarre. Not one but
two people were killed. According to my records, two
people had been killed by the same bear on only three
previous occasions in Alaska: 1) In 1910 two native
boys were following a wounded brown bear near Cold
Bay, when a second bear trailing them struck and
killed them, 2) in the mid-1950s at Nabesna Village a
grizzly killed a woman and little girl, and 3) in 1956
another grizzly attacked and killed Lloyd Pennington
and hunting client Everett Kendall near Snowshoe Lake
at the bear's den.

Marcie Trent, son Larry Waldron, and Marcie's
grandson Art Abel drove the New Seward Highway on
1 July 1995 en route to McHugh Creek. They reached

the popular McHugh parking lot just before noon and coordinated their watches. Their day hike-jog objective up McHugh Creek Trail was Rabbit Lake, some five miles to the east of the trailhead.

At 1:05 P.M. Marcie and Art stopped for a rest and water break, assuming Larry was up ahead somewhere. Below them McHugh Creek tumbled through the thick spruce timber. Devil's club carpeted the creek bottom and thick alder brush spread up the hillside.

Beyond and stretching west to east, Turnagain Arm, a bay of Cook Inlet, captured their gaze. Across the Arm lay the northern tip of the Kenai Peninsula, sweeping west to Point Possession before a southerly plunge that marked Cook Inlet's eastern shore. The mighty Alaska Range thrust its proud head 10,000 feet above the west side of Cook Inlet; old volcanoes Mt. Spur, Redoubt, and Iliamna nestled among her peaks.

Above the hikers the alder brush gave way to quaking aspen, and beyond the aspen a few scattered mountain hemlock clutched the sides of the wind-scoured slopes. The trees were in full growth in midsummer, and green foliage predominated. Five thousand-foot pinnacles poked into the sky, beckoning them onward.

Although the vista was grand, the grandmother-grand-son team moved up the trail. It was nearly 1:30 when Art heard rustling in the bushes above the trail. He saw something running through the brush. He couldn't make out an animal in the bushes and wasn't sure what was happening. Suddenly he heard his grandmother scream.

Art dived headfirst into the brushy gully below the trail. He scrambled downhill, stopping momentarily at the bottom. He wondered if his grandmother had screamed because the animal charged her or only because she saw it. He hoped that she was safe.

Art wondered what to do. He considered returning to his grandmother to determine what had happened. Perhaps she'd been charged by a moose. If that were the case, maybe he could pick her up or move her out of the way so the moose couldn't stomp her more. He thought that she might be dead. At length he crossed the freshet and made his way up the far bank and back to the trail.

Still wondering if she was okay, he yelled back to his grandmother. He got no reply. Art sensed the bushes rustling nearby and thought the moose would attack him. He ran up the trail to a gnarly spruce tree and clambered skyward fifteen feet to safety. He removed his flannel shirt from his waist and put it on for warmth.

Hoping to see his uncle, he looked up the trail. Then he looked down the trail for his grandmother. It was difficult to see the trail from his perch. After a while he climbed down the tree for a better look. He did not see either his grandmother or his Uncle Larry and returned to his treetop perch. He thought about returning to the parking lot for help for his grandmother. Time crawled. Art wanted his Uncle Larry's support. He also wanted to alert Larry and to keep him from going to see Larry's mother.

Forty-five minutes later Art noticed a hiker coming from the direction of Rabbit Lake. Art called out, thinking it was his uncle. The hiker heard Art's call and reached his tree. It was not his uncle, but Jim Blees of Anchorage. Art explained to Blees that a moose had attacked his grandmother and that his uncle was still uptrail.

Art's teenager mind churned. He was scared and nervous. Doubt assailed him. He wanted to go with Blees, but he also wanted to stay to warn his uncle. He couldn't decide what to do. In the end Art stayed in the tree to await his uncle's return. Art climbed higher into the tree and saw movement near the attack site.

Blees went downtrail making noise to alert an animal of his approach. Within a few minutes Blees heard moaning from the brush. He approached the noise and found Larry Waldron. It was 3:00. Larry was bleeding, but he was alive. He lay on his back in shock. Larry managed to tell Blees that a bear had attacked him while he was attempting to help his mother.

Blees placed his fanny pack under Larry's head and wrapped his shirt around him. Thinking there was nothing else he could do for the injured man, Blees left him and ran down the trail for help. Within one hundred yards Blees ran into five hikers. He briefly told them about the bear attack and the injured man. He asked them to stay with Larry until help arrived. Two of the hikers moved downtrail toward the parking lot with Blees, while three started toward Waldron. One of those who went to assist Waldron was Sandra Small, a visitor from New Hampshire. She said, "We were shouting out, 'We're on our way, we're going to help you out.' I started praying right when I saw him."

Waldron was in deep shock and couldn't talk. He was fading when the hikers arrived. Unable to speak, Larry raised his arm slightly and tried to raise his leg. His breathing was shallow, only four breaths a minute.

Sandra Small said, "He couldn't speak to us at all, but he knew we were there with him."

Before long, Larry's breathing tapered off to nothing. The rescuers had some consolation in knowing that they supported him as much as they could, and it may have provided some solace to the family. Small said, "He wasn't alone when he died."

Twenty minutes passed. Rescuers were convinced they could do nothing more for Larry. Fearing the bear's return, Small said, "It was traumatic. I can't think of any other way to explain it. There was a lot of discussion among the three of us, and I was adamant about getting out of there. It was hard. I feel guilty, especially knowing there was a young kid up there."

Meanwhile, Blees reached the parking lot where a man with a cellular phone notified the officials of the attack. Choppers from the Alaska State Troopers and the Alaska National Guard were launched to aid in the search for the victims. At 3:30 P.M. Alaska State Troopers and other agency personnel began arriving at the McHugh Creek parking lot.

The unmistakable thrubbing of a helicopter grew louder. The Air National Guard Pavehawk helicopter touched down in the parking area, picked up Ranger Wesser, and flew up the canyon. Scanning the dense foliage along the trail below, the crew of the Pavehawk spotted Art in his tree. There was nowhere to land so a rescuer rappelled to the ground, where he talked with Art about the mauling (which Art still thought was a moose attack). The rescuer harnessed Art and signaled for his hoist into the chopper.

Art pointed out the attack site, and three men rappelled to the ground. Wesser and the rescue crew found Larry's body immediately. But they could not find Marcie. They radioed requesting the Alaska Mountain Rescue squad to begin a ground search. Not long after that Ranger Wesser discovered a fresh moose kill. Just beyond it and on the opposite side of the trail, the ranger found Marcie.

While officials tried to put together the events of the attack, park rangers, members of Alaska Mountain Rescue, and Alaska Search and Rescue dogs hiked en route to assist the others at the attack site.

Meanwhile, the chopper took Art to the parking lot where he was questioned by a State Trooper at 5:30 P.M. During the time with the trooper, the officer turned off his radio and exited his vehicle. Art wanted to know what was being said and turned on the radio. He overheard comments about finding one body and realized one of his companions was dead.

A police chaplain arrived and asked Art to wait in his car with him until Larry's wife, Rainey, and Marcie's husband, John, arrived. When his aunt and grandfather arrived, Art learned with them that Marcie and Larry were, in fact, dead.

Chugach State Park superintendent Al Meiners closed the trail and posted a notice at the Glen Alps trailhead (the back route).

❖   ❖   ❖

For a few days before the facts were out, confusion over the attack reigned. Some believed the attacking animal was a moose, while others suspected bear. The victims suffered scratches and head trauma. Fresh moose tracks were discovered in the area, and the wound on Marcie's back resembled a moose hoofprint. Yet both victims had been dragged off the trail, which is inconsistent with a moose's capabilities.

Alaska Fish and Game biologist Rick Sinnott theorized, "I'm just a little skeptical. Typically a bear will bite at the head and buttocks, and there are usually puncture wounds on both of those areas. But there was only one puncture wound: one small hole under the jaw of the man."

Alaska State Trooper Sgt. Brad Brown indicated that the culprit was a brown-grizzly bear. Both bodies were discovered within thirty yards of a week-old buried moose carcass. Marcie and Larry had been dragged from the trail into heavy brush. The State Medical Examiner Michael Propst stated, "Each died from the injuries received in a bear attack. No evidence of involvement of a moose was present."

Alaska State Trooper Lee Oly said Marcie Trent was killed almost instantly (Marcie's neck and back were broken, and Waldron's injuries included a crushed pelvis and chest as well as deep wounds), and that Trent had little chance to react to the oncoming attack because of dense brush and alders along the trail.

❖ ❖ ❖

My initial shocked reaction to the deaths of Marcie and Larry was replaced with anger. I was angry that they hadn't been more adequately prepared with some kind of bear deterrent. They would most likely be alive had they been carrying a weapon, pepper spray, or some noise maker. In the midst of Monday morning quarterbacking, I remembered having hiked in the very same locale with our two youngest children.

We had left the parking lot at McHugh Creek armed with nothing. We hiked and played while stopping to take pictures, climb trees, throw sticks, and scale cliffs, all the while giving little thought to the danger of a possible bear encounter. We were guilty of doing what the Trent-Waldron-Abel party had done. It was through no preparation on our part that we did not encounter a bear or suffer a similar experience. We could easily have met with a food-protecting bear, a mother protecting her cubs, or we could have surprised a bear. And the results could just as easily have been injury or death to us. There is a message here for all who would enter bruin's domain: carry adequate bear protection.

Although no official evidence was made public, some people theorize/speculate that the grizzly which attacked the Bonds, could be the same animal that killed Marcie and Larry. The McHugh Creek drainage is but a few miles long, the area comprising too small a range for more than one grizzly. On the other hand it's possible bears were passing through on both occasions.

❖   ❖   ❖

It is always difficult to experience the loss of some-one you love, to adjust to their absence and to try to carry on normal day-to-day activities without them. The people in Marcie and Larry's circle of influence will miss them and mourn their passing.

One of the safest ways to avoid a brown bear's mauling is to climb a tree that the bear can't climb. The Trent-Waldron team did not have time to climb a tree, but Bob Pohl did.

Surveying from a Tree

by Robert Pohl

By now the bear had looked at us and was starting on a lope.

In my quest for bear stories, I flew to Kodiak Island. Our family friend and my former college dorm-mate Frank Morgan, a Kodiak mathematics teacher, suggested that I contact some of the local surveyors whose experience afield should include shoulder-rubbing with bruin. Sounded like a good idea to me. On 19 June 1988 I contacted Bob Pohl, a surveyor for Roy Ecklund.

When Bob came over to Frank's to tell bear tales, I was struck by his persona. Here was a modern-day hunk the girls would go ga-ga over. At six feet and one hundred ninety pounds, Bob is a genuine beefcake. His biceps bulge, complementing his broad chest and robust and congenial personality. It was a joy talking with him.

One of the most interesting stories Bob told me was about his experience with a new hire on the Terror Lake hydroelectric project.

We were working on the Terror Lake hydro project in the mountains, running a power line to Port Lions. My job was surveying out the pole locations for the power line. I had been working for Roy Ecklund for two or three years and been on this project from the very beginning.

We had a new guy, Fred Kowal, who had just started to work for Roy. I didn't know Fred very well. I'd only worked with him once before, and this was his first time out in the bush with us. It was just me and Fred. On the days we didn't stay in camp, the normal procedure was to leave in the morning from town by chopper.

It was a typical Kodiak rainy day, pouring and miserable. We had a lot of stuff. Fred and I loaded the gear in the helicopter. At 6:30 A.M. during July or August of 1983, our pilot, Tony Walker, took us over to the location, right around Barbara Cove, four or five miles from Port Lions. There's a lot of thick brush and grass in there. The only trees you find are down in the gullies along where the creeks run. You might find a few cottonwoods, but most of the terrain consists of alders and head-high grass.

We got there about 7:00 in the morning. It was raining cats and dogs when Tony dropped us off in a gully. We had a pole location down by this creek, so we had surveying gear and everything else, which we unloaded out of the helicopter. It was Fred's first day, and he was asking me if we'd see bears. I said, "We probably will, we usually do see one or two down in the creek bottoms." He was nervous about the bears.

We have radio communication with the helicopter, but a lot of times Tony will be out of range, so he usually comes back and checks on us later in the day. As soon as Tony left us, I noticed that we'd forgotten to get the shotgun. We'd left it in the back of the chopper, but I didn't think much of it because I'd been carrying a gun all these years and never had to use it. I wasn't too concerned.

Twenty minutes after the helicopter left, Fred yelled to me. He was in front, setting up a control point for our traverse. He yelled, "Bob! Bob, there's a bear down there in the gully."

I didn't think much about it and yelled up to him, "How far away is he?"

He yelled back, "A good four or five hundred feet down the creek."

I said, "Don't worry about it. We'll probably be all right."

Excited, he called back, "There's another . . . there's two bears down there . . . there's three bears!"

I thought, *Jeez, I'd better go take a look.* So I climbed up on the hill, and sure enough, there was a sow with three cubs. She was still far away, but she was working her way up the creek. I said to Fred, "Jeez, we better let her know we're here 'cause we sure don't want to surprise her in this tall grass. Watch this, Fred. You start yellin' and they're gonna take off, no problem."

So I start yelling, "Hey, bear. Yeah, bear," trying to let her know we were up there. I've done that in the past, and they've always taken off or gone in another direction. We looked down in the gully. The bear stood up on her hind legs and sniffed. The old hair started to go up, and I thought, Uh, oh. I looked at Fred and said, "We've got a problem now, Fred."

He looked at me as if to say, "What are we gonna do?"

Luckily for us there was a big cottonwood tree about one hundred feet in front of us toward the bear. By now the bear had looked at us and was starting on a lope. I think the only reason she didn't run full speed up the creek is that she was with her cubs. They were fooling around; she'd run maybe ten or fifteen yards and turn around to see where her cubs were. They were young, a year old if that. We saw them moving down in the brush.

We ran down to the tree. The limbs were high. Fred didn't know my personality, and I didn't know his. I was on one side of the tree, and Fred was on the other. Fred's a short guy, 5-feet-8-inches tall and 150 pounds. The limbs were lower on his side. I was on the wrong side of the tree to get to the limbs because they were way up there, probably nine or ten feet.

I had my rubber rain gear on, gloves and everything. I tried to shinny my way up but I couldn't do it. By now the bear was pretty darn close. I looked at Fred and I ran around to his side of the tree. Fred looked at me with wide eyes; he knew the limbs were lower on his side. He gave me a weird look.

I grabbed him by his belt buckle and hoisted him up, and he grabbed on and pulled himself up. Then he reached down and grabbed me. I was able to pull myself up. But when a bear's coming, you lose your strength and your arms go numb. We made it up the tree.

By then the bear had gotten within fifty feet and stopped when she saw us trying to climb the tree. Of course, we were scared as hell. So we tried to get higher. I knew that she couldn't climb the tree, but when something like that's happening—she was snapping her teeth like vice grips, her hair was up, she was pawing at the ground—it scared the hell out of us. We kept trying to climb higher, but those rotten limbs kept snapping off, and our raingear made moving around difficult.

Finally we got high enough to be safe. The bear paced in front of us with her three cubs looking, learning, and watching the whole thing. I'm sure they were thinking, *This is good fun.* From our sanctuary Fred screamed, "I don't care how much we're gettin' paid, this is nonsense."

Finally she got tired of what she was doing and meandered back toward the creek. We couldn't see her because the grass was too thick. I thought, *Well, Jeez, I wonder how long we're gonna have to stay up here?* We were up there probably twenty minutes, and I told Fred, "We gotta get some work done today sometime. I don't know where she is, but I'm gonna go back down and take a look around to see if she's down there."

Fred said, "Don't go down there yet. Wait till we see her."

And I said, "Well, they're probably gone." I climbed down the tree and made my way down to the creek. Sure enough, when I looked around the weeds, there she was probably two hundred feet away. She saw me.

I ran back to the tree. By then I was pretty good at popping back up. Bang. Up the hill she came, right up to the tree, sniffing and doing the whole thing all over again: hair up, snapping her teeth, pawing the ground. This time there was no way I would get out of the tree until I could see her on a far ridge. For another twenty minutes or so we didn't hear anything. Fred thought he saw her on the next ridge where the alders were moving. We decided it was safe, so we climbed out of the tree and went to the creek. The bear was gone. We were relieved. We got lucky. If that tree hadn't been there, I don't know what we would have done.

Fred looked at me and said, "Ya know, Bob, when I saw you comin' around to my side of the tree, I thought it was survival of the fittest because I thought you were gonna throw me right out of the way."

I said, "Jeez, Fred, I'm not that kind of guy." That explains why he had had that strange look on his face.

The worst part was working the rest of that day. After something like that happens, there's a bear behind every twig. Working in the tall grass without that gun was scary. It was a good lesson for I've never forgotten a gun after that. If we'd had the shotgun, I could have shot it over her head. I found out later that apparently the same bear chased a man up on top of a machine one day. She was in the same area and the man said she had cubs. Luckily he was able to get up on the Nodwell, and she left him alone.

We went back to camp and I told the superintendent about the bear incident. You know how word travels about something like that. He said, "How long were you guys up in the tree?"

I said, "Probably about an hour total."

And he said, "I suppose you expect to be paid for that time." What a joker!

Bob Pohl was at work when bears scared him; Stephen Routh was on vacation.

A Thousand Stitches

by Stephen Routh

"I kept my arm jammed into his mouth."

What began as a pleasant day of flight-seeing for husband and wife ended in a fist-to-paw donnybrook between a determined man and a black bear. When the opportunity arose to speak with Anchorage attorney Stephen Routh, I was grateful to get the facts and pleased that he survived his fist fight with a bear.

To better understand this story, you must know that Stephen's Citabria aircraft is a two-seater, with the pilot's seat forward of the passenger's, and the cabin is roughly two feet wide and five feet long.

I was a fairly new float pilot in 1980. July 29 was such a pretty, sunny day that I invited my wife to flight-see with me. I planned to practice landing and taxiing with my Citabria. We were out cruising, landing on a few lakes, and enjoying the weather.

As the day wore on, the weather kicked up with high gusty winds. Since my piloting skills were limited, I thought the proper move was to overnight. It was late in the day, and I had a tent and camping gear on board. We sought a lake with a nice spot to pitch the tent, where we could have some food and return to Anchorage the next morning.

After flying over two lakes, we found one that looked like a good camping area. The lake had nice high banks and level ground surrounding the beach. It appeared to be an adequate place to tie a float plane down, pitch the tent under the trees out of the weather, and spend a nice evening.

I set up for my approach: pulled the carb heat, trimmed the plane, reduced power, and settled safely onto the lake. We taxied to one area where I got out and looked. It was swampy and inappropriate to camp. We taxied to another place and looked that over. It wasn't appropriate either. We taxied to a third place. The bank's height contained the crescendoing noise of the plane's engine as we taxied on step. There was no doubt that any animal within miles would have known that there was an airplane on the lake.

I nosed the airplane in, then heeled it around. With power off, I turned around so the float heels were up on the shore. I had a twenty-foot rope tied to the rear cleat on one float. I grasped the rope in one hand and walked up the little bank, looking for a spot to camp as well as something to anchor the plane to.

I wasn't particularly concerned about animals. Over the years I've followed all the rules to avoid animal problems. My outdoor experience is extensive. I've spent a great deal of time fishing. I have good survival skills. I've been in a lot of bear areas and have avoided bears by making noise and keeping food away.

I looked to the left and didn't see much. I looked to the right. I looked back to the left. Something caught my eye, and I looked back to the right. In my face was a bear. I don't know where he came from, but he was right there. His jaw was a little lower than my chin. It was so startling and so close that I involuntarily screamed. It wasn't the approach I'm used to with bears. Normally man and bear run in opposite directions. But he was within a foot of me standing up on his hind legs, mouth open, nose to nose.

I remember thinking, *This is great. I'll run down my side of the hill, and he'll run down his side of the hill. We're both scared to death. I'll laugh and joke telling my wife. I'll sit in the airplane and probably shake for a while. Then we'll figure out something to do . . . maybe sleep in this airplane in the middle of the lake.*

I turned to run back to the airplane, thinking he was going in the other direction. I also figured the lake would be my salvation should the bear pursue. As I turned to get out of there, he grabbed me. The bear's big, hairy armlike forelegs shot around me literally in a bear hug, *chunk.* Then I felt him snapping at the back of my head. He was all over me. His jaws kept snapping, and I kept moving my head so he couldn't gain purchase on my neck. We were both in a hunting-survival mode. He was snarling and pummeling me. He bit me, grabbing my skull and hair. I felt the back of my head crunch and tear. He grabbed my lower ear in his teeth. I felt my left ear go *huunk.*

At 6-feet-2-inches tall and 195 pounds I was in great shape, but I was no match for this animal. He stood with his forelegs around my torso, and his back legs were hanging on me or clawing me. He was a little shorter than me. Gauging from the fact that my legs buckled with him on my back, and from the length of its legs, the bear probably weighed 350 pounds. The power of the animal was phenomenal. I kept thinking, *This is a black bear; it can't be that strong.*

I couldn't support his weight, and I fell. Since we were heading downhill, we tumbled together to the lake. All the while he snarled and bit and snapped. I thought, *This is a strange way to die.* I was convinced that I wasn't going to make it.

We fought near the shore in ankle-deep water, and I was on my knees most of the time. He was all over me, and I didn't have time to get up. Somehow I got turned toward him and I was staring him right in the eye. I tried to reason with him. Thinking it might calm him, I said, "You don't want to do this."

There was incredible fury in that animal's face. It was in every sense a WILD animal. There was no appealing to him; he had his mission, and that was to eat me. That was all he knew. It seemed that he was just incredibly angry.

I had to get something to try to kill him. I felt that one of us wasn't going to leave there, and I began to fight back. I couldn't stop his forelegs from coming around me. He reached around and raked my back with those claws. I was amazed by the length of the bear's forelegs. I have long arms and wide shoulders (I wear over a size thirty-seven shirt). The bear's outstretched paws went beyond mine. With my arms outstretched I could actually grab him by his wrists, but he still had claws behind them. Even with that leverage and me holding his wrists, I could not stop the arms from coming around, and I'm strong. I could have done that with most people; not many could bring their arms around me if I was holding their wrists from an interior point because I would have the leverage.

Over and over I felt the claws rip into my sides and back as those powerful paws raked me. I reached into my back pocket hoping I could get my Buck knife. I reasoned that I'd kill that bear. He was so busy attacking he wasn't concerned about being counterattacked. I figured I could jam my knife in his throat, or jam it in his mouth. Since I didn't have my knife, I probed for my comb. My theory was that I was going to jam it into his throat and maybe choke him.

But I couldn't stop those arms from coming around, and I couldn't stop that mouth from working on me. And the mouth kept going for my throat. He bit the back of my neck, my hamstrings, and down my spine, where he tried to break the spine to disable me. He was a very efficient killing machine.

I decided that the best way to survive would be to give him something to chew on. Finally I decided to sacrifice my left arm. I jammed it inside his mouth at the forearm (Stephen rolled up his long shirt sleeve and showed me the scar tissue on his left wrist.) He kept busy gnawing on that. He tried to move his head to get around my arm so he could come back at my throat, but I kept my arm jammed into his mouth.

While I was being torn apart, my wife was watching from the floats a mere fifteen to twenty feet away. She had no idea what to do and stood screaming at the top of her lungs.

I had no knife, no comb. I thought I could get a rock from the beach to crush his skull, but the shoreline was silty and muddy. It was covered with organic stuff, with no rocks visible. There was an old log where we wrestled in the shallows. The log had old, moldy, dead leaves on it. At one point I saw a branch on the log. I ripped it off and slashed the bear in the face with it.

He didn't like me messing with his face. He protected himself more than he was attacking me. I hit him in the eyes with the branch. He dodged and backed off. That's when the bear noticed my wife and went after her. Joanie climbed into the airplane and managed to close the door. In two jumps the bear was at the heels of the float. The water was shallow, about six inches deep. There was a bench there before it got deeper. The bear jumped onto a float and ran to the cabin, where he stood up and clawed at the Plexiglas windows, trying to get at Joanie.

I thought about my chances of survival on shore, knowing I might well bleed to death in the water. On the other hand the cold might stop the bleeding. I decided that my best chance for survival was to get into the water so I headed out into the lake. I think it's a deep lake. I was in water twenty to thirty feet deep.

I managed to get one hip wader off, but I couldn't remove the other one. I must have been in shock because I've never had a problem in the water. I've been a champion swimmer, but I couldn't get the wader off. I kicked out in the water to get away.

The bear clawed on the plane for a while. Then he ran to the end of the float and looked up and down the beach hunting me. Suddenly he focused on me and entered the water and headed for me. As much as I had a glimmer of hope before, I figured he was far more equipped than I for this battle. I thought of myself, *This is where you're going to die.* He swam toward me, mouth open and snarling.

I did something instinctual: I splashed water. I would give him the slip—lie back in the water and then push water, which would propel me away from him while sending a wave into his mouth. I'd push, and he would cough—*aarrffff*—and spit the water out, then snarl around, come up, look, and see me. Then I'd do it again. I don't know how long we did that, but I must have poured a ton of water down the bear's throat before he finally gave up and headed back to shore.

I found that I could keep myself up, but I couldn't maneuver well. I realized that I had serious injuries. I determined, *There's no way I'm going back to shore. If I'm gonna die, I might as well die in the water and not be eaten by a bear.*

I was shouting at my wife to start the airplane. If she could get the airplane going and step on a rudder to get to me, I could climb on a float. That would be one positive step. She repeatedly pushed the start button . . . *rrraaahhhrrruuuhhhrruuuhhh*; it wouldn't catch. I kept shouting, "PUSH IN THE RED BUTTON! PUSH IN THE RED BUTTON!" That's all I could think about, the mixture control. (You pull the mixture control out to stop your airplane and cut the engine down. No gas gets to the engine if you don't have the red mixture button in.)

Finally she said, "Oh!" Though she'd never flown alone, she'd flown with me enough to know where the mixture button was. She pushed that in and *vroom*, the engine came to life. Then Joanie came taxiing out. What a wonderful sight!

I had a tough time getting onto the float. Joanie had to drape me over the float, and finally I was able to crawl up. It was difficult getting inside the airplane. Joanie pushed me and I tumbled in, one leg after the other. My left arm was in bad shape. I saw the bone inside and thought, *This is not a good deal here at all.* Then I reached to the back of my head and felt my ear dangling. I touched the back of my neck and it was covered with blood. Joanie tried to figure out how badly injured I was. She lifted up my shirt. Then she put it down and didn't say anything. After seeing the look of horror in her eyes, I thought, *I still might die.*

I was afraid to go to shore because I thought the bear might come back—even though I didn't see the bear after reaching the safety of the plane. I got into the pilot's seat, and she helped get the radio on. I wasn't functioning well. I was messed up, but I got on the radio and started talking, pleading, saying, "Somebody help."

There was a DC-6 flying five miles overhead, and it began circling. We couldn't see him, but I was talking to him. Rescue Coordination Center sent an Otter out. Everybody was looking, but nobody could figure out where I was. I didn't even know the name of the lake, or if I knew it, I had forgotten it because of my condition.

I was a mass of injuries. There wasn't much anybody could do. Where would you start? I was bleeding all over the place. The bear had shredded my new Levi's, causing me to ponder his power (I knew a man couldn't rip Levi's in his hands).

We sat in the middle of the lake, and it got darker and darker. I knew that after a period of time nobody could land: It was too high sided, and you can't see the water, the beach, or the land. People kept assuring, "Yeah, we're on the way. We'll be there any minute." But they had no idea where I was. The ELT (Emergency Locator Transmitter) was going, but it was frustrating observing how the systems didn't come together quite right.

My wife had the foresight to pull out the emergency gear, which included flares. She shot off a flare, followed by another. A pilot flew over, circled, and landed. Since it was close to the Fourth of July, he initially thought this was part of the celebration. But then he thought, *Wait a minute. This can't be right.*

I was in the back of the airplane and too messed up to even transfer airplanes. He took one look at me and knew that there was trouble. He said, "Can you get into my airplane?" Then seeing blood and my condition, he said, "Don't even try."

He decided to taxi my wife and his passenger across the lake to a cabin, then return for me. They knocked on the door. An occupant opened the door, looking half-asleep, and said, "We're on our honeymoon, leave us alone," and slammed the door. They sat outside for a while, and finally my wife couldn't stand it anymore and said, "I'm not going to stay out here anymore." They knocked on the door again, and when the folks realized there was an emergency, they let them in to spend the night.

Meanwhile, the pilot returned, got into my airplane, and took off for Anchorage. We landed at Elmendorf. Because it was so late with no lighted landing areas on water, they had cars shining their headlights across the water so he could see to land. From Elmendorf I was taken to Providence Hospital, about seven miles away in east Anchorage.

AFTERWARD

Our flight-seeing trip was an intended campout. I was in good physical and mental shape. I had planned to fly for a few hours and then spend the night some-where. We had our food and a tent, and everything would be comfortable.

The mauling seemed to last a lifetime but I think the actual attack took less than ten minutes. Things happened so fast but seemed like they were happening so slow. The first phase was probably over in two to three minutes, and the second in the water took a minute or two. If it was ten minutes from the time I first saw the bear until I got on the float, I'd be surprised. It seemed like half-an-hour, but it must have been much less than that.

I survived the shock; I think going into the cold water was the best thing I could have done. The cold water probably saved me, slowing the bleeding substantially. If I had been on that lake another hour or two, however, the loss of blood or hypothermia would have done me in.

My injuries included a severely mangled arm; lacerations to my head, neck, and legs; and a nearly severed ear. My worst wound was to my arm, where I had jammed it into the bear's mouth. I got a deep wound infection. They treated it with a machine that circulated water, slowly cooking my arm in an effort to beat the infection. I was on different types of IV antibiotics. Finally one, Keflex, killed the infection. I was told that the next stage of antibiotic would probably have cost me my hearing.

My dangling ear was sewn back in place. There are a bunch of stitches where three areas come together. They did such a fine job in the ER that people can't even tell my ear was chopped off. I ended up with about one thousand stitches, but if you looked me over you wouldn't know it. I was in the hospital ten days. I was fully insured. To be honest I don't recollect how much treatment was. Five thousand dollars for the hospital bill comes to mind. I signed the forms and the hospital took care of the rest.

I had a .44 Magnum pistol at that time. I guess I'd grown careless and I didn't have it with me on the beach. A month ago I shot a good-sized black bear on my porch at my cabin at Lake Creek. I dropped him at six feet in the shoulder with my .44 Magnum. He ran up a tree and fell out. I tracked him by his blood spoor for three miles and never did find him. My confidence in the .44 Magnum is down to zero now, and I wouldn't use it again, except to shoot myself to avoid the agony.

I'm an advocate of fighting back. I hear people talk about rolling over and playing dead. With this black bear I wouldn't have had to play dead, I would have been dead. I have no doubt that he would have munched on me while I was hiding my head and trying to survive.

I don't think the bear was surprised. Anybody would have known that there was a man out there because there's no missing the sound of a float plane taxiing, especially when you have a high-sided lake.

I received numerous phone calls and input in the hospital and thereafter. One caller said that two weeks earlier on that lake some kids had been taking shots at a bear with a .22 just for fun, not to kill it but just to hit it. And the bear had run off.

I think black bears are more dangerous than grizzlies. Grizzlies will maim you, but there's a chance you'll survive. But the black bear is the killer. He's going to eat your liver. The bite pattern on me is consistent with injuries to animals by bears: sever the spine or cut the hamstring. Bears are far stronger and more resilient than people give them credit for.

I'm impressed with the black bear's strength and survivability. I think they're much underrated.

In the future I'll always be armed. If I'd had my pistol strapped to my side, I could have done more than I did with a twig. I would also carry a knife. Your adrenaline is going so high that you become super human, and I think I could have killed that bear with a knife. I might be the world's biggest fool, but I think I could have sliced the bear's throat or even jammed a knife into his throat and pushed on the end of it so it went into his mouth and he swallowed it. It's good practice to carry a knife.

I have no idea what became of that bear. The fish and game people laughed when I asked them what they were going to do with the bear. They said they never go after a bear unless it kills someone.

Incidentally, today that airplane still has the claw on the back window marks where the bear was trying to get to my wife. But we haven't flown out to Cow Lake for any overnight tenting.

Stephen Routh subdued the black bear with his confidence and a switch. Cal Pappas subdued a brown bear with a rifle.

A Mother's Concern

by Cal Pappas

"She was running at me faster than a racehorse."

Our family friend Cal Pappas told me about his close call with a mama grizzly. I asked him if I could use it in this book, and he agreed.

It was on the fifth day of a caribou hunt, on 14 August 1994 . Two friends from New England had flown to Alaska for their first hunt in the great Northwest. They each had taken a caribou and remained in camp as I went off to search for mine.

We were camped on the north shore of Tutna Lake, which is about two hundred air miles southwest of Anchorage. I decided to hunt the high plateau about a mile from our camp, as hunting the woods and swampy land by the lake had previously failed to supply my caribou.

I came to the edge of the woods and the base of a steep incline, perhaps a five hundred-foot, thirty-degree ascent to the plateau. I dropped my pack and changed my hip boots for my walking shoes as it was a sunny day and the high country would be dry. Since I was to return the same way, I would change back to my hip boots for the mile walk back to camp.

My pack and rifle were on the ground when I stood after I laced up my shoes. I noticed movement out of the corner of my right eye. It was a grizzly bear 150 feet away, and she saw me at the same time my head turned toward her. We looked at each other for ten to twelve seconds. Her face showed curiosity, as if to say, "What are you doing in my woods?"

I felt no danger, remained motionless, and tried to focus my vision on her chest rather than making direct eye-to-eye contact. Just then about half the distance between us, a cub ran out of the woods in my direction. It was small, born that spring.

In an instant mother's expression changed from content curiosity to intense rage. She dropped on all fours and charged. I grabbed the rifle at my feet. Enjoying fine antique weapons, my choice for the hunt was an English double rifle in .500 3-inch Nitro Express—too much gun for Alaska caribou, but a beautiful and well-balanced gun for any hunting adventure.

Mother grizzly was chocolate brown and fat from feeding on blueberries all summer. As she ran, her muscles rippled under a layer of fat several inches thick. When she bypassed her cub, about seventy-five feet from me, I fired both barrels over her head in the hope of stopping or turning her charge. I waited a moment as I would still have time to reload my rifle and shoot to stop her if it came to that.

With the rifle's report, she angled to her left toward the woods and came to a halt about twenty feet away from me. In that time, I had opened the breech, two spent cases had ejected and I dropped two in, snapped the gun closed, and held it at hip level. I didn't raise it to my shoulder as I wanted to avoid as much motion as possible.

Her cub had turned in confusion and had run back into the woods. Mother spun around twice, growled, and swatted the air with her paw, gave me one more nasty look, and turned to join her cub. She looked once more as if to say, "You're lucky this time," and disappeared into the thick.

I went over to the tree where the bear had first stood up. Standing on her hind legs she was about eight feet tall. Being well fed, she weighed perhaps five hundred pounds. Not big by Alaska standards, but when she was running at me faster than a race horse and with the expression on her face (which is permanently etched in my memory) she was big enough! I'm thankful I didn't have to shoot her.

Understanding bear behavior led both Cal Pappas and Jerry Austin to respond appropriately when they each dealt with a sow and her cubs.

Keep a "Bear-stopper" Handy

by Jerry Austin

*"Suddenly the ground erupted in front of us, and
we had a bear at close range."*

*Jerry Austin is a big-game guide in Alaska and has
run the Iditarod Sled Dog Race numerous times. When I
wrote him about some of his close calls with bears, he submitted the following.*

A few years ago I was guiding a Texan south of
St. Michael on flat terrain. We had spotted a large lone
bear about seven miles away and were trying to reach it
before dark. We had heavy packs but didn't want to leave
them behind.

When we got to within half a mile, the bear saw and
winded us. Even though we were walking fast, the bear
was able to walk away from us. Finally I had the hunter
chamber a round in his .375 Remington. I asked him if
he could shoot offhand fast and he replied that he was
pretty good.

By now it was misty, and we finally took off our packs
and started half-running to catch up with the bear. Every
now and then we'd lose sight of the animal for a minute or
two. I commented to the hunter that something was fishy,
we should be seeing it. I chambered a round in my .375
and we cautiously continued.

Suddenly the ground erupted in front of us, and we had a bear at close range. The hunter did a great job of getting off a quick shot, and the bear went down. It got right back up, so I had to shoot it, too. This bear, in the span of a minute or two, had dug a big hole in the tundra to lie in wait for us. We nearly stepped on it before it reared up and lunged at us. We spent a cold, wet night out on the tundra and the next day packed the hide and headed back seven miles, mostly uphill.

On another occasion my whole family was up at our cabin at the mouth of Golsovia River. It was the summer of 1988. My three girls, Dena, Jerrine, and Charlene, were swimming about five hundred feet from the cabin with their friend Wendy Shears. I was behind the cabin when my oldest girl Dena hollered that bears were coming.

I grabbed my rifle by the cabin door, this time an AR-15, and ran down the trail as the kids ran up it. They were throwing off life jackets and towels to make better time. A sow and a two-year-old cub were coming right at me, so I opened up with the rifle, being careful not to hit the children or to shoot in front of them and risk a ricochet. I shot an entire twenty-round clip in the air around them, but the bears kept on coming. I had to run back to the cabin and get more ammo and a shotgun.

By now the bears were getting too close for comfort. I shot another twenty or thirty rounds, and this didn't faze them either. Finally they turned and ambled off. This is common bear behavior; if they are interested in something, gunshots often do not scare them off. Even outboard motors or chain saws often don't scare them at all.

Another time a friend of mine who has a cabin about thirty miles from St. Michael was attacked right in his door by three grizzlies—I assume a sow and two year-old cubs. It got hectic, but he took care of the problem. This was a number of years ago, and recently I asked him about the details. His laconic replies to my questions raise understatement to new levels.

He said the incident had been no big deal. His worry had been for his family inside the cabin. I asked him how many shots it took to defend himself, and he said three. That was all he had with him, one for each bear. Now we all know that this was good shooting, especially in the heat of an attack. I had just recently sold him a 7mm, and believing that he had used this weapon to fend off the attack I mentioned that he must be pretty happy with it. He just shrugged and said, yeah, he liked it a lot, but that day all he had with him was a .243! Three bears with three shots from a .243 in a cabin! This is definitely the kind of friend you want around during a dangerous encounter—bear, human, or whatever!

See Appendix 10

Guide Jerry Austin's outdoor experiences are shared by such guides as Cecil Jones.

Close Quarters

by Cecil Jones

*"The situation was taking on the atmosphere of
a cat-and-mouse game."*

*Another story about a close encounter involved
big-game guide Cecil Jones, of Homer. He tells his
story below.*

It was obvious we were not going to make it. The
small band of rams was traveling too fast and were too
far away for us to cut them off in time to gain shooting
range. We had tried hard and covered a lot of ground
since first spotting them over an hour before. But we
weren't going to make it. The rams had seemed nervous when we first sighted them, but I was certain they
knew nothing of our presence. We sat down on the hillside to catch our wind. As soon as I was able to hold
the glasses steady, I raised them up and watched the
rams as they crossed the skyline half a mile away and
disappeared over the ridge. There was at least one full
curl or better, so it was a bit of a disappointment for
both of us to watch them cross the ridge and drop from
view. Since this was only the second day of the hunt,
neither of us was overly concerned.

As I sat there looking through the glasses, I heard a
rock rattle down the mountain off to our left and across

the ravine. I glanced over, and there coming down a shale slide a quarter-mile away was a pale blond grizzly. Considering the direction from which he was traveling, it was obvious he was the cause of the nervousness we had observed in the band of rams. He was headed in our general direction, so we sat and waited, hoping to get photographs if he came close enough. When he dropped down in the ravine, he went out of sight from us.

I noted that we were sitting on a game trail that led from the ravine right past our position, and I expected the bear would come up out of the ravine following this trail. If this were the case, he would come up in view of us about one hundred yards away and directly toward us across open terrain. It was doubtful he would get close enough for us to get a photo before he spotted us.

Quickly we picked up our packs and moved down the hill and toward the ravine. A fair-sized rock twenty yards below the trail and about the same distance from the ravine would break up our outline to some extent, and perhaps from this point we could get a good broadside snapshot. As quickly and quietly as possible, we gained this position and dropped behind the rock.

Ed got his telephoto focused on the point where the trail came up. We sat there with faint smiles of anticipation on our faces, tensely waiting for the bear to pop up. And by golly he did! Not on the game trail at all but about on our level, which left us sitting at the side of the rock, not behind it, and our camera pointed up the hill instead of at the bear. We stood out like two prunes in a bowl of oatmeal. The instant we moved the bear woofed, switched ends like a cat, and was out of sight in a single bound.

When we last saw him, he was at least a mile away and still running for all he was worth. In spite of our best-laid plans and sophisticated equipment, the animals had won again, but that's the fun of hunting. Though we were returning to camp empty-handed, it had still been a fruitful day.

We made it back to spike camp just before dark. After eating supper, I washed the dishes, and being a bit short on facilities as is always the case in spike camps, I set them on a log, which lay along the front of the tent. We rolled into our sleeping bags well after dark and both fell asleep almost instantly.

Sometime during the night a slice of the moon rose up and cast a slight amount of light on the country-side, not much, but enough so that the inside of the tent was not in total darkness. I appreciated this fact when along about 2:30 A.M. I was awakened by some-one shaking my shoulder.

I looked over and the panic I saw in Ed's face was enough to make my hair stand on end. I sat up and reached for the .44 lying by my pillow. In a high-pitched whisper he explained to me that something was beside our tent. The explanation wasn't necessary because by now I could hear the unmistakable sound of a large ani-mal breathing nearby.

"Probably a wolverine," I lied in an attempt to calm Ed's nerves, but to be honest, my own whisper probably sounded as hysterical as his. About then an object the size of your fist pushed the tent wall in about three inches and slid down the tent wall and away. Either of us could have touched it easily from where we sat. We kept our guns trained on the spot and waited, expecting any minute for a huge paw to rip the tent wall. The heavy breathing noise continued less than three feet way for some time, then everything grew very quiet.

We strained to hear a noise but could not detect a sound, until suddenly there was a loud clatter of plates, pots, and pans along the front of the tent, as if every pan had been knocked off the log with one swipe. The situa-tion was taking on the atmosphere of a cat-and-mouse game, and we were taking a strong dislike to it. A bear that is not afraid of human scent is a potentially danger-ous bear, and this one obviously wasn't afraid.

Our options were few. We couldn't shoot at his out-line through the tent wall. There would be too much of a chance of wounding the bear, and even if we killed it, we could find we had killed a sow with cubs. Besides, I like to see what I'm shooting at and this would be a sound shot. Still, we had no desire to sit and wait for the bear to flatten the tent on top of us either. So for lack of an alter-native action, I stood up and fired the .44 Magnum through the ridge pole hole. It was a relief to hear the brush break-ing as the bear promptly left our fragile little abode.

At daybreak we located his tracks in the mud near the tent, and there on the outside of the tent wall directly over where Ed's pillow lay was a bluish stain on the can-vas. Apparently the bear had been feeding on blueberries and still had the juice on his nose and lips when he rubbed his snout on the tent wall. The width of the track indi-cated it was about an eight-foot grizzly that had visited us during the night.

The bear that visited Cecil Jones' camp left its print on the tent, but Helmuth Port's bear left more than that.

In Without Knocking

Helmuth A. Port

"I would use one bullet for the bear and the second for me."

Many people have spent time outdoors in tents. In vast areas of the world, tent camping poses no threat to human health. Yet other areas exist wherein a camper's life is threatened by the weather or animal inhabitants.

What would it be like waking in the wee morning hours on a mountain ridge with only nylon separating you from vast wilderness . . . waking to the sound of ripping nylon . . . waking to a large, hairy predator clawing you . . . waking to the stark realization that you are this animal's next meal?

Imagine flying into a remote location in a two-seater and landing near a demolished tent . . . discovering that the tent's occupant had just been mauled by a grizzly . . . learning that the pilot will take the victim on a mercy flight to the hospital while you remain on-site alone until the pilot returns.

Helmuth Port experienced such a situation. He was alone, in the wilderness of Alaska's Brooks Range, in a four-man tent. He'd gone to sleep savoring the joys of another day in the outdoors. Tomorrow he thought would find him searching for fossils and minerals.

As he recounts his experience, imagine this solidly built 5-feet-9-inch tall, 170-pound man, with a snap to his walk, a twinkle in his eyes, and a short salt-and-pepper beard. Picture a man in love with the outdoors, a man with a strong German accent recounting his experience of an uninvited visitor.

In the fall of 1990 I was on the upper Eli River enjoying the outdoors. The Eli is 65 miles north of Kotzebue, Alaska, about 475 miles northwest of Fairbanks. I always fly with my friend and guide Johnny Walker when I'm in the Kotzebue area.

Johnny had out-of-state sheep hunters at his base camp. My plans included sheep hunting, hiking, fishing for big char, and searching for fossils and minerals. Since I had a sheep permit and Alaskans are not required to employ the services of a guide for sheep, I hunted alone. I'd been out ten days. Desiring to shower and clean up, I asked Johnny to fly me to his Squirrel River cabin. The cabin provided most of the comforts of home and was only a thirty-five-minute flight in Johnny's Super Cub. After a brief and comfortable stay at the cabin, I went out again to the mountains.

On the way from the Squirrel River to the Eli River we encountered some light turbulence. For the most part the skies were clear, but we saw little spots of clouds to the west.

Johnny's camp was in the Maiyumerak Mountains and part of the Baird Mountains. It was the 26th of August and the fall colors were at their peak. Creeks and rivers provided willow and some spruce tree cover, but other than that the country is wide open. Our camp was located in typical sheep country: rocky ridges covered by caribou lichen and interspersed with valleys.

As we landed, we saw clouds in the distance. Johnny said, "Don't set up your tent. You can use the kitchen tent. I'll get the other hunter and come right back; he's a doctor from San Diego."

It never happened. The beautiful day ended abruptly when clouds moved in. The wind picked up and rain fell. The weather changed so fast that within two hours the temperature plummeted from sunny and sixty-five degrees to the thirties.

Warned by the weather I put my tent up before the snow started. I took a bucket five hundred yards to the river, filled it with water, and returned to the kitchen tent. I wasn't concerned about the weather because I was dressed properly. I wore Timberland hiking boots (Sorrel boots around the tent and for short tundra hikes), insulated hunting clothes, and rain gear from Helly Hansen. Feeling I'd done all I could in preparation for the next day, I crawled into my tent for the night, wrapped in my longjohns.

It was a rough night. The storm blew in and the tent stakes came out of the ground. I spent most of the night outside the tent replacing stakes and putting big rocks on the bottom to hold the stakes down.

When I awoke the next day, the wind was still blowing, and it was still snowing. I went out hiking and saw caribou everywhere. They were moving in from the Kugururok area, across the Noatak River south of the Sekuiak Bluff and into the Maiyumerak Mountains. In that classic caribou mile-eating migration pace, the animals fanned out and never slowed their stride toward the south and the Kobuk River.

Around 5:00 P.M. I returned to camp. Sleep was difficult because high winds hammered the tent, causing the tent fly to pop and snap. The noise was endless and the tent shuddered with each blast. Finally about 1:00 A.M. I got to sleep. Tucked into the cozy comfort of my sleeping bag I slept on my right side, cushioned by three inches of down and Hollofill in my waterproofed cocoon. My right arm stretched out over my head, which rested on my bicep. The top of the sleeping bag covered my head.

About 3:00 A.M. I awakened from a sound sleep. I felt something damp on my face and weight on my chest. I wondered what was happening. It's not easy waking up, knowing that something is happening and not knowing what. You're wide awake feeling something deadly but you don't know what to expect.

I thought, *It's a bear!*

I felt the bear's mouth at the back of my head and I moved my right arm. That's when I felt his wet face hair brush my cheek. The animal instantly went for my right arm. Evidently he saw a danger or considered my moving arm a threat. He sank his teeth into my elbow and tried to rip it apart. With his jaws locked on my arm, his ear was right in front of my mouth. I feared for my life. Knowing that bears have sensitive ears, that I could not move with his weight on me, and that I was locked in my sleeping bag, I screamed into his ear in a loud, shrill, piercing voice.

The noise must have startled him because he pushed me away and jumped from the tent. He had come in the back side and jumped out the same way. It was dusky but light enough to see. He stood ten feet away on all fours with his head down, swaying it from side to side. I thought, *Any second he could attack.*

I tried to grab my .300 magnum. I felt it, but I couldn't lift it. I screamed again. Next to the tent was a bluff maybe three yards high. As he heard my second scream, he jumped up on this ridge, which had been the edge of the riverbed several thousand years before. He stood there and looked at me, continuing the side-to-side swaying of his head.

I would have shot the bear, but I realized that I couldn't use my right arm anymore. I couldn't lift the rifle, aim, and pull the trigger with one arm. I grabbed my rifle with my left hand and opened and closed the bolt with my mouth. Holding the rifle between my left upper arm and my body, I placed the stock on the ground, pointed the barrel straight up, and pulled the trigger. He turned and slowly moved away, disappearing from my view.

I went to work salvaging my gear and preparing for the bear's return. My tent was destroyed. I took my sleeping bag and rifle and walked the twenty-five yards to the kitchen tent. Our food was stored in fifty-five-gallon barrels in the kitchen tent. I rolled one behind me and one to the door, making a fortress. I put my rifle on the barrel for support, pointing it toward the door. I took two other sleeping bags and made a warm area to keep my body temperature up and prevent hypothermia.

Although the bear was not in sight, I was waiting for him. He knew he had me and that nobody could take me away from him. I thought, *He's coming back.* I was protected for his return, sitting and waiting for the bear. I took a ballpoint pen, and on my raincoat I wrote a note for my wife Gisela, letting her know what had happened in case I didn't make it. I told her that I loved her.

After I wrote the note, I took my Swiss army knife and cut my right shirt sleeve open from the wrist to the shoulder. I tied my arm with a tourniquet made of tent rope. I left it on until my fingers got numb. Usually every twenty minutes, I loosened the tourniquet and the arm started bleeding again. I wiggled my fingers until they had feeling, then I tightened the tourniquet with my left hand and teeth for another twenty minutes.

I opened my shirt and discovered serious wounds on my left side. I had enough antiseptic solution made of twenty Swedish herbs soaked in vodka to last for fourteen days. I washed my wounds with this antiseptic solution. Finally I wadded up toilet paper and placed it into the gaping wounds to absorb blood (there were several rolls of toilet paper in the kitchen tent). I cut my shirt into strips to hold the toilet paper in place. Every two hours I changed the dressing, tossing the bloody stuff in front of the door; I wanted the bear to come through the front door, to my face rather than behind me.

I was waiting and thinking, *What now?* As long as I was busy doing something it wasn't so bad, but when I wasn't busy, I thought about the bear. The first bright light of morning came into the tent, bringing hope and emotional feelings. Tears ran down my face. Then I thought about something to drink. I was glad I had the water from the river. I drank honey and water and that was good.

I was not concerned about bleeding to death, but I thought if I didn't get help within three days, infection would set in. Then I would get a fever and die. I made other provisions because I didn't want to die this way. I determined once the fever came I would shoot myself. I had two bullets left in the rifle. I would use one for the bear, and if I couldn't kill him with a single shot, the second would be for me. It was easy to make this decision out there under those conditions. I couldn't make this decision now. I wouldn't have the courage to think it to end.

I reconstructed the mauling in my mind and tried to determine the cause of the attack. The weather had been so nice the last fourteen days that we had not been using the kitchen tent; we'd been cooking under a fly. Two sheep, over forty inches each, had been shot, and we cooked and ate sheep meat. In another wall tent Johnny had fleshed the capes, and perhaps there were some fat strips on the ground. I think the bear smelled sheep from the campfire place. Maybe I smelled like a sheep to him, and he just opened my tent. He ripped the tent open with one paw and came in. This was also a poor berry year in the area, and few salmon spawned in the rivers.

As nearly as I could tell, the bear jumped in and was on me instantly. He first hit my side and held me down by standing on me. He went for my neck (you can see the tooth marks at the head area on my sleeping bag). When I moved my right arm, he bit it. Then I screamed in his ear and he cleared out. It was an old, skinny bear looking for food. Although I never saw the bear after the attack, I kept thinking, *Sooner or later, he's coming back.*

Forcing thoughts of the bear from my mind, I kept up my routine of loosening the tourniquet, wiggling my fingers, and changing the dressing. Thoughts about my life filled some of the time.

After my first trip to Alaska in the 1970s, I decided to quit architecture in Germany and move here. It was neither the fishing nor the hunting that brought me, but rather the closeness with heaven. I was not a religious person. I was raised as a Catholic—Christmas time and Easter we went to church. But Alaska touched me like nothing I'd ever experienced, and I simply had to come to Alaska.

Although I had to participate in World War II and although I came home unhurt, I decided, "No more rifles. I don't touch any gun anymore." I came to Alaska with the attitude "no more shooting, no more killing." When I catch a fish, I can take the hook out and say, "Bye, bye." I cannot take the bullet out of a hunted animal and say, "Hey, go again."

Alaskan friends wanted me to take my camera afield. Of course, you have to take your rifle with you for protection. Then your friends want you to get a bear tag, a moose tag. Before you know it, you're hunting. I've hunted fifteen years in Alaska.

I kept wondering how long it would be before Johnny could come back for me . . . wondering if the bear would return . . . wondering if I'd have to use the last bullet on myself. I knew that nobody would come to me in this weather. Who would? Not Johnny. He was a good caretaker. We were so often together that we know how each would react.

I waited at the tent, where I felt protected. I couldn't move. I kept watching, looking through the tent door to see what was going on. I'd used about six rolls of toilet paper when I heard the first sound of a motor out of the

134

skies. My reaction was, *Calm down. It's only the commuter going to Point Barrow with the mail.*

Then the sound got a little bit louder, and a little bit louder. It took me a while, but I finally got out of the tent. I saw only the tail of Johnny's Super Cub close above me. Now maybe I could forget about the bear's return. I was happy. He was a mighty pleasant sight. The attack took place at 3:00 A.M., and Johnny got back to me at 6:00 P.M.

Johnny dropped in low over the ridge. His flaps were down. He pulled power and glided silently in. His oversized tundra tires skimmed over the tundra and actually rolled through some low bushes on his touchdown. As he flew over camp, he noticed the wall tent up the ridge where he'd skinned the sheep. It was flattened. The bear had been there on its way to me. Realizing that a bear had visited his camp, Johnny had turned around and made a big loop to look for the bear. Thinking that I might be dead and that the bear might return, Johnny said to the hunter, "Throw a bullet in your gun." But they never saw the beast.

He helped the doctor hunter from the plane and said, "You will have to stay here. I will pick you up later. You can stay at the kitchen tent. If you want, you can look around for the bear. I have to fly Helmuth to the hospital in Kotzebue right away."

The doctor didn't want to stay. "Noooo, I won't stay here! I won't stay here."

Johnny's Super Cub was not designed for more than one passenger, and he said, "You have to."

The doctor said, "If you try to leave, I'll jump on the tail." (Only a few days before this the doctor had read halfway through *More Alaska Bear Tales*, and he told John that he would never read it again.) You could see that he was serious. Reluctantly Johnny changed his mind and said, "Okay then, throw all the other stuff out and crawl in the tail section. You can sit behind Helmuth." He flew us both out, with the hunter holding me upright.

We had no problems getting to Kotzebue. En route, Johnny radioed the flight station and made arrangements with the hospital. After landing safely Johnny drove me in his pickup a mile to the hospital, arriving at 8:00 P.M.

They X-rayed me and contacted the emergency doctor at Providence Hospital in Anchorage, who directed them on proper medical treatment. Although the elbow joint was dislocated, no bones were badly broken. The Anchorage doctor instructed them to relocate the elbow. They put it in, then X-rayed it. Ten minutes later, it was out. They relocated it three times. Out, in, out again; they couldn't keep it in. I was bleeding but hadn't experienced any pain the previous seventeen hours due to heavy doses of morphine. I felt pain when they tried to bring the elbow back.

X-rays did not reveal the total damage—all the ligaments and tendons were torn from the bone. There was no connection between the lower and upper part of the arm. The pulse in the arm faded away, alarming the medical staff. A pilot and copilot flew a doctor and two nurses from Anchorage to Kotzebue to return me to Anchorage. The Life Guard unit plus the Leer jet cost me $10,200—the most expensive flight I've ever taken.

During my ten days in the hospital, I was in surgery three times for the elbow and my deep belly wounds. One claw opened the upper cavity on the edge of the lung. The other went in the belly and was close to the colon. Two claws ripped through the ribs, which the bear broke. I had a cast on for five weeks, then I started physical therapy that continued for eight months. At the end I gained half of the normal elbow movement back. I'm back to normal now and no worse for the wear.

I still love the outdoors and spend as much time in Alaska's wilderness as I can. I don't have bad feelings about bears. Bears don't kill for fun. I was not a bad human being. I was in his territory, and he was going for food—me. Although I've had about fifty encounters with bears, I've never been afraid of brown-grizzly bears. But I don't like going close to black bears because I can't deter-mine what they have in their minds.

Going into the bush after such an experience is not easy. When night falls and I crawl into my sleeping bag, memories of the attack come back. My heart beats faster and my ears tune in to the night sounds. When the slight-est noise alerts me, I sit straight up in the tent, a gun in my hand, awaiting developments.

Hunting alone in Alaska is dangerous and foolish. Since my bear encounter, I make sure I don't go out alone. And I'm always on the alert for uninvited visi-tors . . . especially those who enter without knocking.

Some bears visit camps and are scared away. Some bears do not scare so easily and wreak great havoc upon man.

A Grisly Find

by Hank Taylor

*"The three men dug into the mound expecting
to find the body of the trapper . . ."*

*Anchorage attorney Hank Taylor related another tale
about his friend George Brown that was both eerie and
gruesome.*

I believe the time was around 1945. Greg skinned a
cat during World War II and the building of the Alaska
Highway. He worked from the city of Anchorage up to
the highway coming through Canada.

It was fall. Several old-timers were sitting around
on the north side of Turnagain Arm. (This "bay" flows
into upper Cook Inlet from the east. East of the northern
shore from the mouth is southern Anchorage, ten miles
away. The Arm is nearly fifteen miles wide where the two
bodies of water meet.) There was a trapper who lived
alone on the Chickaloon River running into Turnagain
Arm from the south. They hadn't seen him in a while
and got worried. Greg and two others decided to take a
skiff with an outboard and cross the Arm at high tide to
check on the trapper.

Once they reached his cabin at the river, they
"helloed." He wasn't around the cabin, and they went in.
A place setting was on the table with dishes, fork, knife—

everything laid out as if a man had sat down to have a formal meal alone. The food was dried hard on the plate. The rifle was gone from the wall over the fireplace. It looked as if a man had sat down to eat, was alerted by something, rose and removed his rifle, went out the door, and never came back.

They went up the stream on the left bank. A little ways upstream was a clearing, maybe a quarter of an acre, with the ground torn up. Tracks indicated a big sow brown bear with two full-grown cubs. In the middle of the clearing was a pile of brush and leaves and roots and raked-up dirt, a great mound of dirt. The pile was higher than Greg's head.

The three men dug into the mound expecting to find the body of the trapper, and they did . . . what was left of him. But he didn't have a head. They dug all around, but they couldn't find the dead man's head.

Greg went back to the cabin to get something to carry the body in. While walking the eastern bank of the river, Greg noted that the sandy clay bank had eroded. Under the alders the roots had washed out. A sizable clump of alders had washed into the water with their fall leaves trailing out like an alder fence.

Greg said, "I looked down into the water a good ways off shore, and there's my friend's head. His eyes are looking back up at me out of those alder limbs, right in the eye. His skin was white."

"I finally got up my courage and crawled down there and waded out. I was real careful that his head didn't come loose from the limbs it was hung in and got him by the hair. I took his head back to the others and told them they could quit looking: 'Here's the rest of him.' We put him back together again, then went for the Territorial Police."

"We looked real close at what was left of the neck. We figured that when the bear attacked and hit the trapper, she decapitated him. You could see that the bear hadn't pulled his head off. The trapper was hit so hard that the blow ripped his head from his body—and it killed him where the bears buried him. His head flew twenty feet or more and bounced down the bank and into the creek. Where it hung up in the alders was a hundred yards downstream from the body."

The men gathered the trapper's remains, then motored back to Anchorage to report their grisly find to the authorities prior to burial.

The moral of this is: Anyone entering bear country would be wise to have a reliable partner and to be well armed.

Brown bears are ultimately unpredictable and dangerous, as archer Bruce Brown discovered.

Stalk Softly and Carry a Big Stick

by Bruce Brown

"Bruce thrust his hand into the bear's mouth, trying to free his head."

Bruce Brown was eager to bag a grizzly bear. Although the twenty-five-year-old Brown was an avid bow hunter and successful big-game rifle hunter, he had yet to take large game with his archery tackle. Bruce considered harvesting a brown-grizzly with a bow as the ultimate challenge for a North American hunter.

He invited his friend, Dave Delapina, to hunt with him. The men were coworkers at Harborview Developmental Center at Valdez, Alaska. Although tracking a wounded bear was a distinct possibility, neither man expected what was to follow.

After having read about Bruce's bear encounter, I contacted him for an interview in November 1990. We met at the Sea Galley Restaurant in Anchorage, where he told me his story.

The hunter screamed, "Shoot the bear! Shoot the bear!" His hunting partner, fearing for his friend's life, launched a round toward the marauding brown bear. The shot had no visible effect on the animal. Fearing for his own life, the shooter fled the scene, leaving his downed partner at the mercy of the beast.

The hunter, Bruce Brown, lay on the ground fighting for his life. Thoughts flashed through his head and he reminded himself that this was not the way it was supposed to happen. When you walk into the woods, heavily armed, to dispatch a wounded bear, the odds are supposed to be in favor of man. So much for the odds.

Bruce and his friend, Dave Delapina, had followed the blood spoor of the mortally wounded brown, knowing from the frothy blood that it was lung shot. They expected to find it dead but were prepared to finish it if need be. They pressed on. The scenario was far from what they'd expected when they planned their hunt.

They targeted early September 1990 for their outing, deciding to hunt the area Brown had hunted unsuccessfully the year before. They would camp along the Chitina River in the Wrangell-St. Elias National Park and Preserve. They set up camp ten miles from their hunting area where other hunters would be hunting for moose.

Bruce and Dave had driven up the river twice a day scouting. They'd always found fresh bear tracks of single animals, never two or three together. On Thursday, 6 September, Bruce and Dave left camp in Bruce's Bronco and headed up McCarthy Road in the direction of Lakina bridge. A single-lane, rut-riddled gravel strip through the timber, the McCarthy Road connects Chitina and McCarthy. Two miles before the Lakina bridge Bruce dropped off Dave. The plan was for Bruce to drive to the bridge, park there, and hunt his way back to Dave, who would be hunting upriver toward Bruce.

Rain was falling as Bruce parked at the bridge and pulled on his rainsuit. He grabbed his archery gear and shotgun and ghosted into the woods. In addition to their archery tackle, each hunter carried a 12-gauge shotgun. Bruce packed a Winchester Defender; Dave carried a Mossberg 500. Also, Bruce had his Desert Eagle .44 Magnum pistol loaded with 250-grain Full-Profile Jacketed Silhouettes (Sierra).

Twenty minutes passed. The rain subsided, and the vegetation began to dry out. Bruce left the river looking for a spot to remove his rain gear. Ten yards into the brush and about forty yards from the river, he sat down and removed his rainsuit. Kneeling to stuff his rain gear into his daypack, Bruce noticed movement in the brush.

Something brown approached through the trees only twenty-five yards away. Realizing immediately that it was a brown bear, Bruce froze. The animal walked by within fifteen yards of the hunter and continued on to the edge of the foliage. As the animal stood facing away from him, Bruce rose and nocked an arrow. The bear did a 180 turn and walked past Bruce again, completely unaware of his presence. The bear shuffled twenty yards past Bruce and paused beneath some giant cottonwood trees. Bruce waited expectantly for a shot.

Within minutes the bear turned broadside. Bruce drew his bow. The bear then moved behind a tree, presenting an undesirable shot. Bruce slowly eased the pressure on the bowstring and waited. A short time later the animal moved. It stood with its head to the right, giving Bruce the perfect shot. He drew, anchored, aimed, and released his arrow. The speeding arrow sliced behind the bear's right shoulder and exited the left shoulder. The bear spun 270 degrees and rocketed into the brush.

Bruce sat a few minutes before walking to the river. He would take his shotgun and rendezvous with Dave. They could return to trail the bear as a team. He left his bow to mark the spot and walked on. In his excitement to share his adventure with his partner, Bruce stepped quickly along. Twenty minutes later Bruce found Dave.

Bruce poured out his elation, recounting his incident and telling Dave that he needed his help in locating the wounded animal. Dave left his bow and the men started upstream. They reached the scene of the shooting, and within ten feet of the arrow's penetration of the bear, they found blood. Following the blood trail another twenty-five feet, they encountered blood dripping from brush and trees everywhere. Bruce felt a surge of confidence, knowing that the animal was well hit.

Slowly and with shotguns at the ready, the hunters followed the spoor, anticipating finding the animal's body at every turn. Seventy-five yards crept by before they spotted their prey. The bear lay on its side twenty-five yards away. It appeared to be dead, but the men waited just in case.

Suddenly Dave looked at Bruce and held up two fingers, indicating two more bears. Unable to see the animals, Bruce stepped fifteen feet to his right for a better look. The hunters peered through the brush for a couple of minutes. As the men watched, two bears moved off toward the river, leaving the dead bear behind. One bear stopped, turned, and returned to the dead animal.

Bruce stood up and started to step backward toward Dave. Suddenly Bruce caught movement from the corner of his eye. He turned his head. A brown object zigzagged through the trees toward the men. The object's identity registered in Bruce's brain. A bear! He yelled to Dave, "Here she comes!" Bruce shouldered his shotgun and fired a warning shot, hoping to turn the charging bear. She zeroed in on Bruce and never veered.

She came hell for leather, mowing over five-inch-wide alders in her path, never slowing. Chambering another round, Bruce stepped backward and fell. Dave was ten feet away, and Bruce shouted for him to shoot the bear. Faster than it takes to tell it and before he could rise, the bear was on him. She attempted to grab Bruce's head with her jaws. Her power and size overwhelmed him. Dave fired his shotgun, missing the bear. Unable to chamber another round, he retreated from the scene.

Bruce thrust his hand into the bear's mouth, trying to protect his head. The bear bit his hand, breaking it and severing several tendons. Screaming and kicking, Bruce fought for his life. Bruce kicked at her with his left foot, connecting with her nose. The enraged bear bit through his foot, tossed it aside and clamped onto his right thigh with her jaws, then let him go.

The bear recoiled to spring again. As she lunged toward his face, Bruce again kicked her in the nose with his right foot. The bear seized his foot and vaulted over him, rolling and spinning him in the opposite direction. He landed upright on his butt, spread-eagled. He watched as his assailant whirled to attack again!

In that brief moment Bruce freed his .44 Magnum pistol from his holster. He clicked the safety off and fired when the bear was at arm's reach, hitting the bear in the front leg. He instantly fired a second shot, hitting the bear in the neck and breaking it. As the animal collapsed to the ground mortally wounded, Bruce shot it once more for good measure, striking the animal in the shoulder area. The entire attack took less than fifteen seconds.

Bruce quickly rose and looked for the second bear. He hollered for his partner. Seeing neither the second bear nor his partner, Bruce started for the road. He wondered what had become of Dave.

❖   ❖   ❖

Fear for his life overcame Dave. In spite of hearing his partner's screams for help, Dave ran through the trees toward the road. Panic drove him. He heard Bruce shoot, but nothing could persuade him to return to the scene of the attack. He had seen Bruce fire his first round from the shotgun, which had no effect on the animal. (He didn't know it was a warning shot.) He feared his shotgun might misfire, jam, or be an inadequate match for the bears.

Dave didn't want to put himself at risk again. Convincing himself that Bruce was either dead or bleeding to death and that there was nothing he could do to help him, Dave pushed on. He reached the road and clomped along, one foot after the other as fast as he could go. His thundering footfall quickened his heartbeat and his stride. His target was a deserted tree stand. Finally he reached it. With heart pounding, perspiring profusely and harboring little hope for Bruce, he hurriedly scaled the tree.

It would not be long till darkness settled over the woods. Dave didn't want to spend the night alone in the woods, much less in the tree. After forty minutes in the tree, he built up his nerve and climbed down, wondering about his safety on the ground.

He walked to the Lakina bridge and sat down. The only woods sound he heard was the rushing river. Two hours passed before Dave saw headlights from an approaching vehicle. It was the Park Service. They stopped and picked him up.

❖　❖　❖

Bleeding from his wounds but able to walk, Brown headed for the road and his truck. It took him twenty minutes. There was no sign of Dave. He started the vehicle and engaged the automatic transmission. Bruce looked in the rearview mirror and saw only blood. Part of his scalp was loose. Bones protruded from his right hand, looking like nothing more than crunched bone and pulp. Blood oozed from his wounds as he lurched along the gravel thread, forty rough miles from Chitina.

He drove to their hunting camp expecting to find Dave . . . or someone. No one was there so he drove on. Reaching Chitina, Bruce entered a local bar that housed a telephone. Two volunteers with medical training gave him first-aid treatment. After bandaging him, they loaded him into his own truck for transport to Glennallen. At the hospital in Glennallen he was treated and prepared to be med-evaced to Anchorage.

While recovering Brown kept replaying his experience. He was confused and tried to understand the reason for his partner's deserting him. Bruce understood Dave's retreat so he could clear his weapon, but Brown couldn't understand Dave's reason for not returning to help him fight the bear once his weapon was unjammed. Dave later admitted he thought that Brown was either dead or bleeding to death, that he felt he could not help him, and that it was imperative that he save himself.

A number of things individually or jointly contribute to surviving a bear attack: common sense, behavior, will to live, a reliable partner, a deterrent, proper weapon, Providence. Fortunately Bruce had a handgun handy.

Officials representing the National Park Service and the Division of Wildlife Protection investigated the incident. They returned to the mauling scene and found two dead brown-grizzly bears; a sow and a bear of nearly the same size. The sow weighed 700 to 800 pounds and squared 7 feet. The bear Bruce had arrowed was 6½ feet and weighed 600 to 700 pounds.

EPILOGUE

Taken from the "Letters to the editor" section, *Anchorage Daily News*, F-5, 14 October 1990: "Volunteers should get credit"

We would like to clarify Craig Medred's recent stories about Bruce Brown, the man mauled by a grizzly on Sept. 6. Medred's articles consistently lead the public to believe that National Park Service Rangers took care of Brown's injuries, and he even specifically states that they "saw to it that he was evacuated to Providence Hospital . . . ." This is not accurate and certainly not fair to the people who were responsible for the medical care and transportation of Brown.

Brown drove himself to Chitina, but once there, he was cared for by medically trained volunteers. Medred said he went to the Ranger Station, which was closed at the time. Brown arrived at the local bar, one of the few businesses and telephones in town, where local Emergency Medical Services (EMS) personnel provided medical treatment to Brown, arranged for an ambulance to come from Glennallen, and transported him themselves to meet the ambulance. Brown was then transported by ambulance, also staffed by volunteers, to Cross Road Medical Center in Glennallen. There, he was assessed, X-rayed, and provided air med-evac transport to Providence Hospital.

Brown saw a park ranger for just a couple of minutes in Chitina, during emergency medical care, when he asked a few pertinent questions so he could locate the rest of Brown's party and make sure there were no other injuries. The ambulance crew, after hearing Brown's story, also contacted the local Alaska State Troopers with additional information to make sure David Delapina was not injured or lost in the woods all night.

There were a lot of people (providing more than seventy-five man hours on this incident) involved with getting this man to advanced medical care in Anchorage, and they deserve much more than a "Well done!" which is more than Medred awarded them. They would have been happy with a simple mention that he was treated and transported by them.

Please, when you print a story, make sure you include all the facts. One of these days, you may need the local EMS. If it weren't for the volunteers, there wouldn't be emergency medical services in the Copper River Basin and that is true in most communities across the state. A pat on the back goes a long way with a volunteer, any volunteer. A mention in the paper goes a lot further!

—Cherie Conkle-Ansell, Administrator Copper River Emergency Medical Services
—Jay Well, Chief Ranger, Wrangell-St. Elias National Park and Preserve

Bruce Brown met a brownie while hunting, but Ellie Florance was at a work site when a bear came through her tent.

No Way to Treat a Nurse

Larry Kaniut

"Ellie slowly rose to her knees and reached for the pistol."

Traveling to a new environment nearly always involves adjustment. Whether a person ventures from civilization to wilderness or the reverse, change is a certainty. For the city dweller who ventures to the wilderness, especially as a newcomer, surprise often accompanies that change. Such was the case when Eleonora Florance traveled to Alaska in 1994.

Eleonora and her husband Jared are health workers living just outside Washington, D.C., in Manassas, Virginia. Jared is a doctor and public health director in Virginia, while Ellie is an occupational health nurse with the USGS. Eleonora had an opportunity to work in Alaska a second summer and jumped at the chance, even though it meant leaving her husband and children behind.

Eleonora was one of several volunteers. The volunteers worked through the Department of Interior's Volunteers for Science program, which assigned them to the United States Geological Survey. Usually a half-dozen volunteers joined the researchers for the month of July, helping cook and clean as well as assisting in some research. Ellie's primary roles were camp nurse and science assistant at MIAC.

Moose International Airport Camp (MIAC) hugs the shoreline of the Gulf of Alaska, some seventy air miles southeast of Cordova, Alaska. The site, near the foot of the Bering Glacier, houses a group of summer USGS workers and volunteers, fifteen to thirty at any given time. Their activities include studying the Bering Glacier. Their primary concern is that should the rate of advance of the Bering Glacier continue (advancing four miles in eighteen months since 1994), the ensuing icebergs falling into and cluttering the Gulf's waters could choke off the shipping lanes and endanger ships' safety and travel.

MIAC covered a small area with a landing strip scraped out of the bush and gravel. The camp consisted of a half-dozen tents in a straight line. The camp director's philosophy was that a straight-line tent arrangement allowed for better safety should it be necessary to account for a bear intruder. Part of that philosophy assured that the first and last tents were equipped with guns and that they were in the hands of competent people.

In order to minimize the buildup of waste and to negate bear visitors, combustible garbage was burned and noncombustible garbage was bagged and left on the airstrip for daily pickup by a Cordova Fishing and Flying Service. Camp life became routine and was regulated by scientists, assistants, and staff who recorded data for future interpretation. The campers managed to procure necessary data and had no serious problems.

They'd seen an occasional bear. Two days before, an adolescent brown bear had been on the airstrip nosing through the garbage. It was a three-year-old female that appeared thin for her age. A lack of salmon in Lake Vitus nearby no doubt contributed to her leanness. The animal exhibited behavior that constituted a threat to the humans, but she left camp, so no action was taken to destroy her.

The adolescent bear is the most likely bear to get into trouble. Three-year-olds have just been abandoned by their mothers who are about to go into estrus, allowing them to mate again. These adolescents are inexperienced at finding food. Although this bear appeared to pose no problem to the camp, camp personnel took notice and remained more alert because of the bear's appearance.

Should a bear incident develop at the camp, the campers felt confident that they could handle it. They'd engaged in an intense three-day training course in firearms safety, bears and bear behavior, helicopter and fixed-wing safety, CPR, and wilderness first aid (for potential dangers in the deep woods).

Between 6:00 and 7:00 A.M. Friday 29 July 1994, the airstrip adolescent bear started for camp. It ambled determinedly from the south, almost as if on remote control, to the last tent in the line: Eleonora's. In that familiar pigeon-toed shuffle the animal walked a one-hundred-yard straight line. It ignored everything in its path and came within three feet of MIAC's refrigerator, that contained three full coolers of meat, cheese, and milk; and within ten feet of the kitchen tent that contained a large variety of food.

Alone in her two-man tent, Eleonora awakened. She knew that breakfast was at least an hour away, so she closed her eyes. Dozing comfortably, Ellie snapped awake when she heard a swishing sound coming from the tent's walls. She thought the sound was made by the bear's rubbing against the two thicknesses of visqueen sheeting covering the tent as a rain fly. She recalled, "I could hear *swish, swish, swish.* I started screaming out 'Bear! Bear!' and just yelled and yelled. I had no idea if the bear was making a noise. I'm sure I drowned her out."

The bear swatted at the tent walls and broke the tent poles. Then the bear swatted Eleonora from paw to paw. Ellie said, "I was like a little ball in her hands." The bear raked Ellie's right shoulder and hip with its claws. Eleonora's .44 pistol lay at her feet inside the tent entrance. Ellie pulled away from the bear, rose to her knees and reached for the pistol, but was afraid to fire for fear of hitting a fellow camper. "I didn't know who was up at the time or where they might be."

Ellie wanted to shoot but said, "I thought about firing straight up, but I was afraid that if I stuck my arm up there she would get it."

The woman tried to remain motionless, screamed for help, and covered her face with her left arm, which received deep puncture wounds. Whether it was her screaming or something else, the bear backed off. As the bear retreated, Ellie recalled, "I remember standing straight up with the gun in my hand . . . I didn't have to unzip anything so I must have stood up through the tears she had made. I saw the bear walking away, sideways, about thirty feet away."

While Ellie lay in her sleeping bag yelling for help, commercial fisherman, Mike Herder, awakened by Ellie's screams, grabbed his .44 Magnum and leapt from his tent. He looked in the direction of the screams and saw the bear attacking Ellie. Herder held fire for fear of hitting Eleonora. He fired a shot over the bear as it attacked, and the bear moved off. Mike ran closer. Other armed campers showed up, causing the animal to move off momentarily.

The bear began to return, and Mike shot it in the chest. The animal turned and ran off. Mike followed it, picking up a 12-gauge shotgun from the office tent. When the bear turned again, Mike shot it with the scattergun. The slug dropped the bear within a few dozen feet. Herder fired another round into it from fifty feet to make certain it was dead.

Ellie walked the four hundred feet from her tent to the carcass. She said, "I was clutching my side because I knew I was losing blood." The bear had torn the skin between her shoulder blades, punctured her hip, and caused two deep fang wounds in her left arm. She instructed the camp members as to her proper medical care.

Attempts to radio Cordova for help were fruitless because it was "before regular hours." Finally a distress call was made on Channel 16, and the call was picked up immediately by a fishing vessel in the Gulf. The vessel contacted the Coast Guard in Kodiak. They in turn alerted the Coast Guard station in Cordova. Response after that was rapid. A Coast Guard chopper launched from Cordova and churned down the coast; the crew spotted camp immediately. It was fortunate that they arrived when they did, because after that the fog settled in and didn't clear until evening.

In spite of her injuries and blood loss, Ellie was able to walk to the U.S. Coast Guard helicopter. She was flown to the hospital in Cordova and later on to Anchorage's Alaska Regional Hospital.

When Ellie's husband Jared learned of her attack and hospitalization, he was hopeful. He said, "When they told me she had walked to the helicopter, it told me 90 percent of what I needed to know." Jared arranged with his mother Margaret to drive two hours to Manassas to stay with his children while he journeyed to Alaska to be with Eleonora. (She said, "Jerry called me SOS. He said a bear had clawed her arm, and that's all I really know.")

Although Ellie sustained deep flesh wounds, her condition was listed as stable and satisfactory Friday night. Unfortunately, the hospital in Cordova was not equipped for the surgery she needed, so she boarded a commercial airliner as a passenger, loaded with morphine and with a nurse escort, her wounds still open, for the trip to Anchorage.

One bright spot, and a matter of great comfort to both Ellie and Jared, was the professionalism and compassion shown by USGS staff, from the director on down. When Jared asked for help in making reservations, tickets were ready before he was packed. He was met in Anchorage by Paul Brooks, the director for Alaska, and Tammy Bagley, the administrator, arranged for a motel and car, so Jared could concentrate on Ellie's needs. Gordy Eaton, the USGS director, visited Ellie twice in the hospital. And of course, for an agency like the USGS, there was never a question that the medical bills would be covered. Ellie was discharged, and they flew home without incident.

The bear probably attacked because it was hungry. Some speculate that the visqueen cover, an aroma associated with petroleum products, attracted the bear. However, five other tents were covered with visqueen or plastic tarps. Other speculation centered on menstrual fluid. Ellie had some bloodstained clothing in a plastic bag in her tent. She had also just begun her menstrual period. Two days previously when the bear first appeared, another camper was menstrual. The animal approached her visqueen covered tent also. Perhaps the cause of the attack was a combination of the bear's hunger and the odor of the plastic and/or the menstrual fluid.

Upon examining the bear it was discovered that it was two hundred pounds lighter than a bear of its age and height should be. The carcass was ferried away from camp. Although the claws had been removed as a souvenir for Ellie, state fish and game regulations required the hide and claws be turned over to the proper authorities. (However, they disappeared.)

In the end, Eleonora does not fear the outdoors. She said, "I'm lucky to be alive. The bear could have severed my jugular, and I could have bled to death.

"I want to go back. I really do. I think [the attack] was just a freak accident. I hope I feel that way next year."

And so a city dweller met change, was surprised to be the victim of a bear invasion, and adjusted. All things being equal, Ellie doesn't appear to be emotionally damaged or any less physically fit, or enthusiastic after her bear experience.

Ellie did in fact go back to MIAC the following summer. It was a horse she had to climb back on, and she did. And fortunately, Ellie wasn't bitten by anything bigger than a mosquito.

See Appendix 5

Although Ellie Florance did not expect bear problems, Henry Knackstedt, veteran Alaskan, not only expected problems but also took steps to avoid the bear whose path he crossed.

Detour toward Death

by Larry Kaniut

"Henry then began his crawl to life."

*Wily woodsmen know how to stay alive. Experience
has taught them the ways of the woods and enabled them
to conduct their daily activities. Many an old-timer has
had a close call with* Ursus arctos horribilis—*some closer
than others—and lived to tell about it. Such was the case
with Henry Knackstedt of Kenai, Alaska.*

In 1952 Henry was a thirty-nine-year-old fisher-
man-homesteader. Alaska was almost brand new in
1952—seven years shy of statehood. Oil interests, big-
game hunting, fishing, and tourism hadn't sullied the
territory yet. Henry was no stranger to the woods. Like
many of his outdoor brothers he depended upon his
environment for sustenance: They obtained red meat
from big game; they caught fish and picked berries from
sea and field; they trapped hides and prospected yellow
gold from furbearers and streams.

The first day of moose season in September found
Henry a few miles out of Kenai en route to a favorite
moose pasture, daydreaming about moose ribs and past
hunts. He'd left his hunting cabin alone and traveled
upriver, starting into the woods with the wind in his

face. Henry packed a 1903 Winchester with a double safety feature, a mechanism requiring a release before a round could be chambered. Both woods wary and safety conscious, the homesteader always carried his weapon with the safety on but in such a manner that permitted him easy access to firing.

The clearing he sought was a mile away. He followed a well-worn game trail along the moss-carpeted forest floor, wending beneath the canopy of outstretched limbs. Although it had been raining for several days and the brush was sopped, the morning was young, only 8:00 A.M. Before long Henry discovered the lower brush and tall rye grass bordering the trail had been brushed clear of rain droplets. At that point the trail was a good three feet wide. Henry's woods knowledge affirmed that the absence of rain on the trailside foliage indicated recent travel. The "dry" trail was wider than a moose's legs; Henry concluded that the most recent trail user was a bear, more than likely a family of bears!

This was no place to run into a sow grizzly with a litter of cubs. Choosing safety over valor, Henry took a ninety-degree, right-hand turn from the trail, thinking he'd get off the bears' trail and detour a few hundred yards. He figured they were ahead and probably within minutes of him.

After Henry hiked two hundred yards, he broke left, paralleling the trail and expecting to hit his clearing within half a mile. But it was not to be.

Henry had no way of knowing that the bear had also left the trail. His determination to avoid danger was probably the same reason the sow chose to leave the trail. He discovered too late that the sow and her infant cubs were sleeping in the tall grass in his pathway.

Several factors played against Henry: 1) he was downwind from the bear so she probably never smelled him, 2) he was alone, 3) he wasn't as alert as he should have been, partially because he thought he had avoided the bears, 4) he was familiar with the area, had never seen a brownie in the neighborhood, and wasn't expecting one.

Henry soon snapped from his reverie when he heard a growl. The sound triggered his instincts and he automatically raised his rifle toward his shoulder. Surprised, he looked to his left fifteen feet and saw a large sow grizzly. She rose to a half-crouch and pierced him with her eyes. Henry remembered being conscious only three to five seconds after that.

He pulled back on his rifle bolt trying to rack a round, but the extra magazine safety nullified his action. For some reason the double safety feature was on and did not permit loading. With a chambered shell he could have blasted into the sow's ivory-studded maw. Even though the normal time needed to maneuver the bolt required only a second or two, the hunter did not have enough time to inject a round.

In one jump the brute was on him. Henry instinctively swung his rifle up to shield him from her. He held it before his face in an effort to protect him from her hayhook paws and chomping canine teeth. A rotten fish smell emanated from her mouth. She hit Henry like a cement truck, knocking him down and out. Evidently convinced Henry was no threat to her cubs—perhaps that he was dead—she stayed only a few moments.

Some time later Henry came to. How long he lay on the ground surrounded by forest and silence he didn't know, possibly an hour. But when he regained consciousness, he was in bad shape and knew he had to do something to save himself. His trusty old packboard had saved him from more serious injury (it was forward of its normal position on his back and the animal had taken a couple of bites out of it). Henry had no idea what had become of his rifle.

Henry didn't know what had become of the bear, but he knew he needed help. He lay on his face in a pool of his own blood. His left eye was missing, and the left side of his face was a mass of gore. There was a hole in the back of his neck and his brain was exposed to the air, either from claws or teeth. Henry's body was racked with pain. He breathed heavily and shook to such an extent that he wouldn't have been able to feign death had he wanted.

On the one hand it would take all his nerve to move for fear the sow was standing guard over him, watching for any movement. On the other hand he was in such bad shape that he figured movement on his part would send her into a frenzy and she'd finish the job and put him out of his misery. When Henry moved, he discovered that she had gone. About then a wildlife-spotter aircraft flew over him, giving Henry hope of discovery and rescue. However, it did not see him in the clearing below.

Knowing his survival rested on his own shoulders, Henry spent a great amount of time and energy crawling around in search of his rifle before finding it ten yards away. He then began his crawl to life. He fired a few evenly spaced shots, praying they'd be recognized as a distress signal and not a hunter shooting at game. Then he passed out again. When he regained consciousness, he shot the remainder of his ammunition. His rifle reports were answered by gunfire from his neighbors across the Kenai River. Before long helping hands came to Henry's succor. He was rushed from the woods to medical help. Two and a half months later in a Seattle hospital, a doctor told Henry how fortunate he'd been not to have brain damage.

Although others told Henry it was unfortunate that he didn't get a round into the bear, he disagreed. He argued that had he merely wounded the bear—without a spinal or brain shot—she would have made shorter work of him. Evidence of bears' stamina supports Henry's premise. Several documented accounts describe a bear's traveling two hundred yards or more before its mortal injury stopped it.

Neither Henry Knackstedt nor James Erickson expected problems with a mama brown bear, but bears don't play by man's rules.

A Tail Too Close

by James Erickson

"I went limp for what I thought would be the last few seconds of my life."

When I contacted Jim Erickson of Juneau, Alaska, to get a firsthand account of his encounter with one of Alaska's brown bears, he willingly responded with this story.

It was September 1990 when two friends and I planned a hunt for Sitka black-tailed deer on Chichagof Island in Southeast Alaska. The town of Hoonah is located on the northern shore of Chichagof Island and offers unique access to the surrounding forest via the many branches of logging roads that were created to harvest the timber of the island.

The night before our Juneau departure on an Alaska state ferry, I went to Dennis Welburn's home. I work with Dennis, a husky concrete form worker (at 5-feet-10-inches tall and 190 pounds). He's 35 years old, married, and has two children. That night was also my introduction to Ray Rusaw, the third member of our party. Ray was an auto-body man. He was 27 years old and married, with three children. His slender build housed a 5-feet, 11-inch, 160-pound body. Although I was also 27 years old, I was the smallest hunter. My 150 pounds are stacked on a muscular frame 5-feet, 6-inches tall. And unlike the others, I'm not married.

Dennis had successfully hunted the Hoonah area several times, harvesting deer very near the logging roads. Ray had little experience hunting Alaska's big game, but we all envisioned a simple and memorable hunt. Little did we know how memorable it was to become. We felt adequately prepared for the weekend as we loaded Dennis' 1985 Ford Explorer F-250 XL Club cab 4x4 with food, extra gas, rifles, and other hunting gear including sleeping bags, wool clothing, and rainwear in anticipation of damp weather.

The next morning, 14 September, we boarded the ferry bound for Hoonah with an estimated arrival time of 4:00 P.M. With each passing hour on the ferry, our excitement for the hunt grew. We reached Hoonah right on schedule, and decided to drive away from town that night so morning would find us already in deer country. We took a route that led us up Kennel Creek, a dead-end canyon near Freshwater Bay. Although we were well into the fall season, there had been no freezing temperatures yet, and the streams were full of spawned out salmon. Blueberries were also in great supply.

As we prepared ourselves for a night in the cramped confines of the pickup cab, Ray noticed air leaking from one of the rear tires. Since it was now dark with a steady rain falling, we elected to wait for morning to repair the tire. Awakened by first light from what had been a long and restless night, we soon set about to repair the flat tire. To our dismay we discovered the tool set had been removed from the truck and was probably sitting in Dennis' garage in Juneau.

Since he was most familiar with the area, Dennis decided that he'd walk to the logging camp at Freshwater Bay and get any needed assistance or tools. Not knowing how long this could take, he recommended that Ray and I hike up the mountain's near ridgeline to see if we could bag a deer or two. We planned to meet at the truck later in the day. Dennis left his rifle and took his Desert Eagle handgun because he felt safer with his .44 Magnum. He then headed down the road while Ray and I grabbed our rifles and started up the mountain.

The conditions in the woods were dreadful from the start with dense, wet brush and plenty of spiny devil's club impeding our progress. After nearly two hours we reached a subalpine area where the foliage thinned out and provided us with easier walking. We'd reached a point just below the crest of the ridge when the sun came out and bathed us in sunlight. We decided to stop for a breather.

We knew this was bear country. Admiralty, Baranof, and Chichagof Islands, known locally as the ABC Islands, support a healthy population of brown-grizzly bears; the most dense population in the world resides here. We had noticed fresh bear signs on the way up the mountain, but we were now in more open and steep terrain and did not anticipate bears.

We had been sitting approximately five minutes with our backs to the mountain when we heard a snapping sound above and behind us. Sure that I was going to get a shot at a deer, I stood up slowly and peered over the crest of the ridge. I was surprised to see the tail-end of a bear cub as it scooted off behind some light cover not fifteen feet from where I stood! My gaze shifted off to the right about twenty-five feet where I saw a larger bear, obviously the cub's mother, on all fours intently sniffing the ground. Just then Ray stood, spotted the sow, and exclaimed, "Oh, no, what are we going to do!"

The sound of Ray's voice focused our location for the sow as the brown-mini haystack looked directly into our faces. The next second she stood on her hind legs before dropping to all fours and coming for us in a lightning-fast charge.

It didn't seem there was even time to think about raising my rifle. I had both hands on the gun with it stationed at my hip when she was on us. I struck her hard with my gun barrel just as the force of her charge knocked it from my hands. I heard Ray's gun discharge.

In a flurry of activity and fury she bowled the two of us over. Ray tried helping me by pulling the bear off me. The bear bit Ray and pushed him off. I tumbled seventy-five to one hundred feet down the forty-five degree slope. Before I could respond, the powerful animal was on top of me again. I screamed frantically as she came down on me, biting and tearing my flesh. Any pain seemed to be overridden by the terror of the horrible situation.

Ray had lost his gun also, but he tried to help me by pulling and kicking at the bear. She turned from me momentarily and bit deeply into Ray's left thigh. Then she came for me again. As Ray continued trying to help me, the sow bit into his hand and swatted him downhill. When she turned back to me, I struck her on the snout as hard as I could with my fist. This only enraged her further, and I was sent tumbling down the mountain once again.

She was face-to-face with me until I rolled into a tree and managed to get facedown on my belly. In an instant the sow was on top of me and resumed biting me repeatedly along the length of my left leg. She ripped hunks of flesh from my calf. Over and over she bit me in the left foot, calf, upper thigh, and head.

When she seized my head in her powerful jaws and clamped down, I heard crunching sounds. I figured this was probably going to kill me. The realization of being near death seemed to coincide with a sensation of calmness that flooded my body. I went limp for what I thought would be the last few seconds of my life. The minute I quit fighting and hollering, the attack stopped. She must have figured I was no longer a threat to her cub because the sow left me and returned up the hill rapidly.

I lay there motionless for a few minutes, wanting to make absolutely certain that the bear was gone before I moved. When I got up, I looked at my arms, amazed that they were both intact. I knew I had been injured badly from the bite to the head. I wanted in the worst way to climb the tree I had rolled against, but my left leg wouldn't function that well.

Five minutes had passed since the bear left. Unsure what had happened to Ray, I called him. He heard me, but he didn't dare answer for fear that the bear would come back. The sow let out a roar. Fortunately she was with her cub and didn't come for us again.

Within a few minutes Ray rejoined me where I'd come to rest. I stood leaning against the tree I had rolled into. I told Ray not to be shocked when he saw the extent of my wounds. When I moved my head, I heard sloshing sounds inside my skull. Ray told me I had several gashes in my head and that my left ear was shredded. My left leg was badly gouged.

We decided it was best not to leave me alone for fear the sow might return while Ray went for help. Although we lost our weapons and glasses at the attack site, we chose not to return for them—we didn't want to see that bear again.

Ray encouraged me along, and we started for the road. We slowly limped our way down the mountain through the thick brush toward the road. My body continually wanted to give up, but I was determined to live. My life flashed before me, and I kept thinking I might never see my family again. The emotional impact of these thoughts forced me to the ground. But Ray continuously talked to me to make sure I remained conscious. Whenever I fell, he urged me to get up and to keep moving. Our legs continued to cramp and seize up. Not knowing what had become of the bear tormented us as we pushed through the forest.

Ray facilitated my passage by stomping on the devil's club, smashing and knocking it down for me. Nearing the bottom of the mountain, we walked into a clear-cut that had begun to grow back. It was very difficult to cross because the new growth covered tree stumps and logs left behind by loggers. Exhausted, I stumbled several times.

I fell to the ground and dragged myself through the new growth. I pulled myself over logs, tearing my body against the bark and pointed, broken branches. I felt my wounds opening under my clothing. I got up and walked again. By this time we were near total exhaustion, and our blood-soaked clothes were shredded. We stumbled onto the logging road, but the truck was gone.

We started along the road toward Freshwater Bay. Within minutes we saw a vehicle coming up the road. I flagged with my coat. With great relief we saw that it was Dennis. He was returning a second time after removing the flat and taking it to Freshwater Bay to be fixed.

Ray was in better shape than I and climbed into the Club cab, as it was easier for him. I got into the passenger seat. While we were heading for Freshwater Bay logging camp, we met a logger driving a pickup. We stopped and Dennis told him about the bear mauling. He radioed Freshwater's office and told the woman that we were on our way to the camp, needing to be flown to Juneau.

When we reached Freshwater Bay logging camp, the office worker told us that she had called for a plane to come for us. I asked if she could change that to a med-evac flight. The woman called and canceled the plane, then phoned Temsco. Temsco is located next to the runway of Juneau's airport along with Glacier Volunteer Fire Department. Traditionally when there's a med-evac, personnel from GVFD assist Temsco in the emergency med-evac.

We sat in the truck and waited for the helicopter. My body seized up because I had climbed into the truck by myself. I would have been unable to get out alone. Approximately forty-five minutes later I heard the unmistakable sound of a helicopter. I've never been so happy to hear a Huey in my life.

The BH212 helicopter, piloted by Temsco's Dan Maurice, touched down next to our pickup at Freshwater Bay. I was greeted by Alexis Rippe and Jeff Newkirk, emergency medical technicians from Glacier Volunteer Fire Department where I was at the time. I was currently a volunteer firefighter, and I was also an EMT. It was very comforting to have EMTs that I knew. I felt confident that I would be taken care of, as my goal since the mauling was to reach medical help.

Ray told the EMTs to attend to my injuries first. They cut my clothes from my body. When Ray and I were stabilized and bandaged, the med-evac departed for Juneau.

After we left Freshwater Bay, Dennis was left alone. He phoned my sister-in-law Jean. Jean called my brother Dale, who was on shift as an RN in the emergency room at Bartlett Memorial Hospital in Juneau. After Dale had gotten word that I was coming in, and not knowing what he was going to face, he asked if he could be relieved of his duty in order to be by my side to comfort me. Jean also called my sister Sue, who was living in Juneau. She was slightly hysterical thinking about the mauling, knowing how badly a grizzly can shred a person and not knowing my condition. In the lobby of the emergency room my sister and brother agonized for ninety long minutes before I arrived.

After reaching Bartlett Memorial, I was greeted at the helipad by Dr. Urata, my personal doctor; my brother Dale; and two ER nurses. Dale reassured me that I would be taken care of. The doctors and nurses rushed us into the emergency room. Unwrapping the blankets from me, the doctors saw extensive punctures all over my body. They immediately put a neck collar on me to prevent any further possible spinal damage. Next they X-rayed my body to check for broken bones. Determining there were none, the doctors rushed me into surgery. An intravenous tube was placed in my arm, administering antibiotics to ward off infection.

I was in surgery for five hours. The doctors did a fabulous job. My ear needed to be reattached and reconstructed. The calf of my left leg was heavily damaged. The doctors sutured my calf wound, leaving it partially open to allow drainage and healing from the inside out. Drains were put into my buttock wounds to permit fluid drainage.

I have scars from canine teeth puncture marks in my upper left leg and my ankle, heavy scarring on the left calf, and claw marks on my buttocks and back. I lost a slight amount of hearing in my left ear due to scar tissue closing off part of the ear canal. I have a slight amount of numbness in my lower left leg and foot from the damage done to my calf.

Dr. Bob Urata and Dr. Gary Hedges came into my hospital room at least twice a day to check on me. There had been questions at first regarding my ear's chances of regenerating. While in the hospital I became good friends with the nursing staff.

I spent nine days in the hospital so they could monitor the draining of my open puncture wounds and be sure that my ear was not infected.

The charge from the hospital was $12, 989.33. I was also responsible for half the med-evac cost of $1,492.80, plus $200 for the EMTs as I'd been billed for a routine ambulance call. Additional costs included charges for a CRN who had done the anesthesia at a cost of $800, plus lab costs and doctor fees for rehabilitation at my parents' home in Minnesota.

Ray was admitted and released the same day. He had been bitten in the upper part of one of his legs and had puncture wounds also.

It was very difficult for my parents when they first heard of the mauling, since they were hundreds of miles away in International Falls, Minnesota. Hearing my voice and knowing that my brother and sister were at my side helped. Every time my parents told other family members, they broke down because the listener feared the worst. (They knew how bad grizzly-brown bear maulings could be.)

After my release, I stayed with my sister Sue for two days before flying to International Falls, to show everybody that I was still intact and to recuperate under my parents' care. I had a strange haircut from being shaved around the bites to the back of my head. I was on crutches and I was unable to walk on my left leg, which had open wounds that were too large to close without a skin graft. There wasn't enough skin tissue to cover all the wounds, so some wounds were left to heal by themselves, requiring dressing changes daily until they healed.

Fish and Game officers went to the attack site to investigate. They tracked the bear and determined Ray's shot never hit the sow. She was doing a natural thing by protecting her cub. They recovered our guns, eye glasses, and ammunition.

It's five years later and I have been moose hunting with my brother the last two years up north. My nights in the tent are still tough, but I hope that wears off. I'm a carpenter and I lead a very active and happy life. Every once in a while I run into Ray, who tried to save me, and Dennis, who drove us to safety. Ray says that brown bears are a lot more unfriendly than black bears. He has scars on his hand and left leg and continues his autobody work in Juneau.

And every day I wake up, I realize it's a great day to be alive!

AFTERWARD

The following is a portion from a letter from Jim's mother. Jim forwarded it to me.

Shortly after arriving home from a wedding reception, we received a call. It was from the friends we had left that afternoon, asking what we had heard about our son's bear mauling—it was the first we knew of it.

It was a terrifying feeling and our imaginations ran wild. How could anyone survive such a vicious attack? Our concern was multiplied by the fact that we were so terribly far away.

We called our daughter-in-law in Juneau and she referred us to the hospital. There we talked to our son Dale, who told us the extent of Jim's injuries and what had been done for him medically. Then he said we could talk to Jim. The sound of Jim's voice was wonderful and relieved a little of our anxieties. We talked to Dale later and he told us Jim was in no immediate danger, but that things could change with the possibility of infection.

We talked with Jim every day and were assured he was doing well. Dale told us he thought Jim would recuperate better at home, so arrangements were made and he came to be with us. The day he arrived it was a wonderful feeling of relief to see him and know that he was going to be fine. During the time he spent with us he would walk the driveway daily and strengthened his leg so he could throw away the crutches. He went pheasant hunting with us to South Dakota, and three short weeks from his arrival he was on his way back to Juneau and his job.

Only a parent that has had their child hurt or sick and in grave danger can sympathize with the wide range of emotions we went through during Jim's ordeal. We feel sure that the prayers of family and friends were instrumental in his healing.

Deer hunters like James Erickson don't always expect to meet brown bears, but brown bear guides do. What guide Tom Jesiolowski did not expect to find was a surprise.

One Mauling Was Plenty

by Tom Jesiolowski

"The impact of the bear was like being hit by a runaway truck."

Tom Jesiolowski left his home state of Pennsylvania in the mid-1970s for a hunting trip in The Last Frontier. Alaska's vastness and animal life captivated him. He moved to Anchorage, where he owns Northland Arts Taxidermy and is a freelance photographer.

Tom guides with outfitter Richard Guthrie of Anchorage. They hunt the Alaska Peninsula for brown bear and caribou, and the North Slope of the Brooks Range for Dall sheep, caribou, moose, and barren ground grizzly bear.

Tom is no stranger to bear charges, most of which are false or bluff charges in which the animal pulls up short or turns aside. During Tom's days in Alaska's wilderness watching and photographing, he has experienced a number of false charges, each reminding him that a man in bear country must consider the animal's unpredictability, power, speed, and ferocity.

Tom was 36 years old in 1983. He was 5-feet-8-inches tall and weighed 175 pounds. An enthusiastic and tough outdoorsman, Tom guided Norman "Chip" Gerry from Georgia on his first Alaskan brown bear hunt. Theirs was a typical Alaska Peninsula hunt accompanied by fickle peninsula weather. They spent six hours in a downpour, peeking from under slicker hoods until dark drove them back to camp. Getting out of weather and wrapping themselves around warm food and hot coffee ended their day on a better note. They tried hunting the next day, but a storm and low visibility sent them scampering back to their tent for the day.

Chip and I were awake again before the first of light on the third day of our hunt. We fixed and ate some hot grub. We thought it might be another long, cold, wet, windy day. I prepared my hunting pack while Chip got his things in order. His motor was running early as we had spent quite a few hours in our tent the day before, the wind howling and the rain blowing through even the most microscopic holes in our new North Face tent. He was anxious to see if we could find the bear that we had watched leave our valley for a high mountain sanctuary two days before.

We had waited for the big bear six hours that day. I told Chip that as long as he didn't wind us, the chances were good he would come back. It was a well-worn bear trail he'd followed in and out of our valley. There were still some late salmon in the river that drained our hunting area, and it would be awhile before he would take to his den in the high country. The pouring rain never let up, and dark shut us out. He didn't come back.

On day four we left camp before the sky showed much light. I felt the best bear area was several miles back in our valley where we could watch the trail the bear had taken on two days before. I wanted to be back there at the first of light.

I spotted a bear almost as soon as I started to glass that morning. It was a large bear. After we moved closer, we discovered it was a sow with two large cubs. I told Chip they were probably the bears that had made all the tracks around my tent four days earlier.

We watched and admired them for a while. I answered lots of questions for Chip: How big? How old? What would we do if? Before too long I decided we'd better move. They might wind us and spook another bear that we might really want.

The wind was blowing into our faces and quartering up the mountain, following to our right side. It did not spread any scent out into the valley; the wind was good for us that morning. We walked along the river and passed the bears, noting many partly eaten and rotting salmon scattered along the bank amidst lots of bear tracks.

I was headed for a lookout I had known from a previous hunt. It was a small hill, part of the mountain. From there we would be directly across from the place we saw the bear two days before, which would give us a commanding view of the valley.

As we progressed up the hill, I turned several times to check the view. Before we reached the top, there was the big bear again, coming down the same trail it went up two days before! I needed only a moment to study it in my spotting scope. It was a large, lone bear. He was headed for a long narrow alder patch in the valley floor that grew on each side of a stream that tumbled down from his mountain retreat.

We had to move fast. It was a considerable distance across the main valley. There were lots of small alder patches, little sloughs, and ditches to negotiate. I thought the bear would follow the alder patch along the stream till it ended, then head for the larger river and the fish. I figured we could get into a good position if we arrived at the end of his alder patch before he came out. I should have known better. We waited what seemed like hours, but no bear. He either lay down in the alder patch or sneaked out some unknown way. It was going on 10:00 A.M. when I decided to move.

We climbed up on the hill on the downwind side of the alders, hoping to see into his hideout. After watching for just a few minutes, we spied another bear over a mile away up the big valley. If it turned out to be a good bear, I wanted to be on his side of the alder patch we were now watching. We had to drop down and cross a small ravine that the stream had gouged out of the mountain. We lost sight of the bear for only a few moments, but it was gone when we topped out on the other side. There were small alder patches close to the bear, so I figured it walked into one for a nap. That was not unusual at this time of day, as it was 11:00 A.M. now.

Chip and I talked things over and I suggested dropping down on the upwind side of the alders in front of us where we'd last seen the first bear. I left him in position and went down one hundred yards or so. If my scent blew through the alders and the bear was in there napping, it would get him out.

I started back to Chip. When I was halfway, I saw Chip jump up. I turned to see a bear busting out of the alders in front of us. I ran the rest of the way to Chip and quickly calculated the situation. So many things went through my mind that my thought process had to speed up.

The bear didn't appear as large to me as I had thought when I studied it in my spotting scope. Maybe because it was moving so fast now, I felt it was a good bear. Chip was yelling for instructions and asking how large the bear was, was it nine feet? (That was the minimum requirement he placed on the size bear he wanted.) I told him it was close. I also remember saying the bear had winded us and wouldn't be back. If he wanted it, he needed to take it now.

Chip fired, and within moments the bear was down. We moved in on it cautiously to make sure it was dead. When that was confirmed, there was a lot of back-slapping, yelling, and handshaking done.

We had one problem, though. Chip's camera was not working and I had left mine at camp because of the drenching we had got two days before. Chip wanted pictures badly. I said okay. I figured we had just enough time. We could make it to camp, get my camera, and be back to the bear in time to take pictures and do the skinning before dark. Taking the hide back after dark wouldn't be much of a problem.

We would have to move fast. We had quite a few miles to cover. We marked the location of Chip's bear with a plastic bag high on an alder bush. I then checked with Chip on his rifle. I always create an awareness with anyone I hunt with on firearm safety. He had already removed the round from his chamber. It's a rule I maintain when someone is following directly behind me. That way I didn't have to worry about them falling or tripping and shooting me in the back.

I decided to take a shortcut straight through the alders, the same path from where the bear had previously emerged. I knew of a bear trail on the other side that would lead for several miles toward the beach and camp. We hiked toward the alders several hundred yards distant, elated with the good luck we just had and making plans for the rest of our hunt. We needed only to tip over a caribou, and we could enjoy some real good fishing and goose hunting for the remainder of the hunt.

We were soon in the alders, still talking, daydreaming, and trying to soak in the morning's events. A few minutes later we reached a stream running through the center of the alders. The banks were fairly steep, and it appeared to be slippery.

I turned to Chip as a courtesy and showed him I was removing the round from my chamber for safety's sake. I crossed the stream and climbed the bank on the other side, continuing on a few yards after reaching the top of the bank. I then stopped and turned to wait for Chip. Chip was just coming into sight when I heard a bear. He was huffing and popping his teeth.

I turned to see a large brown bear coming down on me with a full head of steam only about twenty yards distant. I realized this was a serious charge, not a bluff. A lot of things were going through my mind. Oddly enough, one thing that stood out was the light coloration of the bear's ears as it bore down on me.

The closer it came, the more I noticed the huffing-puffing, guttural noise it made.

I didn't think I had time to swing my rifle from its hanging place on my pack frame, let alone bolt a round into the chamber. I knew it wasn't loaded, but things were happening so fast that I shoved the barrel at the bear's chest and jerked the trigger on the empty chamber just as he hit me.

What a sick feeling.

He hit me with his mouth open and wrapped both front paws around me before I could get my back turned fully toward him. The impact of the bear was incredible, like being hit by a runaway truck. I felt immense pressures, as if my guts were coming out my mouth.

I was hoping he'd bite into my pack. No luck again! He carried me about a half-dozen yards, where we piled up into the base of some alders. For a few split seconds he tried to get a mouth hold on me. His jaws popped together continuously.

I yelled to Chip to get the bear but not to shoot me. The bear picked me up by the side in its jaws and gave me a few quick shakes, then dropped me just as I heard Chip's rifle crack.

I managed to hold onto my .338 Winchester rifle. The bolt was open as I hit the ground, and I instantly slammed a fresh round into the chamber. I thrust the barrel behind me expecting the bear to get on me again, but Chip hollered that he was circling back into the alders.

When the bear let go of me, I dropped with one leg in an awkward position and I couldn't spring right up. When I got turned around, the bear was moving off just out of sight. Chip said his shot hit the bear for sure. I thought the bear would make a second charge, but he kept his distance. I said to Chip, "Let's get the heck out of here."

We retreated the same way we had entered. A lot was going through my mind now. I had one bear down, another one wounded, and I hadn't yet calculated my own condition. I knew I was going to need medical attention and was upset that this bear had wrecked the rest of my hunt with Chip.

As soon as we reached the open, I wondered whether to check my back first or look for the bear that had just jumped us. I asked Chip again if he was sure he had hit the bear. He said he was. Just then the bear broke out of the alders, turned, and looked at us. I thought for a moment he was coming after us again. He turned, though, and made a break for it, running with a limp.

I ran after him. In a few seconds I had a clear shot and dropped the bear, then gave it one more shot to be sure. I walked over and kicked the bear in the butt. I felt sick. It wasn't a good feeling having to kill that bear, and at the same time I was still upset because I knew the rest of my hunt with Chip was ruined.

Now I had to decide how to handle the situation we were in. We were quite a ways from the beach and our camp. I had two bears that needed skinning, and I still hadn't checked my wound. Already my side hurt quite a bit. When I asked Chip to check my bites, he wasn't even aware that the bear had bitten me.

He helped me get my shirt off. I had a few puncture wounds below the armpit and in my back under the shoulder blade, but they weren't bleeding badly. A hole had been scooped out of my back. My back didn't bother me as much as my side.

The most memorable part of the whole incident was taking the first hit of being run over by the bear. It felt as though all my insides were going to burst. (I found out later the bear broke my ribs when it slammed into me.) It remained a mystery as to why the bear hadn't cleared out, with all the racket and the man scent in the immediate area.

I thought I would skin Chip's bear and leave it to pack out after I got patched up, but before we went back to it, I started getting muscle spasms under my ribs. I didn't know if I might be bleeding inside, so I figured we had better head for the beach. I wasn't in shock and could walk, so we left. Chip would have a lot more problems if I passed out or went into shock where we were.

As we headed for the beach, I couldn't help wondering how long it might be before Rich would come by. The weather could get bad, and we might not see him for three or four days. I soon passed it off. It was a good flying day and Rich is good about checking on us regularly. I was hoping the tide would be out so he could land on the beach. We had a signal worked out in the event that we needed him.

As soon as we got to the beach, I piled the washed-up fishing float high on the bank according to our plans. We scuffed out a "HELP" in the sand. I undressed and Chip tended my wounds. I hadn't felt bad while I was walking, but now I started to stiffen up and hurt. Chip got a charge out of putting the nozzle of the First Aid cream into the tooth holes in my body and squeezing the tube.

We wondered how long we would have to wait for help. I was unlucky that the bear jumped me, but everything else fell into place that day. Rich came by in about fifteen minutes, even before I could get my belongings together. We flew back to where the bears lay so Rich would be able to find them easier from the ground when he returned. Then we headed toward Cold Bay.

In a short time Rich had Cold Bay on the radio and they in turn were diverting a flight from Dutch Harbor, as I had already missed the scheduled flight from Cold Bay to Anchorage. Paramedics met me at the Reeves' Airline hangar and fifteen minutes later I was headed for Anchorage, where by 7:00 P.M. of the same day I was in the hospital getting patched up. My injuries included four broken ribs, and the ribs on the right side of my rib cage were torn from the breastbone.

The next day Richard and Chip returned to retrieve the two bear hides. Chip's bear was in good shape, but the one that mauled me had been torn to pieces by other bears during the night. Both animals were enormous females.

The following spring when brown-bear season opened, I was back at my camp on the Alaska Peninsula. My hunter was Willard Ryan of Jackson, Mississippi. Willard was an old friend, having already hunted with me in the Brooks Range.

We hunted the same valley where my bear incident had occurred the fall before. After hunting this valley hard for ten days unsuccessfully, we decided to move. We would have only two days left in the season, but a fresh area might help to change our luck.

Rich flew us to another spot not far away. Things started picking up even before I got my new camp set up. I was preoccupied with getting the tent up in a light drizzle, when Rich spotted a bear sleeping in some alders only two hundred yards from us. Law prohibits us from hunting the same day we've been airborne, so all we could do was keep an eye on him till dark. This was the boost we needed to rejuvenate our optimism.

We were up before light the next morning. The sleeping bear was gone! I glassed the slopes of the mountains surrounding our camp at first light. The scenery here is spectacular: the mountains form a natural amphitheater and steep alder-grown slopes are rimmed by high, rugged, snowy peaks. Almost immediately I spotted a bear. It was moving from behind the highest peaks directly above our camp. It ran downhill till it reached the first high alders on the mountainside, where it took refuge.

There was nothing tricky we could do here. Geography prevented all but a direct climb up a line that would take us to the bear's elevation, just left of his hideout in the alders. I anticipated the climb would take almost two hours. I knew as the air warmed that it would carry our scent uphill and most likely alert the bear to our presence. I thought we would lose this bear, but we had no other options.

Willard was slightly below and a little to the right of me. I was crossing up to the left, as I figured we were getting very near to the bear's position. Just as I reached the top of the alders, Willard ran up from behind hollering, "The bear is coming!" Willard moved uphill slightly.

I gave Willard some instructions, then remembered thinking to myself, well, the bear winded us like I thought and is probably making his escape. I remember checking my rifle chamber to make sure it was loaded, and turning my scope down from 5X to 1½X. All the while Willard was hollering, "The bear is coming!"

Because the slope of the mountain curved, a small ridge prevented me from having the same view as Willard had. To my astonishment, my first sight of the bear came less than forty yards distant! As he crossed the mountainside, he appeared to run more over the alders rather than through them. I could hear the same guttural chugging of his breathing as the bear from the previous fall. I couldn't believe this was happening again.

The bear disappeared into some thicker alders. As it emerged, my mind was racing faster than normal function allows. I remember thinking, *I hope Willard doesn't need for me to tell him to shoot.* The bear was so close that I didn't know if I'd have time for more than one shot.

We must have fired simultaneously. The bear slumped onto his front elbows and came right back up, hardly slowing down. I was trying to calculate my next shot from the hip so I could turn myself in a defensive posture, when Willard's second shot rocked the bear a full foot to the side. The bear wasn't more than a dozen feet from me. I actually saw the round pass through the bear as it carried dust and debris, exiting the backside of the animal. I'll never forget the relief I experienced the instant I realized that the shot had finished him. Several more shots were fired.

Then several minutes were spent sitting and collecting our thoughts. As I sat there soaking things in, trying to analyze the event, I still couldn't believe it. This bear had winded us. Instead of running away, he circled down-hill till he struck our ground scent, then came on it like a hound dog.

Rich told me later that there was a carcass on the beach on the opposite side of the mountain where the bear came from. Maybe our bear had a confrontation with another bear. Maybe it had lost its meal and was taking its frustrations out on us. Whatever the reason, I still believe most bears will avoid human contact. These instances of bears deviating from what we consider normal behavior keep us aware that we need to always be alert in bear country.

Surprises stalk the forest. Tom Jesiolowski found out, and so did Mark Riccardi.

Sow Swats Soldier

by Larry Kaniut

"You never think it's going to happen to you."

Several people called my attention to the news article about a soldier who had been thumped by a bear. I looked in the newspapers and found accounts of a platoon leader on maneuvers. I was unable to locate the military man, so I rewrote the accounts. While he lay in the mud, he alluded to my first bear book and probably never dreamed he'd be in my third book about bruin.

The soldier was part of a group participating in a three-day orienteering competition. The plan was for each participant to be dropped off in the woods and, through the utilization of map and compass, to find the four-mile distant location before the competition did. It was a good plan. However, a mother grizzly had a different plan.

Second Lieutenant Mark Riccardi of Anchorage's Fort Richardson Army Base was a former New York resident. He was a surveillance platoon leader with the 106th Military Intelligence Battalion. He and his men were on maneuvers at Fort Greely near Delta Junction, 150 miles north. Riccardi was a 23-year-old, 5-feet, 7-inches, 160-pound man experiencing his first year in Alaska. It was 14 August 1991.

Before going into the field, the soldiers were briefed. Mark said, "They briefed us about the bears, all right. But you never think it's going to happen to you. Until today I didn't realize how powerful a bear can be."

While running through the woods toward his distant objective and relying on his training and experience, Mark paused. He recalled, "I stopped running to check my compass. Suddenly I heard something that sounded like a big dog huffing and snorting behind me. I saw it was a grizzly and froze. The grizzly charged me the first time, but stopped about five feet to my left and started to sniff. About five feet to my right, something moved. I turned my head and I saw the three cubs. I think that I startled her when I moved my head to look at the cubs. That's when she attacked."

The 300- to 400-pound sow knocked him to the ground and mauled him. He was amazed by her power. He heard the bear's teeth and claws rip through his clothes and skin. Mark lay on his face in the mud, the sow breathing on the back of his neck. While he lay there, he remembered over and over the quote he'd read in *Alaska Bear Tales*, "The great hunter lay on his back, his stomach and intestines strewn over the ground, his scalp torn off, and his tongue hanging from his mouth."

He later said, "Lying there, along with the fact I was never going to see my wife again, that paragraph was all I could think about."

Part of his training for safety in bear country included playing dead during a grizzly attack. He held his breath until the bear lost interest and ran off with her three cubs. The entire attack lasted no more than ten seconds, which was just fine with him!

Mark recalled, "When the bear finally ran away, I stayed on the ground for about a minute to make sure she was gone. Then I got up, surprised to be alive."

He cried out for help and continued on his way. Another soldier spotted and rescued him. Mark proudly proclaimed, "We walked to the finish line in about half an hour. Officially I finished the race and even made good time."

Mark's rescuers didn't need a compass or a map to direct them to Bassett Army Community Hospital on the outskirts of Fairbanks at Fort Wainwright. His injuries included bite punctures and deep cuts on his back around his shoulders and shoulder blades. He was kept under observation a day or two and discharged Friday 16 August 1991.

Mark wasn't ready to get lost in the woods right away, and he was mighty happy to be alive after his Alaskan bear encounter with the sow that swatted him.

Grizzlies are dangerous, but no more so than a polar bear on a mission, like the one that Scott Haugen tracked.

Terror on the Tundra

by Scott Haugen

"A drag trail left in the snow indicated that the bear had the victim."

The couple walked the familiar street of Point Lay, Alaska, that December 1990 morning. Who would have expected they'd be attacked by a bear in their village? I read about the incident and contacted Scott Haugen.

Scott and his wife Tiffany, both in their twenties, were born and raised by educators in Springfield, Oregon. Her health degree from Oregon State University and his science and social studies degrees from the University of Oregon helped them secure jobs when they interviewed in Portland, Oregon. They knew their teaching assignments would be far from the norm, being two of only four teachers at the smallest school on the North Slope. Following their marriage in July 1990, they headed north to fulfill their dream of teaching in remote Alaska, knowing that they would experience elements of nature found nowhere in the world.

As expected, their lives did change. Tiffany taught grades three through eight in one classroom, and Scott taught grades nine to twelve, as well as coached cross-country, basketball, and volleyball.

Scott had a few months of village living behind him when he experienced a tragic event. He responded to my request with the following story.

When the phone rang at 5:00 A.M., it was my principal requesting my assistance in a village emergency. The village Public Safety Officer (PSO) had requested help over the citizens' band radio. One man had been attacked by a bear, and help was needed to find him and to guard against another attack. Very rarely does a PSO ask for public help, but when he does, you can bet it is a critical situation. That was the case on 8 December 1990.

What ensued in the next two hours was an experience I neither expected nor will forget for the rest of my life. While getting dressed in the three-bedroom home we rent from the school district, many thoughts raced through my mind. I thought perhaps the victim was fine and the whole situation would turn into a simple tracking excursion. *What kind of bear was it?* I wondered. At this point no one knew whether the bear was a grizzly or a polar bear. *Why would it attack someone in the middle of the street?*

With such thoughts racing through my mind and while putting on layers of heavy clothing, I began feeling hot and confined. Other questions flooded my mind. *What if there is more than one bear? What if I am the one who ends up shooting the bear? Not a chance of that; I was asked to assist, not to take charge. But, what if I did go out on the search? Would our group be the ones to find the predator and the prey? What if the victim is severely injured and what type of first-aid procedures might I find myself administering in the subzero temperatures? How far did the bear go with its prey? Maybe it didn't travel very far before it began feeding on its victim. Why else would it attack when and where it did, unless it was provoked? If it was provoked, maybe we were looking for a wounded bear.*

Before I knew it, I was dressed. Getting dressed for early morning hunts is second nature, but never had I gotten dressed so quickly without actually thinking about what I was putting on. Before I left the house, I grabbed my Winchester .30-06 and loaded it with five rounds, pocketing an extra five just in case. I kissed my wife Tiffany good-bye, telling her not to worry about anything. I stepped out the door to walk with Andy Fields, our principal, to the PSO's office.

While walking, my mind replayed information I'd gained in the past two years. The village of Point Lay, Alaska, is situated some 190 miles southwest of Barrow on the Arctic coast, with a population of about 150. Between the current village site and the Arctic Ocean is Kasegaluk Lagoon, which parallels the coastal shore and separates the village and the shoreline by about one mile. According to villagers and regional biologists, the pack ice that annually gathers along the northern shores of Alaska is usually two to three miles off the coast during early December. This past December was different however.

The sea ice did not find its way down until late December, well after the polar bear migration had been under way. Winds and ocean currents were thought to be the main reason the pack ice was not up to its usual accumulation in some places. When polar bears migrate down the North Alaska coast, they usually follow the edge of the sea ice down from the Arctic Ocean and Beaufort Sea searching for seals, their primary diet. Seals haul out on the edges of the sea ice to rest between periods of feeding. This is when the polar bear stalk.

It is not uncommon for the remote Alaskan villages situated on the North Slope coast to have polar bears wandering through during the winter months. It is uncommon for the polar bear to come into the villages in search of food. However, because the sea ice was a mere five hundred yards offshore this year, polar bears visited villages, including Point Lay.

While Andy and I walked toward the PSO's office, we wondered where the attack took place. Little did we know that we would pass within seventy-five yards of where the bear was feeding on the victim. Before I knew it, I was at the PSO's office, three blocks down the road from our house.

The predator was a polar bear. The assisting PSO, Don Grimes from Point Hope, calmly told us the sketchy details. The bear-attack victim was twenty-eight-year-old Carl Stalker.

Carl and his pregnant girlfriend, eighteen-year-old Rhoda Long, were walking from one house to another when they encountered the polar bear at 4:30 A.M. Stalker was walking just ahead of Long when they spotted the bear. Long yelled to Stalker, turned and ran into her sister's house, where she and her sister watched from a window. All she saw was the polar bear disappearing around a corner. Everything happened so fast, for Long and Stalker had no warning signs that a bear was in the area. Activity within the villages at such hours of the night is not uncommon. Stalker didn't follow Long back into the house, but he ran in the opposite direction, perhaps to lure the bear away from his girlfriend.

When Long reported the attack, there were three PSOs in the village instead of the usual one. Point Lay was in the middle of receiving a new PSO, Neil Paskowitz, who had arrived one day earlier. Don Grimes had accompanied Neil to Point Lay to help him get an idea of what his job would entail in the village. Prior to Neil and Don's arrival there was a temporary PSO, Kevin Early, filling in from the village of Wainwright. Kevin was to return to Wainwright the day of the attack. They immediately organized a search party.

As few people were showing up to get involved, it took much longer than I had expected to get the actual search under way. Perhaps people were simply in shock over what had taken place. Instead of waiting at the office, I accompanied Andy and Officers Paskowitz and Grimes to the attack site.

I was surprised to see that the attack had taken place right in midtown in the middle of the road, not fifteen yards from the doorstep of the house to which

Long had escaped. We followed the tracks for only twenty yards to get an idea of which direction the bear had taken the victim.

In addition to the initial attack site, we found one other place, approximately ten yards from the attack site, where the bear had stopped with the body and had apparently bitten the victim about the head and neck as was evidenced by the blood, human hair, and the pieces of scalp lying in the snow. A drag trail left in the snow indicated the bear had the victim.

I had the unnerving feeling that if we found the victim, he wouldn't be alive. The bear seemed serious about obtaining food immediately, not preserving it in a cache for later. The bear had gone straight for the head. The blood in the snow was bright red; small droplets quickly led to larger ones. Where the drops of blood had fallen onto the snow, small splash marks indicated the victim was bleeding as he was being dragged swiftly toward the lagoon. The spattered blood, the indentations of the bear tracks, and the drag marks of the victim's feet were all quite shallow (¼ to ½ inch deep) in the snow.

We found tufts of long, black hair at the initial attack site. Hair attached to scalp was also found ten yards away, as was blood, this time in larger quantities, possibly equaling one quart. We ended the scouting. The drag marks indicated the bear was headed toward the iced-over lagoon, the direction the search would take.

We arrived at the town firehall to find others showing up. Snow machines were being fueled and first-aid supplies were being organized. At 6:10 A.M., the PSOs led the search party out to the initial attack site.

While growing up in Oregon, I had the opportunity to spend a majority of my life in the outdoors with my father, Jerry, who also teaches high school science and is an authority on animal behavior. I spent many years trapping, beginning in grade school, and I learned several fascinating things about wildlife, tracking, and animal behavior. I have tracked several species of animals over the years, including cougar and black bear, whose predatory instincts are not unlike that of the polar bear.

I have hunted small and big game alike. Such outdoor experiences, along with my knowledge of biology and animal behavior, led to my involvement in this situation. When I volunteered to aid in the polar-bear search, the last thing I expected was that I would be tracking the man-eater with a flashlight, on foot, alone. However, I wouldn't have committed to the tracking if I wasn't confident in my tracking abilities.

Seven people assisted in the actual search, but upon arrival at the attack site it seemed many of them were shocked at what they saw. The blood and hair of the victim, their friend and relative, lay in the road, and at this point I'm sure it appeared as a bad dream.

Several minutes elapsed and to the surprise of the PSOs, no one was following the tracks of the bear. A few people headed up the lagoon in search of the bear, some distance from where the tracks were, while others stood in the road looking at the attack site.

Since no one was following the track itself, one of the PSOs asked me if I would take a flashlight and follow the tracks. After getting over the initial surprise of this request, I said I would help in any way that I could.

I chambered a shell into my .30-06 and began following the track. I passed by the place where the bear had dropped the victim to gain another hold. The uniform, flat, frozen surface of the snow was disturbed, smashed down slightly, looking quite different from that of the regular trail. Blood had accumulated in this spot. Beyond this spot the drag trail continued for approximately twenty yards toward the lagoon, as drops of blood were divided by drag marks of the victim's feet. Suddenly I found another site where the bear had regripped the body. This time there was a bit more blood, still bright red but more concentrated.

I was two to three minutes into the solo tracking of the polar bear. For the first time I looked back at the lights of the people still standing in the road at the attack site. I was about thirty yards from them and suddenly realized I was, indeed, on my own. With my heart in my throat I crept cautiously along the drag trail. I followed the track to the crest of a hill, which went down to the shore of the lagoon, approximately seventy yards from the attack site.

In this part of Alaska, the terrain is like a desert. The land is flat with an occasional rolling hill. In daylight, visibility is several miles on a clear day, but on stormy days I have walked and literally not been able to see my own two feet. Luckily, this morning found no wind, only cold, forty-two-degrees-below-zero temperature and the blackness of morning.

The snow depth ranged from three feet to scattered snowdrifts of over forty feet. Fortunately, the cold weather we had been having on the North Slope froze the snow such that not even the bruin and its prey penetrated the surface while traversing the tundra. I didn't have to worry about tripping over brush or limbs or the bear charging out of the trees, because there are none of those things in this region of the Arctic.

While I stood atop the frozen snow at the crest of the highest hill, I shone the light down the trail left by the bear. This was the first time I questioned myself during this ordeal. Approximately five minutes had elapsed since my tracking began, and I thought about what I had seen and what could lie ahead. I knew there was only one set of bear tracks. I also knew that I was the only one on the track, meaning it was likely that I would find the body if the bear hadn't dragged it far. I hoped the batteries in my flashlight wouldn't fail me.

The beam from my flashlight danced off the crystals of ice lying on the crusted snow and made its way down to the lagoon's edge. I vaguely made out an object in the snow fifty yards away on the edge of the frozen lagoon. The fear that I felt earlier was instantly and greatly magnified. It seemed as though every nerve in my body jangled outside my skin, and the only sound I heard was the thundering of my heart.

Immediately a multitude of thoughts assaulted my mind. *Was it the bear or Carl's body? Would I even be able to see the bear? Does it know it's being followed? Does it have its sights set on me as its next victim? Maybe it's a sow with cubs. Be careful not to get caught in the middle. Think! Think!*

I quickly removed my down face mask so I could more freely see everything around me. Despite the extreme cold, I was feeling quite hot. My flashlight cast a strong beam for at least thirty yards. With the added reflection of the snow I could see clearly. But at the extremes of my light, approximately fifty yards away, I thought I had found the body. *I found it, or have I? Don't tell anyone yet. Be certain before you tell anyone. Where's the bear? Why can't I see it's eyes reflecting in the light? Is it now stalking me? Which side of me would it come from?*

The darkened object lay in the snow, surrounded by a radius of darkness as well. My first assumption was that it was the body of the victim, but I was somewhat surprised not to see the bear. As I began walking toward the object, a man approached on a snowmobile from the north end of the lagoon to my right. The snowmobile's light coupled with my light enabled me to focus more clearly on the object. The darkened area changed into red, and the object in the middle was the victim's body.

I yelled to the others to let them know I had spotted the body. As the snowmobile got closer and its light bounced over the landscape, it was obvious that the bear had fed on the victim. Even from where I stood, I could see the victim had been partially devoured.

The man on the snowmobile pulled up to the body and parked so that the headlight reflected off a snow bank near the body and out over the lagoon. It was then that I saw the polar bear on the ice about fifty yards from the body. I yelled a frantic warning to the driver. The roar of his engine and his apparent state of shock at the sight of the victim kept him from hearing me. I rushed to his side.

As I reached the body and the man on the snowmobile, a second snowmobile appeared. I had him focus his machine's headlight on the bear, and I could see that the bear was acting peculiarly. I expected to see it flee or attack. It did neither. The bear's head was stretched outward along the ice with its front paws extended as well. It was pushing itself along the ice with its hind legs, the back half of the body extended upward. This is a stalking position often taken by polar bears while hunting seals in an attempt to hide their black nose and eyes.

As I walked alongside the snowmobile, we closed the distance to about thirty yards. I raised the rifle to my shoulder, praying that the cold weather wouldn't hamper the firing of my freezing gun. My pre-'64 Model 70 performed perfectly. The bear went down immediately as my bullet entered and destroyed both lungs and damaged the spine. I quickly chambered another round, but it wasn't necessary. It was 6:27 A.M.

At this point I became even more concerned with the surroundings, particularly the area that I could not see in the darkness. The bear I had just killed was covered with blood from head to front shoulders, and that, along with the fact that it was acting weirdly, led me to question the presence of another bear.

There was so much blood on the bear that I thought it impossible to have come from the victim. I thought the excess blood was from the killer bear, resulting from a confrontation with another bear, thus explaining the bear's unusual behavior. I expressed this concern to others on snowmobiles, and they promptly began driving in small circles, shining their headlights in all directions.

As headlights scanned the area, I backtracked the bear to the body. Much to my relief, I found only one set of tracks in the area. I was amazed to find that so much blood could have come from the victim.

193

Though I took no direct role in the official investigation, the stories that began surfacing did not make sense to me. I did not offer my opinions based on what details I saw, because I was not asked to do so by the villagers or by the PSOs. Originally the thought was that the bear was stabbed by the victim, which caused its peculiar behavior when I came upon it. This didn't seem right for two reasons. One, when I was tracking the bear from the initial attack site, I found no sign of a struggle. Two, why would a bear eat nearly three quarters of its prey if it had been injured by stab wounds? Also, no knife was ever found.

After I backtracked the bear's trail to confirm that a second bear was not involved, I returned to the bear. Upon closer inspection of it I could see a small hole in one of the bear's hindquarters and a small hole in the lower neck, both about the size of a pencil. I also found marks on the fur of the bear's neck where the victim's blood-covered fingers had grasped the bear and slid down its fur, indicating the victim was not killed by the bear immediately.

The PSOs in the village questioned everyone involved in the search and no one had heard any shots other than mine. It was ruled out that anyone else had shot the bear prior to my killing it. Three days passed before stories began floating around the village about another person shooting at the bear as it fed on the victim prior to my killing it. To me it made more sense that someone else had shot at the bear, thus reasonably explaining its out-of-place behavior. Why no one claimed shooting at the bear, I do not know. In all truth, I'm glad I found out after the fact that the bear was wounded with a small-caliber rifle, for had I known I was on the trail of a crippled man-eating bear, I don't know if my already accelerated state of anxiety could have handled it.

For whatever reason, such a variety of stories seemed insignificant to me. The fact was the victim and the bear were both dead. The only mystery left unsolved was, Why did the polar bear resort to hunting a human instead of its regular seal diet at this time of year? Was it provoked? Was it rabid? Or was it simply a hungry bear in search of whatever food it could find? The bear had evidently traveled down the coast and found itself near the village, a place where it could easily obtain food.

The reports given to me by both state and federal biologists said that the dissection of the bear, which was flown to Barrow for study, showed the bear was emaciated. Even the fat around the heart was gone, which is the last of the fat reserve to go in supplying energy to a bear. Though a polar bear should be covered with fat at this time of year, this bear yielded a total of only one ounce.

The polar bear measured eight feet in length, weighed nearly six hundred pounds, and had an estimated age of six years. Even though it had little body fat, the bear's musculature and organs were in good health and its coat was beautiful. What made this sad situation unique was that it was the first confirmed killing of a human being by a polar bear in the United States. [Author's note: A man was killed on Barter Island and partially eaten by a polar bear before being driven away from the victim with a bulldozer. It is believed this occurred in the 1960s, and I am presently researching that story.]

The initial reaction of the Point Lay residents was that of shock. The elders talked of how none of their people had been killed by a polar bear. People became more cautious about where they went and how they got there. People began traveling in pairs. Two of the six vehicles in the village were being called upon to give rides throughout the community.

Neil, the village PSO, was ordered to drive on polar bear alert from 8:00 to 11:00 P.M. and 1:00 to 4:00 A.M. Some North Slope Borough workers in the village also volunteered to patrol the outskirts of the small village twenty-four hours a day. Such patrols were comforting to people, and continued over the dark winter months.

Fear ruled many of the community's residents. I believe much fear was due to a lack of understanding about bear behavior. I altered my science curriculum to inform students about bear behavior. The Alaska Department of Fish and Game was helpful in supplying me with literature and posters that I not only shared with the students at our school but posted for the public to see as well.

The bear ended up in the hands of the federal government. Despite requests from museums, universities, and myself, who wanted the bear for a life-sized mount, it was released to no one. Instead, the hide was cut into pieces and burned. My request for the skull, a paw, a claw, and even a strand of hair was denied, despite my having risked my life. It was a waste of a valuable natural resource, to say the least.

The last thing I expected when I received that phone call in the early morning was that I would end up finding a dead body and tracking and killing a man-eating polar bear. No matter how many times I tell someone the complete story of what happened or how descriptively I tell it, there are very few people in this world who can relate to the incredible feeling I experienced on that dark, cold, tragic Saturday morning on the tundra.

Wild polar bears are dangerous; so are "tame" ones.

Who Said Zoo Bears Are Tame?

by Robin Paul and Larry Kaniut

"This massive bear coming toward me . . . was like King Kong."

It's not every day that a zoo bear takes a bite out of a visitor. But it happened on Friday, 30 July 1994. Kathryn Warburton, a twenty-nine-year-old dental worker from Sydney, Australia, had planned a vacation in the United States and was having the time of her life. She had arrived in the Last Frontier and wanted to experience as much of Alaska as she could before returning to her native Australia. This spunky blonde embodied the adventurous spirit of our neighbors Down Under.

Several events led to our learning about Kathryn Warburton and her encounter with Alaska's favorite bear. Heidi Baer, our next door neighbor, was getting married. Heidi's uncle, Gary Paul, had brought his family to town for the occasion. In the face of all the preparations, Gary and his wife Robin took their sons to the Anchorage Zoo.

One of the zoo's favorite attractions is the polar bear, Binky. Binky, a twenty-year-old male bear, was brought from the Beaufort Sea after his mother was shot in 1974. When Binky was tiny, zoo workers played with him and rubbed his stomach. But since he has grown in size, age, and cantankerousness, no one goes into his cage any-

more. Binky bit off a worker's finger around 1980 and is one of the more aggressive animals at the zoo. But on this day Binky lazed in his lair.

Gary and Robin Paul approached the polar bear area. Meanwhile Kathryn decided to move closer to Binky's cage for a close-up picture. That's when the excitement began.

We learned about Kathryn and Binky when the Pauls returned to the Baers. I asked Gary if he'd be willing to comment on their experience. Robin mailed me a summary, which she called "Binky the Bear and the Paul Family." Most of her text follows.

In late July of 1994, Gary and I and our three young sons—Garrett, age 9; Austin, age 7; and Carson, age 3— flew to Anchorage from our home in Juneau to attend the wedding of Gary's niece, Heidi Baer. The weather was sunny, the day was young, and we decided to go to the Anchorage Zoo. Our boys had never been to a zoo and were excited as the five of us headed off.

The zoo wasn't crowded that morning and we wandered leisurely. There was a great viewing area of the polar bears, and we stopped and talked about the bear lying near the fence. Binky lay about twenty feet from the tall pipe fence near the shallow drainage ditch, his platter-sized paws facing us. We talked about how huge his feet were and about the fact that even if he looked fat and lazy, all bears have four-wheel drive and can move fast.

As we continued up the path, a motion off to our left caught our attention. We were shocked to see a young blonde woman about to straddle the low fence near the front of the area where Binky was lying. She had apparently looked around and, seeing no one, had decided to go down to the bear for a close-up picture. She had already climbed over the first low fence by the path and had gone approximately twenty feet down the grass slope to the second fence near the bear cage.

There were no warning signs on the pipe fence that rose twenty feet with one-foot spaces between the bars. It appeared she was safe from the king of the Arctic. She was facing our direction, head down, and was lifting her right leg over the fence. Gary was about to yell at her to get away, but instead he ended up yelling, "Look out!" It was too late.

In an instant, Binky was up. Lightning fast, the 850-pound boar rushed to the perimeter of his pen, extended his neck through the bars, and grabbed her with his teeth. Faster than it can be told, Binky jerked his neck back and dragged Kathryn toward the high bars. Binky pinned her to a bar.

With his huge mouth he bit into the soft part of her waist between her ribs and her hip bones on her left side. His bite was massive, and looked as if he compressed that area of her body down to a three-inch girth.

We were the only ones there to witness the bear's action. Gary and I looked around to find something to throw at the bear. There was nothing. Gary told the girl not to fight because it would make the bear madder. The boys were sobbing. I was frantically looking around for help. Gary stayed near the girl while I ran back down the path toward the elephants' area yelling for help.

Mass confusion reigned. People ran down the hill to help. The first zoo employee to get there, Kevin Pickel, who took no thought for his own safety, jumped the first fence by the path, ran across the grass, and grabbed the girl. He had nothing to use against the bear—no one did. He threw his radio (a walkie-talkie that some zoo attendants carry) at the bear's head, and it bounced off into the cage. Binky wasn't about to loosen his grip on the girl's waist. Kathryn tried to push off from the pen and away from Binky with her right foot, but her efforts were futile.

Another employee, Shane Larson, ran for help and to call an ambulance. By then other visitors to the zoo (about five or six feet from her) screamed and tried to pull her away. It was a painful tug-of-war that at times suspended her in the air. A firefighter from Dillingham, Alaska, and another man joined in the effort to free Kathryn. Other people stood in the background, awestruck.

Gary tried to break off a board from the fence, and finally broke off a branch from a tree and handed it to the people down by the girl. Other people helped break off branches and rained huge blows on Binky's head. Finally, as they beat on the bear and pulled on the girl, Binky's grip moved down to her hip, then her thigh (she was wearing shorts and you could see the bites in her leg), then toward her knee, down to her calf, and finally to her foot.

A colossal tug-of-war was occurring. Finally Binky clasped her tennis shoe, which came off, and they pulled her free and out of reach of the bear. During the entire time Kathryn didn't make any loud cries or screams. Perhaps the shock and the force of the bear's jaws prevented her from doing so, or perhaps she realized that the noise might further irritate the bear.

They attended to her on the grass as the crowd, still in shock, cried. After I had run down the hill for help and then back to the area, my attention turned toward our sons, who had been left alone watching in horror. I moved them behind some people where they couldn't see. Garrett, the oldest, was hysterical; at his age he knew and fully understood what was happening. Austin and Carson were crying and shaking.

After the rescuers got Kathryn on a stretcher and we felt we had done all we could do, we quietly but swiftly moved away from the area, still in shock. We thought we could look at more animals and regain our composure. We moved up the path to the next area where the animals were all ears and eyes and obviously agitated and attracted by the smell of blood. We saw three large brown bears standing on their hind legs, looking over the high fence with anticipation. We decided to leave the zoo. Moving toward the exit, I overheard a mother tell her child, "Let's go see the bears."

I blurted out, "You can't go down there, they've closed the area." This intrusion was met with a snotty look as the mother scooted her child toward the path down toward the bears.

We returned to our mini-van, climbed in, and drove off with no direction in mind, each reliving the event. We didn't want to talk to anyone and ended up at Arctic Valley, where we got out for a little walk. Finally we got back in the car and stopped at Carr's in Eagle River for some deli food. No one, though, had much of an appetite.

We went back to the Baers' house and related our story. I was concerned that since we were the only ones to witness the attack, we should let the zoo manager know in the event they needed information. We called and talked with Sammye Seawell, the zoo director, leaving our number.

The boys were subdued for a day or so. Garrett couldn't sleep that first night. Gary and I relieved the scene over and over in our minds. The boys intently listened to any update on Kathryn's status. For their own peace of mind I guess they needed to know she was going to be okay.

I called the hospital, talked to the floor nursing supervisor, left my name (in the event Kathryn needed to talk with me) and explained my reason for knowing how Kathryn was doing. The nurse told me to tell the boys that Ms. Warburton was doing okay. The boys felt better after this and didn't seem as much on edge.

After our family returned to Juneau, things seemed okay. We talked about the incident. The boys couldn't understand why that lady went so close to the bear. The boys firmly believed that the lady was wrong and that nothing should happen to Binky; it wasn't his fault because he was just being a bear. They drew numerous pictures of Binky with signs saying Member, Binky Fan Club.

The most obvious lasting impression on the boys, especially little Carson, was that they were very cautious at our cabin. Carson would not go outside without me or Gary for many months. After a year went by, Carson was observed staring out the window of our home in Juneau. When his father asked him what he was thinking about, he replied, "Are there bears in those woods?" When his father said yes, Carson asked if they were going to come in and get him. He was told no, and looked relieved to know that they didn't want to come into a house.

Looking back, the bear reminds us of a dog with his prized catch. We know that if Kathryn hadn't been bitten on her side and hadn't been in that horizontal position, Binky could have pulled her right into his cage area. The other thing that saved her was that the bars of the cage didn't give Binky room to jerk her from side to side. His massive head was tightly wedged between the two bars and he was barely able to hold on.

AFTERWARD

Kathryn was rushed to the hospital and treated for a broken leg, lacerations, punctures, and infection. Kathryn's bites were up to six inches deep. Her recovery was routine except for the public's response and the concern for infection.

A major problem with ursine bites is infection. Such injuries demand constant monitoring. The treatment she received at Providence Hospital in Anchorage cannot be duplicated in Australia because they have no bear maulings and no infectious bear bacteria. (See Appendix 8 for infection information.) Not the least of Kathryn's concerns was that she had no medical insurance to cover her mounting medical costs.

Kathryn and Binky received worldwide media attention, propelling Binky toward cult-hero status. He had returned to normal within an hour (but in July 1995 Binky and his pen mate Nuka died). A public outcry followed Kathryn's episode with Binky, and emotions ran the gamut.

Some wanted Kathryn to be put into Binky's cage; others wanted Binky put to sleep.

Kathryn said that Binky ". . . just sort of came up from nowhere. . . . I couldn't believe this massive bear coming toward me. It was like King Kong, you know?" She admitted, "Looking back, it was the dumbest thing I've ever done in my life. It didn't occur to me that the bear was vicious. I've been told it had been there since it was a cub, and I thought it was quite tame."

Life after Binky found Kathryn on the mend and thankful to be alive.

See Appendix 6

Kathryn Warburton learned about Binky the polar bear, and so did Josh Huyett.

Mugged in the Zoo

by Josh Huyett

"Josh theorized that the bear was just playing with him, maybe teaching him a lesson about coming too close."

On Sunday, 11 September 1994, Josh Huyett and two of his friends entered the zoo after closing hours. Going swimming they were not. But that rumor spread like a covey of quail chicks chased by a coyote. Unbeknownst to the group, an Australian traveler had been mauled a month earlier at the Alaska Zoo in Anchorage (Josh had been out of town at the time). I contacted Josh, who shared his tale and asked me to put it into the third person.

As soon as he stumbled, Josh looked down to see what had caused him to fall. He felt moderate pressure on his left foot just as he discovered the bear. One of the zoo's polar bears clasped Josh's foot in its mouth. No sooner had this thought registered in Josh's mind when the bear jerked his head back, pulling the young man toward its cage. Josh slammed to a stop when he smacked into the vertical bar at his crotch. Stunned but realizing his plight, Josh screamed for his friend Hank.

Josh wasn't sure how the bear had gotten hold of him, whether it had swatted him with its paw or just grabbed him with its mouth. As the bear held Josh's leg in its jaws, Josh lunged for the bordering three-foot fence, grabbing onto it and pulling as hard as he could in an effort to drag himself free of the bear's grasp. Josh had been in predicaments before, but nothing like this.

Earlier that Saturday evening, he and companions Hank and Wendy had enjoyed socializing with friends. They made the rounds of numerous warehouse parties, where they drank into the night. Some of their friends went home, but this trio decided to stay out longer for more fun and excitement. With Hank behind the wheel, their meanderings took them to Huffman Park. They talked and drank awhile, then moved on. Earlier Hank and Wendy had discussed going to the zoo, so when they moved on Hank headed for it.

A powerline road, accessible by two-wheel drive vehicle, borders the north side of the zoo. Hank drove his pickup along the powerline, where he parked and they got out. At that spot two fences border the zoo: one is wooden; the other is meshed wire. Along the backside of the wooden fence run horizontal nailer braces. These braces form a "ladder," allowing easy climbing. With no plan or purpose the three approached the wooden fence. They clambered over the fence and easily hopped the metal one.

The brown-bear cage, roughly three hundred feet square, lay just below them in the northeast corner of the zoo with a corridor separating it from an eight-foot cyclone fence to the east. The polar-bear cage, home of Binky and Nuka, abuts the brown-grizzly bear cage to the west. Both cages are constructed of three-inch vertical pipe fifteen feet high. The polar-bear house is built into the dirt bank, making it possible to walk right up the bank and onto the roof. The building is surrounded on either end by the pipe fence.

The teenagers were having a good time. Although Josh was quite drunk, he took the lead. Thinking his companions were with him, he walked down the hill toward the front of the bear cage. Unaware that Hank and Wendy had walked onto the roof of the polar-bear house,

Josh continued down the hill and over a perimeter fence to the edge of the cage. Josh turned away from the cage to look for his friends. He thought something had tripped him. Surprised and somewhat confused at his predicament, he looked down and saw a bear.

Josh grabbed the border fence and yelled for Hank. From the top of the bear house Hank and Wendy spotted Josh. He lay outside the corner of the cage at the bottom of the hill. A polar bear's head protruded between the bars. While they ran down from the roof to reach Josh, he frantically tried to pull himself away from Binky.

Earlier in the summer Binky had chewed on an Australian, and it was apparent that he quickly welcomed his new guest. Binky grasped Josh's hiking boot between his jaws. Although there was quite a bit of pressure, Josh felt no pain, partly because the bear's teeth didn't penetrate the leather boots. Binky pulled on Josh's leg while Hank and Wendy held onto the bars and kicked Binky in the head, trying to get him to release Josh. Their blows were ineffectual, perhaps even playful for the huge white bear.

Somehow Binky was able to maneuver Josh's left foot over a horizontal bar that ran along the bottom of the pen and about a foot above the ground. The bar acted like a fulcrum. When Binky pushed down, the leverage picked Josh up, pressing on the bottom of his shin and calf. Hank held Josh up to reduce the pressure on his leg.

His friends continued yelling and kicking the bear, trying to get it to release its grip on his foot. Perhaps their abuse only angered Binky. Surprisingly, the bear made no attempt to grab either of them. And it didn't let go of Josh. Because they were having no success, Wendy took off to find help. As she ran next to the brown-bear cage, the brown bear ran parallel to her on the opposite side of the fence. But it didn't try to reach her.

Hank kept fighting Binky, trying to get him to let go of Josh. Even though Hank yelled and pulled on Josh's leg, Binky refused to give up his prize. Josh didn't think the bear was trying to eat him. He theorized that Binky was just playing with him, maybe teaching him a lesson about coming too close. Pandemonium reigned. Hank and Josh yelled as loudly as they could. Their noise carried into the surrounding neighborhood.

With his right foot against a bar, Josh continued to push away from the bear while pulling on the outer fence at the same time. Hank held Josh and pulled with him away from Binky. The bear pulled; the young men pulled back. It was a tug-of-war between the bear and the young men. Even though he thought he might not get away, Josh determined to try. He wouldn't give up. Yet, as scared as he was and as hopeless as it seemed, he didn't have any ideas about how to get away.

The bear bumped Hank in the head with a forepaw in a movement similar to a backhand blow. The blow was to Hank's temple and not very hard. Had the bear hit him with its claws, Hank's head would have been torn open. Josh kept pushing his right leg against the cage, seesawing back and forth. Minute after minute crawled by. Then Binky released Josh's foot, quickly speared his right leg, and pulled it into the cage. Josh still had muscle movement and instantly pulled his left leg from the cage.

It was a bloody mess. It looked like papier-mâché, with puncture wounds and chunks of muscle hanging loose. Anything that wasn't chewed was covered with blood. Josh had to look away. Binky systematically began gnawing on Josh's right leg.

Although Josh's feet were protected somewhat by his boots, the boys attempted to remove them in order to get Josh's pants off and to free him. Eventually Hank managed to get Josh's pants off, though Josh doesn't know how he did it.

Binky crossed his paws on top of Josh's leg and looked at him. The bear's paws were so heavy that Josh couldn't free his foot from beneath the bear's legs. Then the bear let go of Josh's right leg. Hank pulled Josh back from the pen and flung him away from the cage. Then he hoisted

Josh over the waist-high fence and dragged him up the bank. Hank laid his coat over Josh before leaving for help.

The cage was lit, providing enough light for Josh to see. He saw Binky pacing, doing the traditional polar-bear shuffle with its head bobbing. Nuka, the other polar bear, stood and watched, moving very little.

Josh lay there alone, fifteen feet from the cage. He had no concept of time. He evaluated his injuries. Leg bones were exposed and muscles hung from his leg. There were no broken bones, but the puncture wounds were deep. Everything was covered with blood, though he bled very little now. During the bear's biting Josh had passed out three times. Now his eyes rolled back and he fainted. He then awakened. Even though Josh wore a heavy flannel shirt, he was cold. With his legs exposed and no energy to warm his body, he became colder.

Some time later Josh heard somebody running down the path and yelling at him. Thinking there would be no reason for anyone but a night watchman to be in the zoo, Josh assumed that was who it was. The man did not approach Josh, and it sounded like he was one hundred yards away. He repeatedly asked Josh what he was doing there.

Josh lay there out of breath and in shock. He was unable to say much but told the man that he was hurt and needed help. He told the man that a bear had gotten him, stating, "I need help here." The man asked Josh which bear had gotten him. Then he left, without checking Josh or offering any help. Josh was drained. He lay there thinking that his injuries didn't hurt very much. He thought he should be in pain, yet he felt nothing.

In the meantime, Wendy had reached a house and called 911, contacting rescue personnel. The zoo director arrived and opened a back gate, providing rescuers better access. By the time Hank got out of the zoo, a police officer had arrived, and the firemen were pulling up to the zoo. They entered a gate near the elephant cage.

By the time help arrived, Josh's pain level was such that he asked them for a painkiller, but they said they couldn't give him anything until he reached the hospital. The rescuers put Josh on a stretcher and carried him to the ambulance. Once he got into the ambulance, his pain intensified. They put an IV in him enroute to Providence Hospital.

While Josh rode to the hospital, the police took Hank and Wendy home. At the hospital Josh received the painkillers he so desperately wanted. Because of the deep puncture wounds, Josh was kept in the hospital for nine days. His white blood cells shot up, his red ones dropped, and he got an infection. The doctors left the wounds open to heal from the inside out, and it took a long time for them to close up. Josh has one claw mark on his left thigh, and the remainder of his scars are all bite-shaped.

At the time of the mauling Josh's dad was out of town and didn't find out about the incident until the next day. Even though Josh's parents were upset with the outcome of the evening, they supported him in his recovery.

Most of the criticism Josh received from the media took place when he was in the hospital, and he didn't hear it. During his recuperation at home he heard only a portion of it. Although Josh was taken to task by the media, there was little he could do about it. Josh's parents thought he needed healing rather than reporters bothering him. Josh lost all faith in the media. They didn't have the information they needed so they wrote what they wanted based on the zoo director's comments.

AFTERWARD

Initially Josh was charged with trespassing and possessing alcohol as a minor. The zoo didn't press charges. They might have feared that he'd sue the zoo if they did. Josh returned to the scene later and discovered many alterations as well as some gift shop merchandise pertaining to his mauling (the fences now have razor wire over the top and motion detectors).

Josh was born and raised in Anchorage, graduating from Robert Service High School in 1993. He is the eldest of six children, with four brothers and one sister. The family lives near the Alaska Zoo. Even in a city with a population of a quarter of a million people, bears coexist with people. Bears can't be taken for granted. Josh was fortunate that his injuries were minimal because they could have been so much worse. A polar bear, even in a cage, is nothing to mess with.

Whether a bear is confined in a zoo or roaming free in the wilds, it should be given a wide berth, as Jack Muir discovered.

Eleven Seconds from Disaster

by Jack Muir

"When I hollered, the bear had two choices, run or attack.
She chose to attack."

One Sunday in the winter of 1995, our pastor's son,
Kelly Hood, excitedly approached me at church. Kelly
is a high school senior and an avid athlete and archer.
He wanted to tell me a bear story. Kelly had seen a
video of an archery bear hunt turned bad. He suggested
I borrow the video from mutual church friends Ken and
Linda Witthoeft.

I talked with Linda, who told me the video was taken
by a coworker of hers named Jack Muir. She let me borrow the videotape, and I took it home to watch. I sat before the television watching a man dressed in camo walking in the woods. Grizzly bears came into view in different segments. Suddenly the screen went dark and I heard
"Huuaw! Huuuaa! Huuaw!" (a charging bear) followed
by, "Whoa, bear! Whoa, bear!" Then a series of shots
echoed from the blackened television screen.

Wow! What an introduction to Jack Muir.

I met Jack in March of 1996 and was impressed with
him. He is 48 years old, stands 6-feet-1-inch tall, and tips
the scale at 190 pounds. He's been a sporting goods sales
rep for VF Grace in Anchorage for thirteen years, having
done the same thing in Oregon prior to moving to the Great

Land (what the word Alaska means in the native language).
As he showed me an album of hunting photos, I was in
awe of Jack's credentials. Then he shared his philosophy
and his bear tale.

I've been a bow hunter all my life. I've taken quite a
number of animals with a bow and arrow, including Dall
sheep, mountain goat, caribou, two black bears, seven
moose, elk in Oregon and Montana, mule deer, black-tailed
deer, Sitka black-tailed deer, coyotes, and brown bear. I
went on safari to Africa in 1993 with a bow and arrow,
where I took kudu, eland, and impala. I've spent some
time in the woods.

I like to have a hunting partner with me in camp, but
when I'm out hunting, I want to do it alone because I
think bowhunting should be a one-on-one experience. I'm
not a sitting hunter. It kills me to sit and wait animals
out. Sitting in a blind or tree tests my shooting ability but
does not really test my hunting ability.

I did very little blind hunting, even in Africa. My guide
took me out and let me loose and let me walk. I always
want to see what's on the other side of the next ridge or
around the next bend in the river. I would rather walk
and not kill them, see the country and test my hunting
skills to their survival skills, than sit in a blind and wait
for them to walk by or come to water.

In the fall of 1995, my hunting partner Mike
Manning and I left Anchorage to hunt brown bear. Since
I had arrowed a nice bull moose the year before and my
freezer was full of big-game meat, salmon, and halibut, I
didn't have to worry about chasing moose or caribou.
I was hunting bear.

Hunting the same area five years earlier during a
four-day solo hunt, I saw eight bears and took one, an
eight-footer. I was shooting a 75-pound bow, and the
arrow passed clear through him. It was a one-shot kill
at twenty-five yards. I now shoot a Browning Maxim
compound set at 76 pounds, shooting 2413 aluminum

hunting arrows with Bear Bruin Lites for broadheads and using a fletch hunter release.

I have an eighteen-foot travel trailer that I normally take hunting. I park it five or six miles away from the trail to my hunting area. Traditionally I hunt a ridge above the stream. Five salmon species spawn in the stream, and the ridge affords a good vantage point as well as a means of keeping man-scent from bears. Their noses are so superior that you have to take great care to avoid them scenting you. You've got to get elevation to do it right. The winds along the creek would give you away.

Spruce timber blankets the low hills, while prolific devil's club and alders cover the ground. This year we went in ahead of time and cut a trail that would enable us to get in and out in the dark. I no longer fight my way through the alders. I never go into the brush without my little Sierra saw, made by Coghlands. It's a twenty-dollar saw that folds like a pocketknife, the niftiest brush-wacking tool there is. Cutting a path through the alders might take a bit longer, but when I get to the other end of an alder thicket, I'm not whipped from bending and stooping and trying to drag a pack through the brush.

Mike, who manages Kenai Supply, and I headed up the trail on the opening weekend of brown bear season, 15 September. The first day we sat on the upper end of the stream and saw fish and bear signs, but there were no bears around.

Sunday morning we went back in and sat again. Nothing came by, so around noon we decided to walk downstream to the mouth to see if we could figure out where the bears were. When we got to where the stream flows into the main river, it was obvious that the bears were there. The water in the main river had dropped, and the bears could catch a better quality and quantity of fish in the stream.

I wanted to hunt on the ground from one of the high banks, but my hunting partner wouldn't have anything to do with it. He loves to hunt bears, but he's more cautious than I. He wanted to be in a tree. We also wanted to videotape and felt it would be better if we were both in a tree so we could tape each other shooting a bear. We looked around and found only one tree that we thought we could get up into and shoot from. We then cut a new trail from that spot back to the main highway.

We came back that evening and crawled up the tree. As we were trying to figure out how we were both going to sit in a small spruce tree without tree stands, three bears walked out into the stream about a hundred and fifty yards below us. I got the video camera out of my backpack and videotaped the bears. I didn't want to shoot any old bear because the price of having a rug made is one hundred dollars per foot. I've already got one bear, and I'm looking for a pretty hide. We got some great footage of bears chasing fish.

I let the first two bears go by. On the ridge across the river about one hundred yards away, we heard bears fighting, and we saw a pair of cubs go up a tree. Shortly after that another bear came down to the river and fished his way toward us. He came along the near bank and smelled where we had come out of the water. He then tracked us step-for-step to the base of the tree. I got a video of him as he worked his way there and I've got a picture of him looking up at us, eighteen feet above him. He saw me moving, figured something was wrong, made one "*woof*," crossed the stream, and went up the bank the way he'd come. That was a good-looking bear, light on the back and dark-legged; his coat had some character to it. I should have taken it.

About ten minutes later a sow with two cubs came down to the water about one hundred yards upstream and started fishing. It got dark and, even with all those bears around, we crawled out of the tree, slipped into the water so we wouldn't leave any scent, and quietly left, hoping that we wouldn't run into any bears in the dark.

The following weekend my partner couldn't hunt with me, so I went back by myself and hunted for two days, but didn't see anything. The next weekend we went back. One seven-foot bear came past. It was solid brown, not the bear I wanted, so I passed up a shot at him from about thirty-five yards away.

The fourth weekend my partner was working again, so I went in alone. It had snowed on the mountaintop the night before. The morning dawned a cool, crisp thirty-five degrees. When it got light enough to see, I shouldered my backpack and took off down my trail. There was blue sky and sunshine, an absolutely gorgeous fall day.

As I reached the ridge above the stream, I saw a bear downstream chasing fish where I expected to hunt. It had probably been in there all night fishing. I laid my bow down, took my backpack off, pulled out my video camera, and started videotaping this bear that was about three hundred yards away. He had no idea he was a camera subject. The wind was blowing downstream, but I was eighty yards above him and three hundred yards away, and there was no chance of him smelling me. I was concerned that if I went down to the creek, my scent would blow down to him and he'd disappear.

I was wondering how to get in there without spooking him, when I heard something to my right. I looked in that direction and saw a bear coming along the edge of the ridge fifteen to eighteen yards away. I hollered, "Hey!"

When I hollered, the bear had two choices: run away or attack. She chose to attack. With no hesitation she charged me. A few alders separated us, so she couldn't do a flat-out run. She kept her eyes on me as she threaded her way through the alders, and I never took my eyes off her.

I thought about grabbing my bow, but there was an overhanging three-inch alder limb that would have stopped me from drawing it. I could have done it if I'd gotten down on one knee to shoot, but there wasn't enough time.

Still, on she came. I dropped my camera and grabbed my Ruger .44 Magnum out of my shoulder holster and cocked it (on the video you can hear the cylinder roll). I hollered again, "Hey!"

She kept on coming. I backed up my trail two steps, hoping she would go past me or turn and go down my trail the other way. I stood there looking at her as she continued her resolute charge toward me. I raised my handgun with two hands and looked at the sights, following her with the barrel. She made a ninety-degree left-hand turn onto my trail, only eight feet from me.

She was so close and her head was so big that I touched one off. It hit her in the forehead above the left eye. She dropped like a sack of potatoes. The gun recoiled. It's a double-action weapon, but I drew the hammer back single action again and put it back on her. She was dead still.

By then I realized there were two cubs following her. I hollered at them. They kept coming, so I touched off a round over the tops of their heads. They stopped. I cocked the gun again and swung back on the sow. She hadn't stirred.

I grabbed my bow and started backing up the trail, and the cubs came up along the side of their mother. They were two-year-old cubs. The larger of the two, probably a boar, weighed approximately four hundred pounds. The mother should have kicked them loose by then. They were old enough to be out on their own.

As they moved up alongside, I backed up the trail about fifteen yards to where it made a left-hand turn. From there I could see that the sow had fallen on my video camera. Lying in front of her nose was my backpack full of hunting gear: binoculars, spotting scope, tripod, range finder, still camera, all my bowhunting paraphernalia except my bow.

Bears will chew up anything that has man-scent on it. I could see that they were going to chew up my stuff. One of the cubs walked up and pawed at the backpack while the other sniffed at the camera.

I hollered at them and shot my gun again. They just turned and looked at me, not showing any signs of aggression. They were probably still waiting for their mother to lead them, because up to this point in their lives she had been in control. The mother wasn't doing anything and they weren't either.

After seven minutes (timed on video) I decided I wanted my camera and hunting gear back. I reloaded my gun, yelled, and I fired two rounds. If they attacked I needed at least four rounds. I kicked the alders and made noise to sound as big and bad and nasty as I could. I hoped my bluff would work.

I got very close. I never showed any hesitation and kept coming right at them. I began to think I had made a mistake because I got closer than I thought I would have to get before they started backing off. Finally they turned and backed off the way they had come.

I was able to grab the camera out from underneath the sow's head. I grabbed my backpack, opened it up, dropped the camera in, and headed up the trail. I walked ninety steps and stopped. I put the backpack down, reloaded my gun, and put it back into my shoulder holster. I pulled the camera out to see what damage the bear had done and realized that it was still on. The camera had landed on its side facing in the direction of the river rather than down the ridge, but the sounds of the entire bear attack were recorded. It was then that I realized there was a piece missing off the end of the camera. I shut it off, put it in my backpack, and headed back to camp.

I reached my truck and drove to my trailer. My camp companion and camp cook was still in her sleeping bag in the trailer house.

She said, "Why are you back so early?"

"Well, I had a little problem with a bear."

"Did you get one?"

"Yeah, but not the way I wanted."

We made a pot of coffee and I explained what had happened. Finally about 11:00 I said, "Let's go in. We gotta get this hide off of her. By law you have to turn the hide into the Fish and Game." I grabbed my Model 70 Winchester .375 H & H Magnum that I had bought as a backup for my brown-bear hunting with a bow and arrow. We drove up there, parked the truck, and headed down the trail.

I gave her a can of bear spray because I didn't figure she could handle a rifle. When we got to the bend in the trail where I could see the downed bear, we started videotaping. As we walked in, we heard something off to the right-hand side, and one of the cubs was back in the brush about ten yards away.

I videotaped it and decided we'd better chase it off. I walked around the sow in an open area. I wanted to stay in the open in case I had to move the gun around quickly and shoot. I tried to chase the cub off. It started to move off and I was following it along, when suddenly the larger cub got up to my left. He was standing broadside looking at me.

He was twelve yards away. And boy, he got my attention. I put the .375 to my shoulder. There was a downed alder between us. We looked at each other for a minute as I talked to the bear in a conversational tone, trying to convince him to leave. He just stared at me, eyeball to eyeball. I leaned into my .375, so that if I touched it off the recoil wouldn't tip me over backward. I looked like a shotgunner ready to take him on.

Finally the boar started to move. I told him, "Don't come around that alder. You come around that alder, I'm gonna kill ya." He started to come around the alder, then stopped. He slowly turned and went in the direction the other bear had gone. They wandered off just out of sight, which was about twenty yards into the alder thicket.

By that time I had a charge of adrenaline. The long eyeball-to-eyeball encounter with the big cub had me charged. We took some still pictures and video. While we were doing that, the larger cub suddenly came walking in behind me. I jumped up, grabbed the .375, and confronted him again. He stood and looked at me. I took a few steps toward him, and he turned and reluctantly moved off.

I took two more still pictures, and he walked in again. That did it. This bear wasn't going to leave. There was no way I could get the hide off the sow safely. I didn't want to shoot the cub or put the woman with me in jeopardy, so we packed up our stuff and got the heck out of there. Later that evening I went back. The cubs were still there. I couldn't get them to move away.

The next morning I circled, got in the creek below them, and shot more video of them as they looked down on me. I returned to camp, loaded up the camp, and got ready to head out. I decided to go once more about 4:00 P.M. to see if the cubs had left.

This time I was in luck: The bears were gone. I scouted within twenty yards in all directions. I cut some alders down, opened the area up so I could see better, and started skinning. I did a record job of getting that hide off.

I had the hide about three-quarters of the way off when a bear came walking down my trail. My friend was holding the .375. I jumped up, grabbed that .375, hollered at the bear, and it turned and went charging off through the alders. I don't think it was one of the cubs because it shot out of there.

It surprised me that the bear had walked down the trail we had just left, because of the fresh scent. Obviously, the bears in that area are not afraid of human scent.

I finished getting the hide off, tied it onto my packframe, and we boogied on out of there. I threw the pack into my pickup, and we headed back to Anchorage. The next morning I took it down to Fish and Game. I told them my story. They said I had some forms to fill out. I said, "Well, let me tell you a little more about it. I got it on film."

"What. You got the film with you?"

I had the film in my hand, so we went to the back room to a VCR and watched my film. Eleven seconds had elapsed from the time I was videotaping the distant bear until the sow was dead—only eleven seconds!

The sow was a 7 to 7½-foot bear. I'm a bow hunter, and because it was taken with a handgun I didn't want it as a trophy. I know taking a trophy with a handgun is a challenge, but that's not the way I intend to do it. I'll be back in this area next year, and I hope to arrow a pretty bear for my wall, and maybe on film as well.

I do a lot of hunting in Alaska without carrying a pistol. When I'm in the woods, I figure I'm the king of the beasts and they need to watch out for me more than I have to watch out for them. After this incident, I realized an attack can happen with amazing speed, so I won't go into the woods without my handgun. That Ruger Red Hawk has earned its trip with me from here on out. It's not because I'm afraid, it's just that things happen quickly.

My Red Hawk has a 5½-inch barrel. I had two loads in the gun. One was a handload done up by my hunting partner. It's the locally made hard-cast, lead bullets made by Ace Dooby. It's a 328-grain hard-cast bullet loaded with 21½ grains of H110 behind it. The other load, made by Arctic Ammo, is specifically for our Alaskan bears and is a 265-grain Barnes solid with a velocity of about 1,400 feet per second. It's a bullet machined out of solid brass, designed for breaking big bones or shooting through the head.

The bullet penetrated the skull and shattered the first vertebrae on the neck where the skull and neck are attached. When I cut her head off, that area was a mass of bone fragments. The bullet was lying underneath the skin on the right side of the neck. It weighs thirty-nine grains less now than when it was in the pistol.

My ultimate Alaskan hunting thrill was arrowing a 35-inch Dall sheep. I was the most excited about that because it's a tough animal to hunt with a bow and arrow. It takes a lot of effort, skill, and dedication to

Some Bears Kill

Brooks Falls, Katmai National Park, Alaska—4 July 1995.

Grizzly charges Tom Jesiolowski and friend in Denali National Park. Bear actually charging toward squirrel colony the photographers happened to be filming—and bear probably heard squirrels and thought men were hybrid "squirrels." Bear backed off when men shouted and waved.

Moose International—Bering Glacier Camp, where Ellie Florance was mauled.

Coast guard helicopter that rescued Ellie Florance.

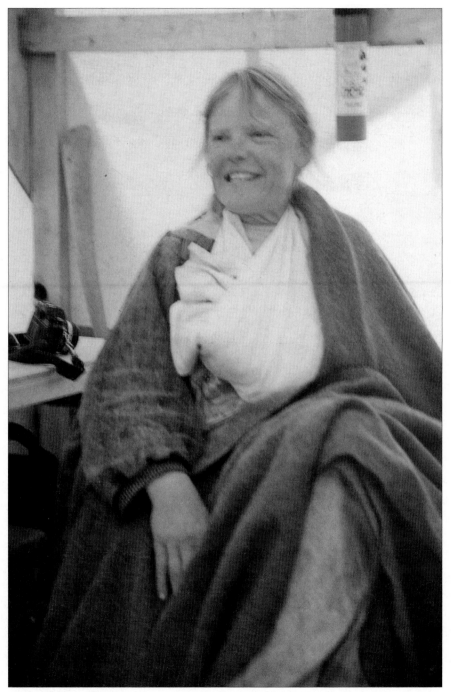

Ellie Florance after her Bering Glacier brown-bear attack.

Bull moose (58° inches) taken by Jim Erickson, September 1995, in south-central Alaska. The hardest part of being outdoors for three years running is sleeping in a tent every night.

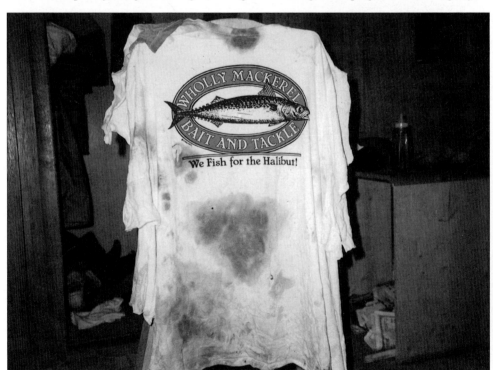

Jim Erickson's bloody shirt after the bear attack.

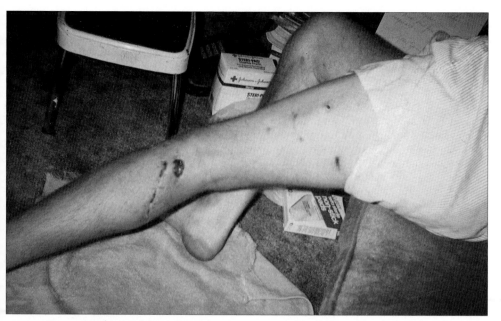

Jim Erickson and the injuries to his left leg.

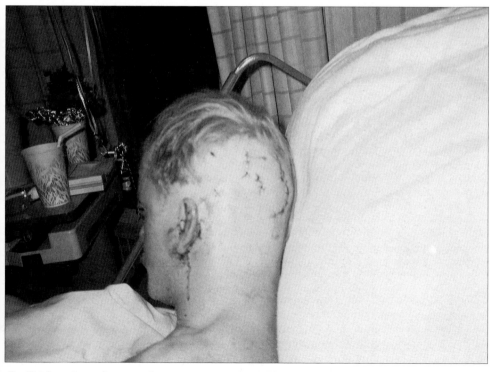

Jim Erickson's scalp wounds.

Some Bears Kill

This is the black bear that stalked Marti Miller.

Hunter Willard Ryan and the bear that he and Tom Jesiolowski shot as it charged within 40 yards.

Some Bears Kill

Jack Muir and his eight-foot brown bear, shot at twenty-five yards in 1990.

Darrell Thompson's furnished this photo to the author of his giant brown bear. Darrell Thompson shot this bear near Port Heiden, Alaska, in the spring of 1954, with one shot in the chest from a .375 H & H. Thompson took the hide to biologists at the Fish & Game Department in King Salmon, Alaska, and they determined the following statistics from the nature of the hide:

> *Estimated weight: 2,200 pounds*
> *Estimated age: 35 years*
> *Hide squared: nearly 14 feet*
> *Ear tip to ear tip: 25 inches*
> *Front paw: 13 inches across*
> *Skull scored at 34 9/16 inches—not entered into any record book*

bowhunting to arrow an animal that survives in the high open mountains of Alaska.

From what I learned about Jack, he's tougher than the critters he hunts.

Scalped Alive

by Paul Sargent

"The bear grabbed him by the top of the head."

I met Paul Sargent at an autographing of More Alaska Bear Tales *(for Debbie Reifenstein and Susan Hickey, owners of Hearthside Books) in Juneau's Nugget Mall on Saturday, 12 August 1989. Paul agreed to meet me later to tell me of the scalping of Earl Hirst.*

Paul is a spry, gray-haired gentleman who will never see sixty years old again. His ruddy complexion gives witness to his active years in the outdoors. He readily shared in a comprehensive manner the story he heard first-hand from Earl Hirst.

Ever since I first came to Alaska in 1933, I've heard the remarkable bear-mauling story about Earl Hirst, and how he had his scalp on backward.

Earl had been prospecting in the Chisana country when the mauling took place. My opportunity to meet Earl came when I took an Alaska steamship bound for Seattle where I was taking my son for burial; he had drowned at Chitina. Earl was on the same ship. There was a writer on board named Betty Loman or Lomen, who now lives in the Queen Charlotte Islands.

We knew that Earl always went for a mug around 10 P.M., so we cornered him to see if we could get his story firsthand. I told him, "Earl, I've heard all these stories about your bear mauling, all different versions. Can you tell us exactly what happened?"

He said that he and his partner had been hiking all day in to prospect, and they were very tired. He was in front and his partner brought up the rear. He heard his partner say something about a bear, but Earl didn't pay much attention.

His partner yelled louder about a bear. Earl turned around and the bear knocked him down and grabbed him by the top of the head. He was in shock and dazed when the bear dropped him and headed for Earl's partner. Earl grabbed his rifle and shot the bear dead with one shot before it got his partner. Earl collapsed and drifted in and out of consciousness. During one lucid moment he noticed a patch of red bear hide on the ground.

He told his partner, "I thought I saw a piece of bear skin on the ground."

His partner said, "It's okay, Earl. I got it all back on."

The patch of "bear skin" was Earl's entire scalp.

In those days you had to go on the highway to Valdez and then by ship to the Cordova Hospital because there was no hospital in Valdez. They waited in Valdez, caught a ship, and went to Cordova. They unwrapped bandages from Earl's head and discovered that the scalp was on backward but growing, taking root. Under it they found moss or gravel. They turned the scalp around (he was a redhead) and sewed it straight.

He had a jagged scar just above the eyebrow and all the way around his head. He said to me, "Feel the top of my head." There were grooves in his skull from the teeth; you could feel definite ridges.

I never saw him again.

Some Bears Kill

One must wonder about the mysterious meaning of human skeletal remains found in bear country, as the next story illustrates.

Eerie Tale from an Old-time Guide

by Larry Kaniut

*"Fifteen or twenty years later, the surviving hunter returned
to the same area to look for his partner."*

When I first glanced at the two pictures, there was nothing about them that was out of the ordinary. I was reminded of the many photos of giant bears I'd seen since my youth—photos that riveted the eyes and the heart to Alaska. I was reminded of photos of Kodiak Island brown bears and bear camps that I'd poured over in Outdoor Life *and other hunting magazines in my early teens.*

One picture that I remember in particular was the three-bear ad depicting Pinnell and Talifson's success, showing three monster brownie hides tacked to their cannery hunting base in Olga Bay. Other photos depicted hunting camps (which I learned were those of Alf and Charlie Madsen on Kodiak Island). The cabins were wood framed, with batting covering the gap between the vertical siding. These dwellings appeared to be twelve-by-sixteen feet. The cabins were outlined by tall, broad frames. To these frames giant brown bear skins were attached, skins so large that they nearly obscured the view of the cabins.

I studied the two photos in front of me and I noticed that the first showed a hunter before a Madsen cabin. He looked to be in his twenties or early thirties. A Levi's jacket and brown hip waders covered his body. A red baseball cap crowned his head. He knelt on the ground in the center of the picture. Spread behind him on a bear frame was a huge brown-bear hide. To the right center of the picture and in front of the kneeling hunter lay a large flesh-covered bear's skull, jaws agape.

The second picture captured a much older hunter clad in a full length, khaki raincoat. He wore hip waders and knelt in winterkilled brown grass, with leafless Alaskan alders in the background. He held a broken-stocked, rusted rifle in his left hand. Before him a few feet to the right foreground lay a weathered brown-bear skull. Between the bear skull and him lay a human skull. A human skull? A human skull!

I saw these two pictures 7 June 1995. I had stopped at Time Frame in Anchorage to get some photocopies. Mike Bennett, a former student of mine, asked, "Did I show you the pictures the bear hunter left?" I answered no, and Mike went to get the pictures. I asked him if he knew the hunter's name, and he said no. I told him I'd really like to query the hunter about the photos, to which Mike responded, "I thought you would. He comes in all the time. I'll get his name for you next time he's in."

Then Mike told me the story.

The first picture represents a hunter who shot a large brown bear on Kodiak Island, probably in the 1950s or 1960s. His hunting partner had gone out alone after another bear and failed to return. A search was conducted, but the partner was never found. The lost hunter was listed as missing and in due time considered dead.

Fifteen or twenty years later, the surviving hunter returned to the same area to look for his partner. The second picture shows him kneeling with his partner's rifle where he found it. The bear skull and his partner's skull were located close to the rifle. Evidently his partner had wounded the bear before it killed the man. Then the bear had died.

The two pictures started the wheels turning in my mind: What was the actual story, and how did the hunter find and shoot the bear? Where was the animal hit? How did the hunter become the hunted? Did the animal attack the man, or was the hunter trailing the bear before it turned on him? What was the time frame involving the shooting of the bear and the deaths of the man and bear? Why did the search party fail to find the man? A very puzzling set of pictures.

❖   ❖   ❖

My curiosity was piqued. I wanted to discover the derivation of the photos and the story behind them. I contacted a number of people, and the trail led me to Russ Knight in the winter of 1996. Russ is the owner of Knight's Taxidermy on Arctic Boulevard in Anchorage.

Russ told me that the second picture—the one with Pinnell, the rusty rifle, the brown-bear skull, and the human skull—was a hoax. Bill Pinnell was considered by many to be the talking partner of the P & T brown-bear hunting team of Kodiak Island fame. His longtime partner was Morris Talifson. Jeff Hall, a former assistant guide for P and T, had given Russ the second photo and shown him a video of Pinnell, who appeared to be in his late eighties or early nineties.

Russ said that Pinnell, known as a practical joker, had found the old rifle in the bay in front of their cannery home, stumbled onto a human skull, and had an unclaimed brown-bear skull. He posed with the rifle and the two skulls.

I wondered if Bill's wife could shed any light on the photographs or the story I'd heard from Mike Bennett. Having spoken with her in 1988 about visiting P & T at Olga Bay, I contacted her in Palmer, Alaska, in March 1996 and asked her if I could pay her a call. She kindly agreed to talk about her late husband, and I spent a pleasant time visiting with her. She didn't know about the photo involving the mysterious missing man, but she confirmed that the man in both pictures was her late husband and prankster Bill Pinnell.

Bill Pinnell was joking, but C. W. Mulford wasn't laughing when he met his bear on the river.

Whispering Close

by C. W. Mulford

"We were now one to two seconds from brown death."

In January 1996, C. W. Mulford of New York called me long distance, wondering if I'd be interested in his bear story. I told him I was.

By way of introducing himself, he stated that he was employed from November 1979 to May 1981 at Prudhoe Bay. He worked with an engineering-construction firm called Santa Fe. He hitched a ride down the haul road in June to Fairbanks. He became so enamored to the beauty of Alaska that he determined to return to the Brooks Range.

In 1995 my wife, Kathy, and I made our second Alaska float trip, traveling from the Gates of the Arctic south to Bettles via the North Fork of the Koyukuk River. We knew our guide, Randy Keller, from a previous three-day float trip with Isuma Guideworks. Randy knew and loved the vicinity well, as he used to live, mine, and run dog-sled trips there. Our friends, Dave and Dorothy Gille of New Jersey, chose to tag along.

A beautiful, warm day in mid-July met us on our fourth day on the river. We had made camp the night before on a large gravel bar, the farthest end of which bordered on a small inlet. Rising before the others the following morning and not wanting to wake anyone, I decided to try my luck fishing at the inlet. Approximately ten minutes after my first cast, a tremendous cracking and thrashing sound erupted from the woods across the bank as a large cow moose and her offspring emerged. Seeing me, the moose and calf headed up the inlet away from me at a trot. Looking toward camp, I hoped others might be up so I could get their attention, but they were too far away.

When I looked back toward the inlet, I discovered that for some unfathomable reason the moose had reversed her direction and was charging me. She was at a full gallop with her eyes fixed on me. Bravely I stood my ground until I recalled that you're supposed to run from a charging moose.

It's odd what goes through your head in the one or two seconds it takes to react, but I remember complete shock and disbelief. I hadn't provoked her; she had already put enough distance between herself, her calf, and me; why on earth did she come for me? My predominant reaction was "this isn't fair." However, I soon realized that I was not in a position to rationalize this thought with an oncoming moose. Therefore, I turned tail and ran as fast as I could toward the river, with mama and calf in hot pursuit. I was in no hurry to be swept downstream in a fast-running, icy-cold river. As I prepared to jump into the river, I looked back to see if she was still following. That's when I fell flat on my face.

My fishing pole clattered away, and I realized I had never thought to drop it. As I scrambled up and over to the river's edge, the moose veered downriver from me and started wading across. Figuring at last I should be safe, I tried to catch my breath as I watched her wading the river.

Wrong. As soon as she saw that I had stopped running, she changed direction midriver and started coming toward me again. This time, I told myself, I wasn't looking back until I got to camp. I estimated that I could beat the moose to camp by three to five seconds, and I counted on Randy to shoot if necessary.

So off to camp I raced, yelling and screaming as though being chased by the hounds of hell. As I neared camp, I saw my wife emerging from her tent. In a very unconcerned manner she waved her arms slowly back and forth like a runway attendant giving directions to a parking plane. Randy looked at me with a bemused expression.

As I neared my wife, I heard her say, "Thank you dear, you don't have to run anymore. I see the moose crossing the river." As far as she was concerned I had just given her a game wake-up call! Randy, on the other hand, had guessed what had really happened by looking at me. But all he had to offer was, "So what were you planning to do, let her follow you here to stomp on the rest of us when she finished with you, or did you figure she'd make a nice breakfast if I were a good enough shot?" Dave came out of his tent, shook his head, and politely asked me if I could hold down the noise the next time I went fishing. Did everyone have to be a comedian on this trip?

Later that morning, we crossed the river, fished for a while, and were about to return to camp when our guide pointed out a grizzly on the opposite bank, walking along the sandbar toward our camp. We yelled and the bear turned, looked at us, and started a casual lope away. He threw us a few over-the-shoulder glances before finally breaking into a faster run up the inlet.

Our guide suggested we follow his tracks to ascertain that he kept going. So we crossed the river and commenced tracking. The inlet area was muddy, and the bear had left well-defined prints. At the end of the inlet the ground got sandier and drier, and it seemed like the tracks were going in every direction, including a more recent set that headed directly away from camp. Satisfied that he had left the area, we followed what had now become a dry creek bed in a slow, lazy, left-hand U-turn heading back to the river.

We reached the river, hiked a short distance upstream, and then started back to camp. When we reached the creek bed again, we decided that instead of following the horseshoe route to camp, we would take a more direct route through the woods that paralleled the river.

The going was slow, pockmarked with small ravines, thick brush, and uneven footing. We'd gone only seventy to one hundred yards, making our normal bear calls, when our guide turned around to ask if this was too rough, and if we'd want to return to the easier route. At that moment I noticed a flicker of brown movement about thirty feet ahead and heard David say, in the calmest voice I've ever heard, "Uh, Randy, there's a bear ahead of us."

There sure was! An adult grizzly weighing about six hundred pounds was slowly making his way toward us. We were now one to two seconds (at bear speed) from brown death. Randy whipped around, positioned himself nearest the bear, and yelled for us to hold still and talk for all we were worth so the bear would know we were there. The bear stood up to check us out, then slowly ambled away deeper into the woods.

We were just beginning to breathe again and nervously joke about which way we'd continue, when I spotted the bear coming back. I anxiously told Randy, who told us not to stare the bear in the eyes; to keep talking to him in a commanding voice; to back out slowly; and to keep retreating no matter what happened, all of which we did (although I'm sure that my own voice didn't sound any more "commanding" than Minnie Mouse's at the time).

The bear kept coming, I thought he was intent on bringing one or two of us down. When I saw Randy raise his rifle (which I knew he wouldn't do unless it was absolutely necessary), I thought some of us might not survive this encounter. Randy fired a round by the bear's ear, and I wondered if I'd lost my hearing. Sadly for us, "ol griz" was either deaf or determined not to give ground to us interlopers.

During the longest minute of my life while we backed out of the woods onto the flat creek bed, every fiber in my body felt as though it were electrically charged. I hoped that the feeling was an "adrenaline rush" so I might not feel his claws or teeth as much as I was expecting. Maybe he was just curious. Although he followed us all the way to the forest's edge, he never charged.

After considering my earlier "this isn't fair" thought with the moose, I considered that maybe all's fair concerning wildlife. I realized that the poor moose had turned on me probably because she saw or smelled that bear, giving her a choice between me or the bear—and I can easily understand the direction she chose as her path of least resistance! [Author's note: Perhaps the moose smelled the bear and thought Mulford was a bear walking erect.]

I would like to add that our guide did everything a person could humanly do to protect us. He kept himself between the bear and us while giving instructions. Fortunately, we had just spent three days in Katmai National Monument prior to this trip, and thanks to the "Bear Etiquette" program the rangers require all new arrivals to watch, as well as Randy's constant reminders, we all kept our heads and "did the right thing."

We were fortunate because that bear could have had us if he'd wanted. It seems reasonable to say that if that bear had chosen to charge, he would have wrought considerable damage unless Randy had made the shot of his life (and he wouldn't have had time for more than one).

We had been told repeatedly that it's best to climb a tree because grizzlies can't climb. However, there was no time to climb and either the trunks of the trees we passed were wider than we could grasp, too small to hold our weight, or rose no higher than a bear's ability to reach. I agreed with my wife's observation. She asked, "What tree?" It was just like a comment from one of Larry Kaniut's previous tales: an encounter will usually occur under the worst circumstances.

Because bears are unpredictable and more powerful than an unarmed man, a bear-stopper is essential for survival in bear country. Carrying a rifle is good preparation, but even a pocketknife, though highly inadequate, may save your life.

A Man, a Bear, and a Knife

by Larry Kaniut

"Dirt and moss flew in every direction as she came straight at him."

The likelihood of being attacked by a bear is very slight. When an attack is imminent, however, an adequate weapon will often stop a bear. In the annals of history, man has employed such crude weapons as knives and arrows for defense against a mauling bruin. And in a handful of cases these weapons have prevented death.

On 5 September 1975, Jim Heine, a Colorado big-game guide, ran into a black bear that had death in her eye. She attacked him with no warning. He saw her before she saw him, anticipated her movements, and made for a tree. Other than the snapping of her jaws, her attack was as silent as the inside of an empty silo.

As the big, black sow ran him up the tree, Jim lost his bow but managed to hang onto a fiberglass arrow from his quiver. While clinging to a limb and jabbing the broadhead into her face, he stared at instant death. One jab struck the bear in the left eye and blood poured from it. Within seconds she slid down the tree trunk and left. It was not the last he saw of her, however, because she returned when he gave a primordial scream. But the arrow made the difference between his otherwise likely death and his eventual survival.

Another outdoorsman called upon his only weapon, a knife. Art LeGault was a seventy-one-year-old plywood cutter with a heart condition when he encountered his bear near Engadine, Michigan, in June 1960. It was the first time he'd run into such an animal when he wasn't adequately prepared.

He fought the bear in an upright position, face to face, for twenty minutes, in a two-hundred-foot area. It was quite a slugfest as she pummeled him and he shoved her away time after time. As the battle heated up, Art's vision became blurred. Nearing the end of his stamina, Art thought of his knife and pulled it from his pocket. He worked through her front paws and stabbed as often as his failing strength allowed. At one point he felt the knife blade sink its full length into her head. Because he had hit her eye, she left, allowing him to stumble to safety.

A knife against the formidable weapons of a bear—four-inch, razor-sharp claws and one-inch canine teeth—is not much of a weapon. Should you wish to consider your chances with such a foe, view a video that shows the incredible speed and strength of our ursine neighbors. (Many people have told me, "I had no idea they could move so fast.") However, in a few instances a knife was not only adequate to stem the attack, but the knife also proved fatal to the attacking animal.

In May 1983 Larry Reimer faced a black bear with only a fillet knife. Larry and his friend Keith Ecklund were fishing a creek in Nipawin Provincial Park in northern Saskatchewan, Canada. Their enjoyment was interrupted by a menacing bear. It grabbed Keith, who cried out to Larry for help. Larry ran to assist his pal, but the bear had left Keith and taken refuge in the brush near Larry.

Keith shouted to warn Larry of the approaching bear. Larry dived into the creek. The creek was slightly over his head, and his hip waders hampered his effort to swim away from the bear. The bear caught Larry and a face-to-face fight to the death ensued. Larry thrust his fillet knife toward the bear's throat. Larry's knife found its mark, and blood poured from the brute's wound. The animal swam to shore and died on the beach.

Still another man, Carl Stalker, called upon his pocketknife in a moment of desperation. Carl was not as fortunate as Larry Reimer, but his courageous effort allowed his sweetheart to escape. (See "Terror on the Tundra," chapter 26.) A knife may not be the best choice of weapons, but it certainly has saved a few lives. Take Robert Nichols of British Columbia, for instance.

Robert James Nichols of Maple Ridge, British Columbia, is a forty-nine-year-old longshoreman and father of three. He's a lifelong outdoorsman and a tough customer at 5-feet-10-inches tall and 200 pounds.

Bob wanted to bag a moose with his brother, so he agreed to a week's hunt. The hunting trip was a good excuse for family members to get together since they hadn't seen each other for years. The hunting party consisted of Bob's brother, Darryl Nichols of Fort. St. James, and four cousins: Leonard, Morris, and Albert Ross, and Albert's son Randy.

They would hunt out of Darryl's cabin on the Ocock River, eleven miles north of Fort St. James. Darryl said, "It was the first chance we had to spend time together at my cabin. It was as much a family vacation as it was a hunting trip."

On Friday, 20 October 1995, at 4:00 P.M., Bob was returning to his brother's cabin after a fruitless day of searching for moose. He knew the rest of his hunting party would be at the cabin and that Darryl would have dinner ready. Bob crossed a beaver dam, then sat on the ground and removed his boots and stockings and wrung out his socks. After replacing his footwear, Bob rose and pushed on.

He'd walked but a dozen yards when he detected movement with his peripheral vision. A grizzly charged out of nowhere. The sow ran past him a few feet to his right. The speed of her charge was such that although Bob carried a rifle, time did not permit him to release the safety.

The sow leaned into a hard turn and threw her legs to the outside. Dirt and moss flew in every direction as she came straight at him from twenty feet, never slowing. She ran low and fast and lunged at the last second, hitting the hunter on both shoulders and knocking him down. His rifle flew from his grasp, leaving him his only defenses: his fists, his mind, and his knife.

The sow stood on Bob's legs with her hind feet, pinning him to the ground. She bit into his left leg. Then she held him down with a paw, bit him, and pulled back while twisting her head and tearing chunks from his thigh. She attacked his abdomen next. Her efforts to get hold of him there failed, so she sank her teeth into his right arm and shook him like a rag doll.

Bob tried repeatedly to reach his rifle, but each time he tried to bring the weapon into play, the carnivore lunged for his throat, causing him to abort his actions and cover his face with his arms. An animal that can break the neck of a barnyard bull or drag an adult moose three hundred yards uphill through alders is a formidable foe. However, not many grizzlies meet men with Bob Nichols' determination and zest for life.

Bob Nichols is no stranger to danger. He was fighting this bear for all the marbles, and he didn't want to be left holding the bag. He knew that only one would survive this episode. It was a primal struggle: man versus beast. Which would prevail?

Bob was determined not to die. He freed his left hand and pulled his knife from its belt sheath. It was razor-sharp and had a five-inch blade. Bob swung at the animal with his left arm, but the knife was knocked free and it fell onto the moss-covered ground.

Bob didn't give up. He retrieved the knife. The bear bit at the man. Bob thought he could blind the sow or hit its jugular vein. He cut himself while picking up the knife, then stabbed at the sow over and over again. Bob stabbed the sow above the eye, igniting rage in the beast.

The bear went nuts. She bit him in the chest, biting into the rib cage. She tore his pectoral muscle away. The bear never made a sound, just kept biting, ripping, and tearing. The animal continuously slipped her paw under him and attempted to turn him over.

Bob frantically stabbed the bear in the same spot. Blood poured from her wounds and filled her left eye. After a while the bear broke off the attack and rocketed into the woods, running erratically down the trail in an S pattern, perhaps hampered by the blood in her eye or a greater injury. The entire incident lasted less than a minute.

Bob sat against a tree. He figured he had killed the bear with all the stab wounds in the throat area. Bob fired the universal three-shot distress signal from his rifle. He smoked a cigarette and waited twenty minutes for responding rifle fire. No one answered, so he fired again. This time there was a response.

Bob managed to get a stick to use as a crutch. He hobbled nearly a quarter of a mile down the trail before he realized he'd lost a large quantity of blood and decided to stop. He fired his rifle again and received another answer. He awaited his rescue.

It was some time before the rescuers reached Bob. His brother Darryl had driven half a mile in his truck toward the sound of Bob's gunshots, then ran the rest of the distance. Bob was covered in blood and unrecognizable. The others couldn't figure out what had happened. As they got closer, Bob yelled, "It got me. It got me good. But I got it good, too."

Morris Ross, a former scout leader, told the others to remove their coats. They strung the coats onto tree limbs, constructing a rough stretcher. The temperature was near freezing, so the men also removed their shirts to cover their injured pal.

They were concerned that rescue would be delayed because the sun had gone down and it was nearing 6:30. They carried Nichols to a clearing, hoping for a helicopter pickup. Bob was fully conscious and coherent the entire time.

In the meantime, Darryl had run to his pickup to radio for a med-evac. The Kamloops dispatch didn't think they could get a helicopter out because of the lateness of the hour: It was 6:00 P.M., and 6:40 P.M. was ground time. However, Pacific Western Helicopter launched a chopper.

The predicament was compounded by the chopper crew's inability to see the men in the heavy growth on the ground. Morris turned on the pickup's headlights, but the flyers didn't see the lights. The helicopter passed overhead a few more times but failed to see them. Albert grabbed a small flashlight from his pocket and pointed it skyward. In a desperate final flyover, the chopper crew spotted the light and descended three hundred yards away. Bob's shirtless relatives carried him to the helicopter.

The helicopter transported Bob to the Stuart Lake Hospital in Fort St. James. Doctors in the emergency room went into high gear. Local doctors Denis Brown and Tony Hatchwell were given critical support from Prince George doctors, who happened to be in town sharing their medical expertise in a workshop. They pumped plasma into Bob and stabilized him. The team of doctors worked on Bob for three hours before transferring him to Prince George Regional Hospital.

He had sustained severe wounds to his right wrist, both legs, left groin, buttocks, chest, and abdomen. Ninety minutes and eighty-seven stitches later, Bob's nineteen wounds were closed. Within days of the attack, Nichols was in satisfactory condition.

On Saturday morning, conservation officers from Prince George and Vanderhoof flew to the mauling site to search for the bear. The men observed three grizzly cubs on the ground near the site. A ground search located the dead sow grizzly, 150 yards from the site of the attack.

Bob hadn't realized it, but in his effort to move down the trail, he had passed within arm's length of the dead bear off the trail to the left. She weighed 350 pounds and was between ten and fifteen years old. She had thirteen knife wounds in her neck and four above her left eye.

Evidence suggested that the bear had recently been feeding on a moose carcass, although conservation officers believe the attack was predatory rather than defensive. But regardless of the cause, Bob Nichols was mighty happy to have a well-honed knife, which made the difference in his survival of a terrible ordeal.

AFTERMATH

In British Columbia, the lack of bear hunters has allowed the population of grizzlies to increase. This increase, in addition to six bear attacks in the summer and fall of 1995, has fueled a concern for people's safety.

Elk hunters Shane Fumerton and William Caspell were killed by a mother grizzly near Radium Hot Springs. They'd dropped a large bull elk on a remote mountain nearly two weeks before Nichols' encounter. One of the hunters may have chambered a round but didn't have time to fire.

The British Columbia government issued a warning to outdoorsmen 20 October, detailing the need for caution in bear country, particularly advising hunters to be vigilant when handling fresh-killed game (suggesting hunters abandon their meat if approached by a bear).

Vanderhoof-based conservation officer Bob Lay admitted that, "In my opinion, hunting regulations have become so strict that people don't want to bag bears anymore. Five years ago it was rare to spot a grizzly and her cubs. Now the sight of a sow with three or four cubs is getting to be routine."

The number and size of cubs with the Nichols' bear was unusual. Leonard Ross indicated that there was a difference in the cubs' sizes. The sow's tracks were wider than the length of his hand (about five inches) and the three larger cubs' tracks were wider than the width of his hand, whereas the one small cub's tracks were only two to three inches long. Earlier in the hunt, Morris Ross had seen five grizzlies in a group: probably a sow, three two-year-old cubs, and a cub of the year.

See Appendix 1

Canada moose hunter Nichols faced a grizzly, as did Alaskan cowboy and moose hunter Steve Malaski. But the results were very different.

Cowboy up a Tree

by Larry Kaniut

"I was so scared that I wasn't afraid."

In 1988 I spoke with Steve Malaski about brown-grizzlies and Arctic Valley. I told Steve that almost every moose hunter I know of had had a run-in with bruin in Arctic Valley. Steve said, "There's a lot of bear up there. Everybody warned me that after the first five or six days, when there's a lot of moose down, the bear come down. Ya gotta watch 'em. They hear a gunshot, and they're gonna come toward that gunshot 'cause they know there's a dead moose."

Steve told me it was his first hunt in Arctic Valley and his first encounter with bears. Here is Steve's story.

Jim North and I took three horses eight miles into Arctic Valley—most guys who go back that far use horses. It was the first time we had taken all the horses hunting, and they were plumb give out. It was the first week of the season in September 1987.

On the first day Jim and I made camp and Jim went down toward Ship Creek. He noticed sheep running on the side of the mountain, and he said, "Hey, we might have a moose or somethin' here. Let's take a look at it." So we got our glasses out. Fifteen Dall sheep—lambs and ewes—were on the west side above timberline. We couldn't see any big rams. But he did see a grizzly sow and two cubs scare the sheep. I watched them all that day while we were setting up camp.

On the fourth day of hunting, we walked down to the creek. On the way down, we ran across a moose kill about a quarter of a mile from our camp—almost a mile on the trail by horse. There were a lot of moose down at that time (dead moose).

When we reached the creek I said, "Well, I'm just gonna lay down on this log here with my binoculars." The clouds were rolling by. Then, between alder patches, I saw a massive gray animal walk across a clearing. The clouds lifted so that I could see that it was a gray bull.

The man who shot the moose a quarter of a mile from our camp had told us there was a sixty to seventy-inch bull there. This looked like the one. We started up the mountain after him; we left our horses in camp to stalk the moose on foot. The clouds were coming in and we lost him, but we ran across a forty-two-inch bull, which we shot.

At 2:00 P.M. we skinned him out, quartered him, and got him ready for us to pick up. We then went down to get the horses. We had forgotten our survey tape to mark our trail back to the kill site, so we used toilet paper. It started raining. By the time we had loaded our horses with the moose, it was getting dark. We started following our toilet paper trail back to camp, but it had washed off the trees.

On the river there are rapids. We were at the third set of rapids up Arctic Valley. It got dark on us, and since all of our horses were loaded with meat, they were trying to run over us. We were afraid they were going to break their legs in the swampy area, so we stopped. Jim said he would stay with the horses if I would go to camp and get our sleeping bags and something to eat. I said, "Sure, okay. I can hear the rapids, they're just to the right of us."

When I left I could see only twelve to fifteen feet. By the time I found the trail, it was almost pitch black because of incoming clouds. We'd gone too far. I found the trail only about twenty-five feet from us. I made a right instead of a left because I was disoriented. I went down the mushy, muddy trail, fell twice, and got wet. I decided, "Well, I'm lost, I'm goin' the wrong way, and I can't see to go anywhere." So I got underneath a big spruce tree. It was at least fifty feet tall, with large boughs reaching almost to the trail—I could get out of the rain under them. It was a good tree.

I had toilet paper underneath my raincoat, and I tried to start a fire with dried spruce. A cloud passed, the moon came out, and it got light. It also got very cold. I was sitting about ten feet from the trail. I looked up and saw the shape of a bear. I thought, "Well, that's just . . . it looks like a bear."

I tried to get my fire started again. I looked back up, and I still saw the bear. But the bear had stood up halfway and was looking at me from behind the tree. I thought, "You're not seein' things, Steve. This is a bear."

I climbed the tree. I had a Bic lighter and a .44 Magnum with three shells in it in a shoulder holster. The sow paced around the tree a few times grunting and swatting. Then I saw her two cubs. She must have made a few passes around the tree earlier while I was trying to make the fire. She didn't pay me much mind, and she lay down about eight feet from the tree. The moon was out and I could see her clearly. The cubs played. I was only halfway up the tree.

Then one of the cubs went back to mama who idly played with the cub as she lay there. The other little cub would come up the tree, look at me, and growl, and I'd flick the lighter at him. He'd go back down, run over, and jump on his mama who would turn around and knock him for a loop. He'd go rolling, then he'd come toward me growling and going around the tree. I kept flicking the lighter at the cub. I figured, "Man, if I piss off these cubs, mama's gonna come and take me outta this tree."

At first I was fifteen or twenty feet up, but after the cub shimmied partway up the tree, I climbed all the way to the top, at least forty feet in the air. By this time I was scared to death. I'd never been so afraid in my life—I was so scared that I wasn't afraid. I figured, "Piss on it. Let's get it over with. I've got three shells here; one of 'em's gonna be for me—she's not gonna eat me. If she comes up the tree after me, I'm gonna shoot two bullets and I'm gonna shoot myself. I'm not gonna be eaten alive."

But the sow never did harass me. The little cub was the one that gave me all the trouble and had me scared to death, because I knew if I shot at him and wounded him, hell would break loose and the mother would be on me. The sow knew I was human, yet she acted indifferently toward me. The cubs were of the year and were more curious. They were ornery little critters.

They hung around the tree for about an hour, then wandered in the direction of Jim and the horses. I'd left Jim my shotgun. I could hear him shooting a round every twenty minutes.

I tried to stay awake as long as I could. I took my shoulder holster off and tied myself to the top of the tree. After a while I fell asleep. I kept waking up all night because I was on a two-inch limb and my butt was sore. Once I awoke to find that I was leaning back with the holster strap holding me in the tree. But I had decided I wasn't coming down. I didn't know where the sow was.

I spent the whole night in the tree, and the next morning I felt great. I had climbed the tree so fast that I hadn't thought of the danger. At daylight, I looked down and saw that if I had slipped or a branch had broken, I would have died. I was at the top of a tall tree.

I got out of the tree about 8:00 A.M. and started up the trail looking for Jim. I was surprised to discover bear tracks all over the trail. When you leave the rigs to go up Ship Creek, normally all you see are horse tracks. But when you get up early in the morning and are the first one on the trail, all you see are bear tracks, BIG bear tracks. As I plodded along looking for Jim, hypothermia set in.

In the meantime, Jim was looking for me. He didn't know what had happened. He had unloaded the horse I was riding and used my saddle blankets for a bed. He started a little fire. Later on in the morning he thought he was going to die, too, from hypothermia. It wasn't below freezing, but the wind was blowing and we were both soaked to the bone. We finally met on the trail. Jim had been scared during the night because he heard something in the brush. But he never saw anything.

When I made it back to camp, I climbed inside my sleeping bag with all of my clothes on and I fell asleep. The next night I hallucinated. We kept a Coleman lantern lit, which we checked throughout the night to make sure it was burning. We had our horses with us, too, and we knew they would raise a ruckus if a bear showed up, so we weren't too afraid. I never do sleep well when I'm up there. I always have my slug gun and my flashlight ready, and I'm always listening to my horses.

On the last day we broke camp and took the horses and the meat out. We went back for our camping gear. The sun was out, and I saw a big, long-haired boar on the eastern side of the valley. The sun shone on him as he sat there. I'd seen four bears in Arctic Valley in seven days, and I'd seen two live moose bulls—and we got one of the bulls.

I can smile about it now, but I was afraid at the time. I learned two things: Never split up with your hunting partner, and always take sterno cans in case you need a fire.

Some Bears Kill

Steve Malaski escaped a bear by climbing a tree; however, a great many questions arose over the tree-climbing blackie and Darcy Staver.

It Didn't Have to Happen

Larry Kaniut

"There was flight—God-fearing, heart-pounding, panicky flight."

When two college co-eds were killed by two different grizzlies twelve hours apart in Glacier National Park in 1967, people were stunned. There had never been a double bear killing in the national parks. Although the shock was not as extreme, Alaskans were surprised twenty-five years later in July 1992 when two people were killed by bears in the same week. There was greater shock in 1995 when a single bear killed two well-known Anchoragites.

I felt stunned disbelief when I read about Darcy Staver in the newspaper 9 July 1992. Not another death by a bear! Only two days later I read about another bear attack. This time an adolescent brown bear struck on the Alaska Peninsula, killing a little boy named Antone Bear.

I know of only three other times up to 1992 that two people in the same party were killed by bears in Alaska (and only a few incidents throughout North America where black or polar bears killed two or three people in a party). In 1910, two native boys were following a wounded brown bear when a second brownie struck them from behind and killed them. At the village of Nabesna in the 1950s, a grizzly fatally mauled an Indian woman and a young girl.

In April 1956, Lloyd Pennington and Everett Kendall ran into a grizzly at its den site near Snowshoe Lake, and the animal killed both guide and client.

My concern was that someone should get the details and present the public with information to avoid such incidents. With proper education and practice, these things could be prevented. Of course, in 1992 I had no idea that I would ever compile another bear book.

However, it seems almost futile to chronicle bear encounters and dole out the appropriate advice. It doesn't matter how many books are written or read, people will still think they're invincible or that maulings couldn't happen to them. People do their own thing, but if they fail to practice safety around bears, they become the ones we read about in the paper. Yet, I hope people learn about the danger the wild presents and practice safety therein.

❖   ❖   ❖

Michael and Darcy Staver returned to their cabin 7 July 1992. Darcy enjoyed spending time at the two-bedroom cabin, located between Eureka Lodge and Tolsona Lake Resort, a few miles west of the Lake Louise turnoff. Her brother Eric had spent a weekend at the cabin a few weeks earlier without seeing bears.

Early in the morning of 8 July, Darcy was awakened by a noise. She woke Michael and told him there was a bear on the porch. Michael was not wearing a watch and did not know the exact time. Upon investigation they saw a cinnamon black bear prowling about. The Stavers, and other local residents, had not seen this small bear in the area before.

They attempted to chase the bear off, pounding on pans and making noise. The animal, however, refused to leave. Sometime later the bear became more aggressive and broke through a rear visqueen-covered window, entering the cabin. The couple fled, with the bear in pursuit. It took a swipe at Michael while he was still inside, but the bear missed him.

Darcy ran outside and ascended a ladder to the roof, pulling the ladder up behind her. Michael climbed a railing to the roof as well. The bear went outside by breaking through a closed screen door. After seeing the people on the roof, the bear returned to the interior of the cabin and ransacked it. Before long the bruin was outside again, circling the cabin. Michael fired several rounds from a .22-caliber pistol in an effort to scare the animal. He took great care not to hit the bear in order to keep from further antagonizing it.

Michael and Darcy debated their options atop the roof. At length they decided that Michael would make a run for the boat, fire up the outboard, and race across the lake half a mile to Al Lee's Air Taxi for help. He would also be able to procure another weapon there, one that would be more effective against a bear. Without further ado, Michael made for Lee's.

Around 9:00 A.M. Michael told Gregory W. Talley, an assistant guide and laborer for Lee's Air Taxi Service, that a bear had Darcy trapped on the roof of their cabin. Talley and Michael returned to the cabin armed with two rifles.

Only ten to fifteen minutes had passed while Michael crossed the lake and returned with Talley. Leaving the boat at the dock, Talley approached the cabin and observed a bear feeding at the southwest end of the dwelling. The animal briefly glanced toward the man with an air of nonchalance, then resumed feeding.

Talley fired a .375-caliber rifle fifty yards from the bear and dropped the bruin. It died where it lay. Michael approached the animal and discovered it had fallen on his wife, who was deceased. Her arms and legs were severely mauled, and the bear had been feeding on her body. They pulled the bear off Darcy's body and Michael shot the animal in the head.

Michael told Talley to summon the troopers while he remained at the site. About 9:25 A.M. the Alaska State Troopers in Glennallen received a phone call from Talley reporting Darcy's death. Arrangements were made for

Talley to meet the troopers at Lee's Air Taxi, and Trooper Sgt. G. Tanner left with Trooper Roscovious of the Division of Fish and Wildlife Protection. Fifty minutes later the officers met Talley, who told Sgt. Tanner of his rescue efforts.

The officers left Lee's in a wooden skiff for the Staver cabin. Upon their arrival Sgt. Tanner observed Michael Staver near the cabin with a rifle. Tanner saw that Staver was in shock and asked him to return to Lee's with Trooper Roscovious. Tanner then began an investigation of the scene.

He noted that the cabin was large and consisted of a bathroom, kitchen, and living room, in addition to the two bedrooms. A porch was adjacent to the front door. Tanner noticed the dead bear outside, near which lay the victim, covered with a blanket. He identified Darcy, formerly of Palmer, Alaska. He discovered no trash or food items in the area of the cabin's exterior, nor did he detect any aromas that might attract a bear.

The bear carcass was examined to see if it was rabid or had other abnormalities leading to the unusual behavior. The bear tested negative for rabies. An analysis of the bear disclosed no physical characteristics that would account for the bear's extremely aggressive behavior.

Darcy was a woodswise woman, competent in her outdoor ability. She had shot big game and packed moose and caribou. She knew how to take care of herself outdoors. She was a regular Mrs. Grizzly Adams. Under normal circumstances, this bear would have posed no problem for her. But these weren't normal circumstances. According to Tanner, the bear had climbed a tree adjacent to the cabin and jumped onto the roof. He noted broken limbs, indicating the bear's presence. Tanner believes Darcy was killed in a fight with the bear or in her attempt to flee.

❖   ❖   ❖

Antone Bear was a six-year-old boy killed by a brown bear at the edge of the village of King Cove on the Alaska Peninsula. The bear that attacked Antone's family was also a healthy animal. It was an average-sized two to three-year-old Alaskan boar brownie. It weighed 450 pounds and squared seven feet. It had moderate body fat, a full stomach, and no injuries. The major difference between it and its wilderness cousins was that it was a village bear, eating whatever garbage it could find. Antone was an Alaskan native lad of average size. It wasn't even a close match!

Lillian Bear of False Pass and her children, Antone and two-year-old Janet, walked on the edge of King Cove at 6:00 A.M. Friday, 10 July 1992. Antone heard a noise and proclaimed that a bear was following them. Antone cried when he saw the bear. Lillian and her children panicked and ran from the animal, becoming separated in the tall grass. Lillian found Janet and ran to a nearby house. Responding to its predatory nature, the bear chased little Antone. There was no battle. There was flight—God-fearing, heart-pounding, panicky flight. A primeval effort to survive prevailed. A young bear and a child raced, but the child had no chance.

The result was a gut-wrenching, tragically sad statistic and lasting grief for the human survivors. (Later the bear was hunted down and killed, the usual punishment for a man-killing bear.) Fear spread throughout the community. Night patrols were mounted around the village dump to provide human safety. An effort was made to dissuade villagers from killing bears.

Darcy Staver and Antone Bear were loved and are mourned by their survivors. Although the bears that killed Darcy Staver and Antone Bear were two different species, they were both in good condition. Both victims fled their pursuer. Both humans were killed and partially eaten by the bears. Sadly for the victims and their loved ones, both deaths could have been avoided. Having an adequate weapon, preferably a high-powered rifle, would have deterred or killed Darcy's black bear and, in all likelihood, Antone's bear as well.

See Appendices 3 and 4.

A bear-stopper is a necessity for saving lives, as Bill Poland relates.

Close Calls Call for Big Guns

by Bill Poland

*"She was twenty-five feet away and leaping twelve to
fifteen feet . . . like a racehorse coming after us."*

*Entering bear country is like being immersed in shark-
infested water: there always exists the possibility of an
encounter with a hostile animal. Sharks patrol their waters using their senses to apprise themselves of intruders.
Bears also sense intruders in their environment.*

*Fortunately, not all sharks attack man, nor do all bears.
Some bears merely bluff while others attack only to investigate the situation. A few attack with more serious intent.
Regardless of the bear's reason for attacking, the possibility of serious injury or death always exists.*

*Many guides are at a loss when asked about their bear
attack stories because they have never been attacked. A
respected and veteran guide is Bill Poland, who is also one
of the oldest living Alaskan guides. I visited Bill in Kodiak
in June 1988.*

I've only had two close calls with bears. I had the first
one in Spiridon Bay in 1953. I had a hunter from Texas,
and we were ambling along in a draw. He was behind me.
I heard a sound from him, so I turned around and saw a
bear coming out of the alders toward me. The hunter had
his rifle up. I signaled for him to shoot, but he didn't. So

I turned around and shot the bear right in the chest. It was twenty-one feet away. He was a big son of a gun, almost a ten-footer.

There was still snow on the ground, and we tracked him back into the alders. He had been lying in a bear bed, a depression six or eight feet long and two or three feet wide and filled with ice-cold, snowy water. He'd either been mating (they take quite a beating from the sows sometimes), or he'd been fighting with something. His face was cut and festering. I think if there had been a railroad train coming along he would have tackled it. He was mad.

Fortunately the hunter had made enough noise so that I was able to shoot. He explained his reason for not shooting: He told me that he had brought a 6X scope, disregarding my instructions to bring a 3X one. At that range he couldn't see anything but a big ball of fur. He couldn't see where to shoot.

After fifteen years without a close call, I was hunting on the Alaska Peninsula when I saw a good-sized bear in a stream. We went after him, and just before we got there, we ran into a sow and a cub. She was about an eight-foot bear. The hunter took some pictures of her, and we went a long way around to avoid any problems with the sow and cub. We kept walking to where we thought that big bear would be.

Suddenly I felt the earth shake as though a train were passing by. I turned around and the female bear was coming. She was twenty-five feet away and leaping twelve to fifteen feet. She was like a racehorse coming after us. It was as though somebody had thrown a bucket full of ice-cold water on me: I gasped in shock. I couldn't do anything wrong; if I did, I would have had it. I only had time for one shot. I shot her in the chest with my .375. I think the hunter shot too. She went down like a punctured balloon.

This is about the only serious encounter I've had except for some stupid ones. We were up at Little River Lake on Kodiak Island. The hunter and I were sitting up on a little bluff glassing the country, when we spotted a big bear coming. He must have been three-quarters of a mile away coming down the river. He disappeared from sight and we ran after him.

We came to the river—we could see far down that river—and there was no bear in sight. We figured he must have gone by. We ran back upriver and couldn't see him. In order to get to the river, we had to go through alders six or eight feet high, and we couldn't see anything. That was a dumb move.

We heard a crackling, and there was the big bear. And so help me, he couldn't have been more than twenty-five or thirty feet from us. He stood up and looked at us. I told the hunter to go ahead and shoot him. The bear stayed there, watching us. He didn't have any idea what we were. We both shot at one time, and the bear went down.

That was a big bear, pushing ten feet.

If I had been thinking I never would have gone into the brush like that. If that bear had gotten down on his four legs, he'd have been on us before we could have done anything.

Strange things happen with bears. One of the strangest was a polar bear on Kodiak Island that Clara Helgason told me about.

Believe It or Not

by Clara Helgason

"I think you're mistaken. It's an albino bear."

Our friend Frank Morgan told us about a Kodiak polar bear that Kris Helgason had shot. I contacted Clara, who told me the story

One Sunday morning 1943, we were having breakfast when Charley Ahonan, a Finnish fisherman and neighbor four miles from us, landed in his skiff at our gill net site. He ran up to our tent on Seven Mile Beach, between Karluk and Uyak, where we lived in the summertime. He said in broken English, "Kris, come shoot the bear."

I asked my husband, Kris, "What's he talking about?"

"He wants me to go shoot a bear."

Kris asked him, "Where is the bear?"

Charley answered, "It's down the beach coming this way."

Kris was going to go in the skiff with him. I said, "I want to go too." So I went along with my .22. Kris had his .30-06.

I sat in the bow and saw a white thing moving along. I said, "What color is that bear?"

Charley said, "Oh, it's kind of white."

I said, "Daddy"—what I call my husband—I think I see it." The banks on Seven Mile Beach are gray clay. The bear was off-white. The bear came to an old dead sea lion, half-buried in gravel. It stopped and tried to dig it up.

Kris told me, "Mamma, you stay in the skiff and watch it."

I said, "Okay."

Kris, his partner, and Charley went ashore. Kris took two shots at the bear. He hit it, but not in a vital spot. It ran up the bank and went into the brush. They followed it by the blood spots. It had gone quite a ways into the brush, so they came back.

We went home, and Charley went with us. Charley told us that the night before a terrible storm had hit and he hadn't been able to get out to his net. In the morning he had gone out to clear his net up and put it in his skiff because the season was closed. Once there, he saw a polar bear on shore. It tore his tent trying to get his food.

The bear saw Charley out in the skiff, not too far from shore. The bear started swimming out to him. Charley got scared and had a few fish that he'd picked from his net, so he threw them at the bear. The bear grabbed one of the fish and swam back ashore. Charley got his net in the skiff, and that's when he came to our place.

Two weeks later our other neighbor, Jacob Lou, came over and said, "You and Kris better be careful. Don't come down to our place. That bear comes down every evening and eats on that sea lion."

One day Jacob came over and said, "Kris, that bear is around." So Kris and Jacob went to the beach and looked with their binoculars, and they saw the bear eating the sea lion. Kris and his partner Joe went to the beach, and Kris shot him that time.

We were surprised to see that it was a polar bear. I never had seen a live polar bear, but Kris knew what it was. It had hair all over its paws—a distinguishing trait—and Kris had seen a lot of polar bears in Iceland. When we told Charley Madsen about it, Charley laughed at Kris and said, "I think you're mistaken. It's an albino bear."

Kris told him he was crazy. "You don't know what you're talking about. I've seen a lot of polar bears in northern Iceland where I'm from."

Even to this day we don't know how that polar bear got to Kodiak Island. Perhaps the bear got on an iceberg and drifted out to the Shelikov Straits. It's about fifty miles from Seven Mile Beach to the mainland on the Alaska Peninsula. A lot of people don't believe us. Even to this day, if we talk about it they look at us as though we're crazy.

We skinned the bear out, but we didn't have any salt. The neighbors didn't have any salt either. We couldn't preserve it, but Kris applied fly spray to keep the blowflies away from the hide. Without the salt, however, we couldn't save the skin. Kris cut it in half and said, "We probably can save the head and have a head mount." We took it to Seattle, where Kris was going to see a doctor. Moths got into it in the basement where we were staying. All the hair fell off the head before we could take it to Jonas Brothers, so into the garbage it went. I felt terrible about it.

One of the most incredible encounters with a bear ever recorded was experienced by Forest Young.

Where Danger Lurks

by Larry Kaniut

Fifteen hours after the attack, Forest finally felt free.

Alaska's vast playground beckons, but her siren song belies the danger that she spawns. One age-old hazard is wrapped in fur and festooned with claws and jaws. Unfortunately, people stereotype all bears as dangerous, often branding the entire tribe as bad. Bears can be dangerous, often engaging people in life-and-death struggles; however, not all bears are bad. But one that Forest Young ran into in 1955 was a bad, nasty bear.

A patchwork of green and gold mantled the hillsides, signaling winter's approach. Hunting buddies Forest H. Young, Jr. and Marty Cordes shot two respectable bull moose in late September 1955. They dressed the bulls, cached the hides and some meat in a birch tree, and packed part of their take two miles to the cabin.

The following day they loaded the canoe with meat and Marty headed for Haines, Alaska, forty-five miles down the Chilkat River. By the time Marty returned the following afternoon, Forest had everything except Marty's moose hide in camp. On 2 October, Marty took the shotgun for a batch of grouse, while Forest targeted Marty's moose hide. They would rendezvous at the cabin around noon.

Two mounds of debris covered the moose remains at the kill site, indicating that bears had taken over. The discovery didn't scare Forest because he'd encountered bears for years. He reached the cache, glanced back at the kill site one hundred yards away, and saw two grizzlies.

One of the grizzlies ran toward him. Assuming it was a bluff charge, he waved his arms and shouted. At the last moment Forest realized this was no bluff. He lunged for a tree limb to climb out of harm's way. He never made it.

The grizzly snatched him from the tree. Forest landed on his back but rose to a sitting position; the bear's left foreleg pinned his legs. Man and beast were nose to nose, the hapless hunter at the bear's mercy as its blood-red eyes bored into his. Expecting the beast to grab him by the throat and snap his neck, Forest pummeled the bear's face until he broke his hand. Forest felt his clothing grind into his flesh while the bear chewed. Every bite registered intense pain as the animal stripped flesh and clothes from the hunter.

Forest tried playing dead and the bear immediately broke off its attack. But then Forest groaned, and the bear nailed him again, slashing a hole in his side that exposed his bladder. Forest remained motionless while the bear ripped three ribs from his spine and tore a hole in his chest cavity. Then the grizzly left. Although he hoped the beast would not return, Forest suddenly heard a strange panting noise and felt the muskeg shake. The bear stood only a yard from his face. Time crawled. Finally the bear moved off.

In spite of the pain, Forest managed to roll onto his stomach, allowing body fluids to drain from his nose and mouth and facilitating his breathing. Later Forest heard that queer panting sound and felt the ground shake again. No sound could have caused him greater fear.

Perhaps the animal sensed he'd moved. It bellowed in rage. The bear lifted Forest off the ground in its jaws and shook him until he thought his back would break. As abruptly as he'd appeared, the bear dropped Forest and departed. The brute had ripped out one rib and left two exiting the skin, mangled his right hand, opened a hole revealing his lung cavity, tore flesh from the inside of his legs, and ripped his buttocks.

Cold water filtered up through the muskeg and chilled Forest to the bone. He agonized . . . *even if Marty finds me when he returns, I might be dead.* Believing his plight hopeless, he determined to take his life. He cut his left wrist, exposing tendons. Seeing no blood and fearing a crippled hand should he survive, Forest stopped. Next he considered cutting his jugular vein. As Forest felt for his jugular, Marty hailed.

Shocked and unable to carry Forest because of his injuries, Marty hastened to camp. He returned and made Forest as comfortable as possible, easing him into a sleeping bag, hanging his outer clothing from limbs to fend off the drizzle, laying the loaded shotgun beside him, and lighting and placing the lantern within Forest's reach. Marty immediately left for Haines.

Cordes had fifteen river miles to cover by outboard, and another thirty by truck. He'd have to round up a rescue party, then cover the same mileage on his return. The river was low, and they'd be traveling in the dark. Forest didn't expect Marty until midnight. Worse, Forest wondered if he'd live that long.

An hour after Marty's departure, Forest began feeling better. *Maybe I'll make it.* He'd nearly forgotten the bear and had fought the urge to doze, when he heard that queer panting and felt the ground shake. Forest lay motionless in the bag, the top covering his head. His tormentor approached. Perhaps confused by the light, the sleeping bag, and Marty's clothes, the animal lumbered off, venting a bloodcurdling roar. Sweet relief flooded Forest.

As darkness fell, the lantern burned out and Forest panicked. He fully expected the bear to jump him once it realized the light was gone. And his fear was realized.

Forest heard the beast coming for him. Then it was there, near his head. Forest pointed the shotgun in the bear's direction, held high so no pellets would strike it, and fired. Flame stabbed the darkness, the recoil jolted Forest to the core of his being, and the bear fled, a strangled bawl trailing off into the night.

As Forest focused on Marty's expected midnight return, the bear came back. Forest decided that if it got within ten feet, he'd shoot it; if that wouldn't kill it, maybe the shot would drive it off. For ten minutes the bear snuffled twenty-five feet away, then left. Just after that, Forest heard the welcome sound of an outboard. Figuring rescuers had reached the cabin, he prepared to strike matches. He heard voices and lit all the matches. Voices responded and he quickly felt the hands of succor. Fifteen hours after the attack, Forest finally felt free.

Carl Heinmiller injected him with penicillin and morphine. Marty, Carl, and Walt Dueman struggled nearly four hours carrying Forest to the cabin in the dark. The next morning Forest was loaded aboard a Royal Canadian Air Force helicopter and flown to Juneau's St. Anne's Hospital. He arrived in critical condition twenty-seven hours after his ordeal had begun. Forest spent nine weeks in the hospital, lost thirty pounds, three ribs, and half an inch off his third finger on his right hand. He also acquired some nasty scars.

Forest's misfortune was compounded by the fact that he had minimized the significance of the bear's presence at the kill site and had gone unarmed. Had he climbed the tree immediately when the bear charged, he'd have been safe. There is a time to play dead; there is a time to resist. Playing dead probably saved his life. Forest survived his ordeal and spent many enjoyable years in Alaska's great outdoors, where danger lurks.

Appendix 1

Bob Nichols

When I telephoned conservation officer Cam Hill for more information about this mauling, he sent me the following bulletin:

Province of British Columbia
Ministry of Environment
Lands and Parks

INFORMATION BULLETIN

PROVINCE ISSUES SPECIAL ADVISORY TO HUNTERS

—Extra Caution of Grizzlies Urged—

VICTORIA—With the number of recent grizzly-bear attacks, the B.C. Wildlife Branch is asking hunters to be extra cautious this autumn while out in the wild. This is the time of year when bears are on a constant lookout for food as they attempt to fatten up for hibernation. It's also the most popular time for hunting.

There have been many recent incidents of bear attacks on hunters and other outdoors people in remote areas. Grizzly bears recently killed two hunters near Radium Hot Springs, apparently while they were dressing freshly killed elk. Earlier this week, another hunter was mauled by two grizzlies in a remote part of the East Kootenays.

With their keen sense of smell, bears can easily find freshly killed game, and are not hesitant to claim it as their own. In the Kootenays, where there are many hunters and bears, some bears are so used to eating the remains left by hunters that they appear to have come to associate the sound of a gunshot with their next meal.

The Wildlife Branch is asking that hunters be extra cautious around killed animals and take precautions when returning to a kill site to pick up meat. If approached by a bear at a kill site, the hunter should abandon the meat, back away from the bear, and report the incident to a conservation officer.

Bears can be found in most parts of the province. British Columbia has up to 160,000 black bears and up to 13,000 grizzlies. Black- and grizzly-bear attacks in B.C. have resulted in about six deaths in the last ten years, and there are usually between three to five maulings a year. So far this year, bears have caused two deaths and at least eight injuries in B.C.

Bears are especially dangerous if they are defending a fresh kill, if they are used to human food, or if they are with cubs. Anyone in the wild should be alert, make their presence known by making noise, and watch for signs of bear activity.

For more information, call your nearest B.C. environment office and ask for a copy of *Safety Guide to Bears in the Wild* or *Safety Guide to Bears at Your Home.*

Wildlife Branch
Public Affairs & Communications
British Columbia

Appendix 2

In Memoriam
Marella O. Trent and Larry A. Waldron

Marella O. Trent was born in Hutchinson, Kansas, in 1917 and moved to Alaska to homestead in 1946. An inspiration to both young and old, this tiny 77-year-old lady, who weighed less than 100 pounds and stood five feet tall, was matriarch to Anchorage's running community. She and her husband, John, pioneered running in Anchorage, forming the Pulsators Running Club (an informal group that logged their running mileage and received awards for attaining certain levels) in the 1970s. Marcie logged over 70,000 miles and finished seventy marathons.

Marcie will be remembered by all who knew her.

Larry A. Waldron was born on 11 August 1949, attended public school in Anchorage, and graduated from East Anchorage High School in 1967. He received a degree in arranging and composing from Berklee School of Music in Boston, Massachusetts.

Larry was a popular saxophonist, playing the local jazz scene. He was an avid long distance and marathon runner (competing in many of the same races as his mother). He was a gifted and popular teacher, and he will be greatly missed by all whom he influenced.

❖ ❖ ❖

I visited Chugach State Park Superintendent Al Meiners on 15 May 1996, at the Potter Marsh park headquarters. We discussed the Trent-Waldron tragedy and the park's action based on the Alaska Department of Fish and Game's bear policy and the need for education. We discussed the report on pepper spray, and wildlife-human conflicts proposals, and Al gave me the following information.

CAUTION
You Are Traveling in Bear Country
Bears Don't Like Surprises

Make noise, sing, talk loudly, or tie a bell to your pack. Avoid thick brush. When possible, walk with the wind to your back and travel in a group. Do not camp on trails or bear routes. Avoid or detour areas where you see or smell carcasses of fish or animals or when you see scavengers such as ravens or magpies congregating. This is an indication that a bear's food may be there. If a bear is nearby, it may defend the cache aggressively.

Don't Crowd Bears

Give bears plenty of room. Bears have a sense of "personal space," and, if you get within that zone, a bear may react aggressively.

Bears Are Always Looking for Something to Eat

Don't let bears learn that human food or garbage is an easy meal. It is both foolish and illegal to feed bears, either on purpose or by leaving food or garbage that attracts them. Cook away from your tent. Keep food smells off your clothing. Store food away from your campsite in a tree or bear-proof container. Pets and their food also may attract bears. Keep a clean camp. Wash your dishes. Avoid smelly foods. Food and garbage are equally attractive to bears, so treat them with equal care. Do not bury garbage.

Close Encounters: What to Do

Identify yourself—Let the bear know you are *human*. Talk to the bear in a normal voice. Wave your arms. Help the bear recognize you. A bear needs to gather information to identify you, so it may stand on its hind legs or move closer to you. A standing bear is usually curious, not threatening. You may try to back away slowly and in a diagonal direction, but if the bear follows, stop and hold your ground.

Don't Run—You Can't Outrun a Bear

Running will only encourage a chase. Bears often make bluff charges without making contact. Continue to wave your arms and talk to the bear. If the bear gets closer, raise your voice and be more aggressive. Bang pots and pans. Use noisemakers.

If Attacked—
If a Bear Actually Makes Contact, Surrender!

Fall to the ground and play dead. Lie on your stomach, or curl in a ball with your hands behind your neck. Most bears will stop attacking once they feel the threat (you) has been eliminated. Wait as long as possible or you may provoke a renewed attack. In rare instances, particularly with black bears, an attacking bear may perceive you as food. If the bear continues to bite you long after you have assumed a defensive posture, it is likely a predatory attack. Fight back vigorously.

Be Bear Aware—Remain Aware of
Your Surroundings

Don't wear headphones. Avoid running in dense vegetation. Pay attention to wind direction. A wind from behind you will carry your scent ahead of you, which will inform bears of your presence. If the wind is in your face, be extra alert and make noise. Travel in a group whenever possible.

Bearanoia!

Follow these precautions, but enjoy yourself. Given the amount of outdoor activity and the infrequency of attacks, the statistical risk of being killed or injured by a bear is very remote.

❖   ❖   ❖

Research into Pepper Spray

Stephen Herrero and Andrew Higgins
Environmental Science Program
Faculty of Environmental Design
University of Calgary
Calgary, Alberta, Canada T2N 1N4

Some conclusions from our research into the use of pepper spray in man-bear encounters are:

1) Capsicum spray appears to be reasonably, but not 100%, effective against aggressive brown/grizzly bears in sudden encounters

2) Use of the spray against brown/grizzly bears searching for people's food and garbage was generally effective in causing the bears to stop and leave the area in the twenty incidents studied

3) Because of the small number of incidents where the spray was used in sudden or possibly predaceous encounters with black bears, it is not possible to draw conclusions about the effectiveness of the spray in this type of encounter. Analysis of the four incidents available in this class suggests the spray is less effective than in sudden encounters with brown/grizzly bears

4) Use of the spray against black bears searching for food and garbage had mixed results. In half of the cases, the bear either did not leave, or left and returned a short time later. The spray appears ineffective as a means of deterring black bears that are strongly conditioned to human foods and garbage

5) In at least some bears, there is not an overwhelming, innate physiological response to the spray that drives all behavior subsequent to spraying

6) Sprays containing capsicum appear to be potentially useful in a variety of field situations; however, variable responses by bears occur. Because the database is composed of diverse field records, the results should be viewed with caution.

Appendix 3

Darcy Staver

Four years ago I read about Darcy Staver in the paper and red flags went up. Other people suspected foul play. How could this happen? A healthy woman. A healthy husband. Two grown people against a small black bear. Something seemed amiss.

Although a public safety report and an autopsy were completed and this incident was wrapped in a tidy little "case closed" package, the case report raised questions that remain unanswered. Many people have told me "there was something fishy about the incident." There is a lot of doubt about the actual events at the cabin surrounding Darcy's death and Mike's story.

In an effort to ascertain the facts of the attack on Darcy, I attempted to contact Michael Staver. So far I have been unsuccessful. Only a couple of the other principals in the story have responded to my queries. Only one person was able to tell what happened that fateful day in July, which only raised more questions. I contacted Trooper George Petry, and we discussed the case report in detail. Some of the concerns and questions follow:

1. If the couple lived at the site, couldn't they have appeased the bear long enough with food to allow them to get to their boat?

2. Since they lived at the site, why did they have only a .22 caliber for a defensive weapon, and a pistol at that?

   a. Wasn't a better weapon accessible?

   b. What became of the pistol?

3. Since Darcy was both statuesque and a formidable woodsperson, and Michael was an army ranger, what kept them from jointly fighting the bear so that they could escape to the boat?

4. Why would the bear attack the roof dweller rather than the more accessible person on the ground?

5. What was the size of the tree and how far was it from the roof.

    a. Could the tree support the bear?

    b. Was any bear hair found on the tree?

    c. What types of bear marks were on the tree and how far up the tree? (One witness said the tree that the bear climbed to get onto the roof bore no scratch marks, broken bark, or any sign that a bear had climbed it. The same witness said Michael cut down the five-inch tree within a few days of the incident.)

9. Was Michael tested for drugs or alcohol? Given a polygraph test?

10. How thorough was Propst's report?

    a. How did he explain rigor mortis within an hour-and-a-half of the decedent's passing?

This incident left many questions unanswered and gave rise to much speculation concerning the appropriateness of Michael's response during a dangerous situation.

Appendix 4

Antone Bear

Dick Sellers, wildlife biologist in King Salmon, responded to my query for more information about this mauling. He wrote, "As you indicated, this tragic incident is particularly sensitive because of the circumstances. But it does emphasize the futility of trying to outrun a bear."
The investigation and a necropsy report follow.

INVESTIGATION OF FATAL BROWN BEAR ATTACK OF 10 JULY 1992 AT KING COVE, ALASKA

The brown bear involved in this attack was a sub-adult male (estimated three years old). It had been seen several times in the general area between town and Ram's Creek, usually in the company of another sub-adult bear. While these bears were undoubtedly getting human garbage, no serious or threatening behavior by these bears toward people was reported prior to the morning of 10 July 1992.

About 5:45 A.M. on 10 July 1992, Mrs. Lillian Bear and her three-year-old daughter and six-year-old son (Antone) were walking east on South Ram's Creek Road, headed out of town. Antone noticed a bear following them at some distance (described by Mrs. Bear as "two houses away"). In an attempt to escape, the family climbed over the guardrail and fled down the hill toward the bay. The bear gave pursuit. Antone got separated from his mother and was overtaken by the bear. Mrs. Bear and her daughter kept running and eventually got back to their house and summoned help. The police and several citizens arrived, and the bear was soon spotted about twenty to thirty yards from the road. When the bear stood up, it was killed by simultaneous shotgun blasts from two citizens. The bear was still on the boy's body. It is clear that the bear's natural chase response was triggered when the family began running away.

As with virtually every village on the Alaska peninsula, King Cove has experienced conflicts with bears, and, as is the common theme, the conflict stems from bears being attracted to the village dump by human garbage. King Cove has already taken several measures to reduce these conflicts, and the suggestions made here are not aimed at detracting from their efforts and are not offered as a quick or easy fix.

Dump—There are several steps that could be taken to reduce the availability of garbage to bears, and thereby reduce the number of bears that frequent the area around the village. The present dump is located east of town, and is only about ½ mile from a subdivision. Ideally the dump should be put as far away from human residential areas as possible. Plans for refuge disposal will continue to use the current dump, but future deposits will expand away from town. Efforts will increase to minimize the amount of waste material that is exposed each night. This may help reduce the amount of garbage that is available to bears. In addition to this, it would be prudent not to allow future residential development any closer to the dump than the present dwellings are.

Dumpsters—The city of King Cove has a number of dumpsters distributed around the village. I understand these are emptied at least every other day. This is a very progressive step and should go a long way toward reducing bear problems around houses. It eliminates the problem of having household garbage stored on porches or in pickups, assuming residents are not lax about taking their perishable garbage to a nearby dumpster. The following are several general suggestions that will help to the extent that they are practical to execute.

1) Put dumpsters in locations that are exposed (i.e., away from cover such as alder brush, junk, crab pots, etc.) and well lit. Although bears can become rather bold and oblivious of people, their natural tendency is to seek

cover and be secretive. A dumpster that is well out in the open and near a strong light will generally be less attractive to a bear than one that is next to an alder patch.

2) In addition, if the dumpster is exposed where a vehicle (e.g., police car) can actually run off a raiding bear, this can be an effective and safe deterrence. If a dumpster does become a consistent target for a bear, move it (at least temporarily) and empty it every evening until the bear moves off.

3) Aversive conditioning (a fancy term for punishment—e.g., bird shot or rubber bullets) may also help break a bear from using a dumpster.

4) Although it may be too costly at this time, more secure types of dumpsters (e.g., using sliding doors that can be latched) are available. Perhaps the state prison system could be persuaded to begin making such bear-proof dumpsters as part of an inmate vocational training program.

5) Assuming people will cooperate by not leaving garbage around, the other in-town attractant is hanging fish. This may be harder to secure from bears, but perhaps some communal areas could be developed where bears would have a hard time gaining access (e.g., inside a sturdy fence).

Education—A comprehensive education package on how best to live amongst bears, including video and written messages, should be made available by the state to residents of King Cove (and other villages). Much of this material is already available or in production.

❖   ❖   ❖

FIELD NECROPSY REPORT
BROWN BEAR INVOLVED IN FATAL MAULING
Bear Certificate #75567
Skull Seal # 9204675
Case KC 92 - 071
Date: 10 July 1992
Time: 22:30 - 23:30

Location: Center of King Cove

Circumstances: This brown bear was killed at approximately 6:00-6:30 A.M. on 10 July 1992 as it was feeding on a six-year old boy. Antone Bear and his mother and sister were walking east on Ram's Creek Road at approximately 5:45 A.M. Antone noticed a bear was following them on the road. The family immediately jumped the guardrail and fled down the bank. The bear gave chase and caught the boy who had become separated from his mother. The bear was killed by a total of five shots from two 12-gauge shotguns. The first two were fired simultaneously from about thirty yards as the bear stood up and faced two local citizens. The bear immediately fell over. The two men approached the bear, which still had some leg movement, and fired three more shots into the side of the chest and neck (both 00 buckshot and No. 4 shot were used).

Conclusions: This bear appeared normal and healthy, and previous injury or debilitation was ruled out as a contributing cause of this attack. Evidence from subcutaneous fat deposits and a stomach nearly full of garbage suggest this bear was not starving and had eaten a significant amount of food prior to the attack. Thus it is unlikely the attack was provoked by hunger. Rabies test was negative, as reported by Dr. Don Ritter over the phone about midnight on 10 July 1992. In my professional judgment, this attack was the result of the bear's instinctive response to pursue fleeing animals (in this case, the family).

Submitted by

Richard A. Sellers
Wildlife Biologist

Appendix 5

Eleonora Florance

MEMORANDUM

Office of International Geology—Mail Stop - 917

3 August 1994

To: Bonnie McGreggor, Jim Devine, Tom Ovenshine

From: Bruce F. Molnia

Subject: Bear Attack at Bering Glacier Camp, 29 July 1994

The purpose of this memo is twofold: first to formally report on volunteer Eleonora (Elly) Florance's attack by a grizzly bear, and second to discuss volunteer training and preparation for work at Bering Glacier.

Bear Attack

On Friday, 29 July 1994, just before 7:00 in the morning, a three-year-old female grizzly bear attacked Elly Florance while Elly was in her sleeping bag, in her tent at our Bering Glacier Camp (also known as Moose International Airport Camp (SAC). Elly, who is a public health service nurse, was working in my project as a camp health-care person and science assistant through the Department of the Interior's Volunteer for Science Program. This was the second year that Elly had participated in my program. As are most of my volunteers, Elly had taken the three day "Firearms Safety and Bear Behavior" course taught by the USGS. She also had training in helicopter and fixed-wing aircraft safety, CPR, and wilderness first aid.

As I reconstruct the situation, the bear entered the camp from the south and went directly to Elly's tent. Retracing its footprints, it appears that the bear went in a straight line to her tent from at least three hundred feet away. It ignored everything else in camp, walking within three feet of MIAC's refrigerator pit, which contained three full, partially buried coolers containing meat, cheese, and milk, and within ten feet of our kitchen tent that contained a very large selection of different foods.

The bear had previously walked through the camp two days before (Bureau of Land Management (BLM) wildlife biologist John Payne's "Incident Report . . ." is attached), ignoring the food tent and coolers and exhibiting no aggressive or threatening behavior. Closely watching the bear, John and I, armed with shotguns, both decided that the bear's actions were not life threatening to our people or property (as dictated by Alaska law and Alaska Department of Fish and Game policy, and as taught in the USGS firearms safety and bear behavior course). Hence we decided that there was no provocation to kill the bear at that time.

On the morning of 29 July, Elly, who was just awakening, described hearing a swishing sound from outside her tent. Elly, who was the only occupant of the tent, was located in the western-most tent in our line of sleeping tents. She thinks that the sound she heard was made by the bear rubbing against and touching the exterior of her tent, which was covered by a double layer of visqueen plastic sheeting. Then, within seconds, the bear was on her, swatting her with its upper paws and claws. It appears that the bear leaned on the top of Elly's tent, breaking the fiberglass tent poles and collapsing the tent. Hence while she was being attacked, she was partially in her sleeping bag and covered by the tent, the tent fly, the poles, and the layer of plastic. Elly had her tent covered with plastic to keep out rain, as a result of having gotten very wet in a major storm that we had experienced more than a week before.

Fortunately for Elly, all she received were deep flesh wounds. She was raked by the bear's claws on her right shoulder and her right hip. She also had puncture wounds on her left arm, which she was using to protect her face. These may have been caused by the bear's teeth. Elly said that during the attack, she tried not to move, but she screamed for help and covered her face. When she started to scream, the bear backed off. Elly told me that she then slowly rose to her knees and picked up her gun. She did not shoot at this time as she did not know where other people were. She then rose to her feet and stood up through the hole that the bear had made in her tent. She said that she saw the bear at the most distant work tent, about fifty feet from her tent, but did not shoot at it. A USGS press release (29 July 1994) describes Elly as being dragged from her tent. This is not correct.

Other people in camp, responding to Elly's screams, came out of their tents with guns in hand. Mike Herder, a commercial fisherman from whom we were renting a boat, was the first to chase the bear. He fired one .44 Magnum round into the hip of the retreating bear. He quickly grabbed a loaded 12-gauge shotgun from the office tent and continued to pursue the bear. He caught it and killed it with rifled slugs from the shotgun.

After the bear was killed, Elly walked the approximately four hundred feet to where the bear lay and looked at it. She directed camp members in the dressing of her wounds. She later walked to the U.S. Coast Guard helicopter that evacuated her to Cordova.

We can only speculate as to why the bear focused on Elly's tent. John Payne believes that bears are attracted to plastic and that the visqueen cover on Elly's tent may have been the critical factor. However, at least one other tent had a visqueen cover and at least four tents were covered with plastic tarps. Elly told me that she had just, unexpectedly, started her period and that she had some bloodstained clothing in a plastic bag in her tent. Whether this was a factor in the bear attack is also not known.

When the bear first entered our camp on Wednesday, 27 July, the only thing in the main part of the camp that the bear touched was the tent of another woman who was also having her period. This tent was also visqueen-covered. It is quite possible that the plastic concentrated or held the scent of menstrual blood, and that this combination of plastic and menstrual blood, or the scent of menstrual blood is what the bear was attracted to. Again, this is speculation.

Volunteer Training and Preparedness

Several years ago, I prepared a series of safety guidelines for participants in my Bering Glacier Project. A copy of these "Guidelines for Field Program Participants for a Successful Field Season at Bering Glacier, Alaska" is attached.

In preparation for this year's field season, I sent a copy to each of my volunteers. Additionally, each year as many volunteers as are able to attend participate in the survey's three-day gun- and bear-training program. This year, five took the course. Last year, four completed the training. Hence, the majority of my people at MIAC were formally gun trained. When I talked to the five BLM personnel who were in camp, all who live and work in Alaska on a full-time basis, I was surprised to learn that only one, John Payne, had received formal firearms training.

One of my camp practices is to put all sleeping tents in a straight line, with the people in the two end tents being armed, trained, knowledgeable individuals. Elly was serving in this capacity when she was attacked. The straight line permits a wide field of fire in the case of necessary response to a bear in camp.

Another camp practice is to make sure that at all times, every field party and the camp have at least one trained gun-carrying individual at all times. On 27 July, a day when the five BLM people were in camp, John Payne and I were surprised to learn that we were the only two people in camp with firearms training. Consequently, I canceled a planned outing for the two of us to ensure that the camp had a gun-qualified individual. That evening only after other gun-trained individuals had returned did we leave camp.

I make every effort to provide a safe work environment for my volunteers. This year, as we were going to be using a helicopter as our primary means of transportation, a special Office of Aircraft Services (OAS) helicopter training course was presented at camp to maximize the volunteer's knowledge about safe helicopter use and survival. The course, taught by an OAS safety inspector, also covered fixed-wing aircraft. Some of my volunteers have had small-boat handling training, wilderness first-aid training, CPR, seismic blasting and explosives handling, and safety training. Every effort is made to prepare my volunteers for a safe and successful field program.

In closing, I want to mention that this is the first time in twenty-one years that a camp I have run has had a bear incident. As John Payne's report suggests, this bear was an abnormal, unusual, and possibly sick bear. Our food stores were not its target in either of its visits to camp. Its behavior on 27 July, although unusual, was not such to result in our taking its life.

We will learn from this experience and tighten some of our camp procedures with respect to food, trash, and the distance of sleeping tents from our food area. I sincerely hope that the Volunteer for Science Program does not suffer as a result of this incident. Elly, who plans to return to Bering Glacier for a third year, next July, feels the same way.

Appendix 6

Kathryn Warburton

In Support of Kathryn

While completing this research, I asked Edythe McCuaig to contribute her comments about Kathryn. McCuaig's reply appears next.

Kathryn possesses a thirst for knowledge and a strong sense of responsibility for herself and her actions. A well-educated dental worker, she loves travel. Her work ethic and thrift had already afforded her journeys into the Middle East and much of Europe prior to her Alaskan trip from her native Australia. She knows as much about Alaska and polar bears as we know about New South Wales, dugongs, and, it would seem, polar bears.

Although facing months of pain and expense, Kathryn had no intentions of making anyone but herself responsible. We live in a time when the majority of people blame everyone for everything. Her attitude is refreshing. It was this attitude that caused me to pick up the phone and offer her a place to recuperate for as long as she needed.

She has lived a nightmare. I watched her be misquoted in the press and be blamed for "upsetting Binky." Those who didn't make money from ridiculous T-shirts found other ways of giving this fine person perhaps more pain than Binky had inflicted. She was expected to be available at all hours for radio and TV fillers, which she did graciously. She seldom heard a sincere "Thank you." And she never received monetary help from these sources.

Just as the people at the zoo came forward to help (at great risk to themselves), people came forward to cheer her. These people included the author, Larry Kaniut, and his wife Pam.

The group of Australians in the area came forward and helped plan her trips to and from the doctors, and her friend from the hostel and others who helped will be there in her mind to ease the nightmares. Without these people I would never have been able to help. It was a busy six weeks. People came to discuss Australia's medical care (medical care was one reason Kathryn needed to leave Alaska and return to her country) and others from the news media came to the house to film.

About five weeks into this situation we decided we had to have a cookout in appreciation for those who had become part of the solution. Kathryn tried to contact everyone who helped at the zoo, including the gentleman from back East. We had a great time and found ourselves invited to a cookout in Eagle River.

She will always be overwhelmed by Binky's huge, smothering size, power, and smell. Her one hope is that her experience will give reason for the small guard fences to be heightened so children and others will be safe. It took another person's tragedy (six weeks later) before anything was done.

Kathryn is still fighting problems from that day. The doctors continue to check the progress of the broken leg just recently freed from casts, and she is able to work. Her love of all animals continues. I believe she should be proud of herself.

❖ ❖ ❖

Zoo Bears

Numerous polar-bear maulings have taken place in zoos throughout the world. In March 1995, a 28-year-old psychiatric patient, who leaped into a polar-bear pit, was clawed by a 700-pound animal in Buffalo, New York. He had climbed the waist-high fence and jumped into the fifteen-foot deep pit. "The bear went right after him . . . like he wanted to play. The bear had one paw around the man and was licking his face," said Jon Gallo, a zoo visitor. Zookeepers lifted the clawed man to safety after which he was taken to the hospital and treated for minor injuries.

In May 1994, a Chinese tourist was hospitalized for bites after he jumped into the Beijing zoo's polar-bear pit. The man said he had wanted to play with the bear. . . .

In 1992 at the Karkov, Ukraine, zoo a polar bear mauled and killed an eleven-year-old boy who had been taunting it with a stick.

In 1990 a Cincinnati zoo animal keeper Laurie Stober, 30, was attacked by Icee, an 800-pound polar bear. Icee grabbed her fingers with his teeth and chewed his way up to her elbow. The beast chewed off and swallowed Laurie's arm. The zoo claimed that Stober violated zoo policy by sticking her fingers inside the cage. Stober claimed she'd held out a grape, which the bear took, along with her arm. Stober was awarded nearly $3.5 million resulting from the injury.

In 1987 two polar bears killed and partially ate an eleven-year-old boy, when the child entered the Prospect Park Zoo in Brooklyn, New York, to go swimming. Both animals were put to death.

Appendix 7

Marti Miller

Steve Nelson's Weapons Training Program

After talking with Marti and knowing about Cynthia's lack of a weapon, I thought it would be good to talk with Steve Nelson about his weapons-training program. Marti introduced me to Steve and I spoke with him on 2 May 1995 in Anchorage.

Steve was born in 1945 and graduated from San Jose State with a bachelor of arts in geology followed by a master of science from the University of Nevada. He served three years in the U.S. Navy and worked twenty-three years with the USGS, primarily in Alaska, before retiring in September 1995. For the last eleven years he was the firearms trainer for the USGS.

Our current program is twenty-four hours of training, emphasizing safe gun handling and safety in the field because we feel that the hazard is much greater that somebody may have an accident if they are untrained with firearms. The topics covered in four lectures are safety, ballistics, maintenance, and bears and other animals.

Our USGS bear safety course evolved after Cynthia Dusel-Bacon's 1977 attack. After Cynthia's attack there was a recommendation that we give a training program. Prior to that time most of the geologists in the field were men who were probably more familiar with firearms than the present generation. To my knowledge, there was really no training other than just what people did on their own. The first courses were conducted by two people— a local FBI officer, and a Fish and Game protection officer. These courses were really good in the bear description, but the shooting exercises tended to be focused on police or FBI-type activities. Self-defense against humans has similar attributes, but we don't want to get into those just to focus on bears. Through time, the USGS developed a firearms-safety program that focuses our concerns on the field work situations.

The instructors for the courses must go through pretty extensive training themselves—they must have participated in a USGS class as a student and taken the NRA firearms instructor class and a USGS firearms instructor class. In addition they must take a nongovernment-accredited firearms training class in either rifle, pistol, or shotgun.

By the time the instructors are through, they've had well over sixty hours of training in firearms. This gives them credibility as being experienced with firearms, and it exposes us to some really topnotch instructors who provide good training.

I offer training once a year, although the government requirement is that they only need to take the training once every three years (which I find unacceptable). Most people take it yearly.

Probably half of the students are reasonably familiar with firearms before the course. The other half may have fired a .22 at the most sometime when they were kids. There were twenty-four in my class this year, and there were two who had never fired a firearm.

The best training is a simulated and stressful situation. I try to emphasize to the students that this is not enough; they need to shoot more on their own. The people who have gone through the class and have faced bear situations emphasized that what went through their minds is almost instinctive handling of their firearm based on their training (such as what Marti or Elizabeth, who happened to be working with Marti, said of their encounters).

Their minds focused on the bear—"'Oh, I need to move back" or "I'll drop my lunch sack" or some other kind of thing to try to make the bear go away. But their firearm was ready, and the whole manipulation of it was almost instinctive. What you've been trained to do is what you will probably do.

I am still uncomfortable with bear spray. I and one of the students listened to Mark Matheny who was mauled in Montana by a grizzly bear at the Sportsman's Show recently. He had a partner with him. While I was not there, my reading in the way he described it was that the bear was reacting to him and his partner exactly as it would had there been no bear spray there.

I tend to agree with the philosophy that if you have a buddy or a partner with you who is being mauled, maybe it would be better in that situation to spray a bear to get it off your partner than to try to shoot it off. But, and I emphasize this, the bear's going to come after the sprayer (just like it did with Mark Matheny of Montana). The sprayer must be ready to deal with a charging bear. I've also discovered that the propellant of the bear spray in a distance of four feet or less is so diluted from the other materials in the can that it's much less effective.

In our class we go out in the backyard here, and every student gets to try the pepper spray. Commonly there's a little breeze out here. With a slight breeze the pepper cloud is dissipated. I point out to them, "What if the wind was blowing from the bear to you?"

The antidote for the spray is water, so if it's raining heavily or if the bear's charging from across a creek, the pepper spray's effectiveness will be reduced.

There are two situations where I suggest they might consider using spray. One is in a mauling situation. The second is in a camp situation where the bear is in your camp in a nonaggressive mode. It's probably curious or looking for food. If it sticks its head into your tent and you give him a good shot of the spray in its face, it will probably go away.

I've sprayed several dogs when I've been walking my dog. I've been amazed at how they react to the spray.

I've hit them really good in the head-shoulder area. In every case they left but showed no intense reaction to the spray.

I've been in a cloud of this spray myself. It choked me and my eyes watered. These dogs just turned and went away. I was expecting a more dramatic reaction.

People who have gone through our bear safety training have indicated that their training made them feel more comfortable. They had a sense of confidence with a firearm. They would handle it safely and be able to hit something out there.

I started in the early 1980s doing a little training unofficially. This was a pretty crude program by the standards we have now. There were a lot of people carrying firearms who had very little or no experience, and I felt very uncomfortable with this. We'd go out to the range and maybe shoot a hundred rounds—and that was about the extent of it.

As the program developed and all of us learned a little more about self-defense shooting, we then began to apply techniques. A couple of things I'd like to emphasize too is that the use of the firearm is only one of several possible solutions with a bear encounter. We tell the students that they should do everything they can to avoid attack, and we recommend reading Kathy Etling's book. I recommend reading some of your books. I say, "Read these stories to try to understand what we can learn from them. What would you do differently if you were in that situation?" The main thing is try to avoid having a problem with a bear. If you have a problem animal and you've chosen to use a firearm, then here's how to go about it.

Most of the shootings that I'm aware of (and we've had something like 25-30 over the last thirty or forty years), the shooters were all ready for the bear. No attacks that I know of were a total surprise—they all saw the bear, were aware of the bear, tried to make the bear go away, but it didn't and they had to shoot it.

I also emphasize that learning to shoot a firearm effectively is not a hard thing to do. But what they need to work on is up in their head. We emphasize awareness and their mind-set. They must start, once they've spotted a potential threat, to develop a plan. Do I need to retreat? Do I need to climb a tree? Do I need to drop my lunch?

Then at the highest level what you're really focusing on is . . . if the bear comes to that bush or shows an aggressive sign or something to activate your trigger response, you will shoot the bear at that point. You need to have a spot that keeps you from mentally retreating and never doing anything until it's too late.

[The author] I'm convinced that the older I get and the more I learn about man-bear situations, most of the maulings are due to "pilot error." This training is a neat concept because it gives people experience through simulated attacks and hands-on experience—before an attack.

Appendix 8

Some Medical Aspects of Bear Maulings

I talked with outdoorsman Dr. James T. Scully, M.D. about injuries suffered at the paws and teeth of bears, and he provided the following information.

"I have experience with two bear attacks. Both occurred while the individuals were hunting alone. The first attack could have been avoided, while the second attack, in my opinion, was provoked by the hunter. In both cases the bear(s) went for the head. I believe that this is an instinctual reaction since most large meat-eaters go for the neck so as to either choke the animal to death or to break the neck. In the case of humans, the neck is relatively short, so instead of biting the neck the bears will grab either the face or the cranium.

"The skull is a difficult area for the bear's teeth to gain purchase, so they frequently scrape and tear. This leaves grooves in the skull, which allows the bear to avulse [forcibly pull off] the scalp. A puncture of the skull or an actual skull fracture does occur, but this happens predominately in the thinner bone of the temporal area. I believe that it would take an especially large bear with a large bite to encompass a human head, and it is doubtful, in my opinion, that a bear could totally crush a human skull.

"Injuries to the face generally involve puncture wounds and crush injuries to the facial bones—primarily the maxilla (upper jaw) and the mandible (lower jaw). Naturally, damage to the eyes may occur if the teeth enter the orbit. The bear's teeth may also go through into one or more of the sinuses. This is not usually a large problem as the sinuses will heal spontaneously once the facial bones are put back together.

"Evidence suggests that escape is generally not possible during a brown bear or grizzly attack and therefore running or turning one's back is not advisable. It has been stated that dropping to the ground and curling in a ball is a correct response. The exposed areas would be the hands covering the face and/or head; the back of the neck with its fairly substantial musculature; the back itself; and the legs.

"Curling into a ball will protect the face and the anterior neck, where the trachea and esophagus are located. A person in the fetal position will also protect abdominal organs, the chest, lungs, and heart—although they are not commonly at risk.

"The anatomy of the neck is relatively straightforward. The so-called "Adam's apple," more prominent in men than women, is technically called the thyroid cartilage. The name thyroid is derived from the Greek word for shield as it is shield shaped. It protects the vocal cords and the upper portion of the trachea or windpipe. Below the thyroid cartilage, the trachea is a firm cartilaginous tube that extends to and below the sternum. All of these structures are at risk in a bear attack. However, if the chin is tucked securely to the chest, they are adequately protected.

"The large muscles on either side of the neck running from behind the ear and attaching to the sternum and clavicle are called the sternocleidomastoid muscles. Each of these overlies the common carotid artery that divides in the upper neck to form the internal carotid artery, which goes to the brain, and the external carotid artery, which goes to the face and scalp. The external artery is the one most at risk in a bear attack. Once again, the head in a tucked position with the arms over the neck will protect this area.

"The back of the neck has fairly heavy musculature over the cervical spinal column and the spine is not especially susceptible to damage. The muscles of the back and buttocks when in the curled position are more than adequate protection for the vital organs.

"The skull and head area in general have the most blood vessels, and thus blood flow, of the entire body. Therefore injury to this area can result in relatively rapid bleeding and serious blood loss in a short time. Attempts should be made expeditiously to slow down or stop the bleeding. If there is enough blood loss, it will lead to shock, which is a serious consideration. There is also an increased risk of hypothermia given the fact that we live in Alaska. Loss of blood and shock will definitely speed up the process of hypothermia, resulting in confusion, disorientation, and cardiovascular compromise.

"The bear's immense muscularity of the forelegs and chest could easily tear skin from bone, limb from body, or face from skull. It is possible that worse damage would occur if the victim were standing rather than lying curled up. The bear in the latter case could roll the victim around much like a child swatting a beach ball.

"While it is recommended that any bits or pieces of tissue torn loose by the bear be carried with the patient to the hospital, the likelihood of reattaching a large piece of the hair to the scalp without sophisticated microsurgery is remote. Pieces of skin from the scalp and face can, however, be used as free grafts to at least temporarily cover raw or denuded areas. If they take, well and good. If they don't, then further skin grafting would be needed. The potential grafts should be kept cool and moist but not frozen. (I was once requested to replace a severed tongue that had been placed in formaldehyde for "preservation.")

"I think that it would be equally dangerous if the bear were to attack with the claws instead of the teeth and jaws. One bear victim had six different organisms cultured from his scalp wound. Bear saliva and dental debris left over from previous meals can and are inoculated into the wounds. In addition, if the bear rolls the victim around, then twigs, dirt, and leaves are commonly deposited in the wounds. Immediate sterile irrigation of the wounds is mandatory as well as appropriate broad spectrum antibiotic coverage."

❖   ❖   ❖

In addition to the dangers of infection that Dr. Scully alluded to above, he told me that he had gotten an infection once while gutting a moose. He said that he had nicked his finger and within twenty-four hours the wound was infected, and his hand became the size of a softball. He spent four days in the hospital, which he said was "no fun."

As indicated, the dangers of bear hunting are not limited to an attack or mauling by the animal or traversing the terrain it inhabits. Another danger that is greatly overlooked is the risk of infection. One hunter who bagged a 9½-foot brown bear suffered from his experience.

Ron Cone was a 34-year-old airman in the U.S. Air Force when he shot and killed a brown bear in mid-October 1991. A few days after returning from his hunt, he noticed that one of his fingers was swelling. The next day he discovered the finger had swollen to twice its normal size, and the lymph nodes under his arm were swollen.

Ron immediately went to Elmendorf Air Force Base hospital for a diagnosis. At first the doctors diagnosed the illness as tularemia, an infectious disease carried by rodents. The bacteria can be transmitted to people handling infected animal flesh and is generally carried by rabbits, thus affecting rabbit hunters.

In Ron's case the doctors thought it probable that he contracted the disease from the bear he'd shot. They prescribed antibiotics to treat the disease, but Cone did not improve. Although the swelling went down, the pain intensified. Ron returned to the doctor, telling him that his symptoms were getting worse. The doctors conducted more tests. They inserted an 18-gauge needle into Cone's hand and withdrew a cottage-cheeselike substance. The doctors assumed it was a staphylococcus bacteria infection and admitted Ron to the hospital. The infection had reached the tendons and nerves, and the doctors feared it might get into the bone of his arm. They surgically removed the infection.

Ron and his doctors remain mystified as to the bacteria's intrusion into his system. Cone had no open cuts. However, doctors explained they'd treated other patients whose scabbed-over wounds permitted bacteria to travel into their bodies. However, Cone had punctured the bear's gut in the process of skinning it. The stomach contained numerous rotting salmon. It was a big bear, and it was covered with dirt and stinking salmon residue.

Cone was not the only hunter to suffer from a bacterial infection as a result of skinning a trophy. Cone's taxidermist has been infected twice as a result of hunting, and a goat hunter Cone talked to also had an infection after cutting himself while cleaning an animal. An assistant guide picked up an infection from another bear. A biologist from southeastern Alaska cut his knuckle while skinning a deer in 1991, and it became infected.

Hunters who engage in the removal of offal from their animals need to be aware of the dangers of contracting a disabling infection. Perhaps the infection is more prevalent than we understand. A staph infection can lead to blood poisoning and death, if untreated. Great care is needed in butchering or removing the skin of game. Wearing latex or surgical gloves to reduce or eliminate contracting a serious infection is advisable for those intent on enjoying the great outdoors.

Appendix 9

Bear Attack Prevention

Bears and Man

Since time began, man has faced foe, be it a saber-toothed cat, lion, crocodile, or bear. For thousands of years, bears have attacked, maimed, or killed other beasts in defense or predation. Bears attack mankind for the same reasons.

Man's confrontation with bruin seems to remain constant—it may even be on the increase given that more people are in the woods, that more bear habitat has been converted to people territory, and that there is less negative conditioning of bears due to less hunting. As long as man encroaches into bear country, we will continue to hear and read about man-bear encounters.

However, people who seldom enter the woods have little to fear from a bear mauling or even an attack. My research reveals that in the past hundred years there have been 230 documented maulings in Alaska's wild, resulting in 49 fatalities. That's two maulings a year, with one fatality every two years. (Lee Miller, retired Alaska Department of Fish and Game bear expert, reviewed this appendix and suggested: "Before 1960 records were poorly kept. Might check for past 35 years." Lee has tagged over 500 bears and affixed the state's seal to 4,000 or more, including polar bears in the Arctic and brown bears on the Alaska Peninsula.) The numbers for North America are incomplete, but there have been something like 375-400 maulings and 100-150 fatalities (including all three species of bear). Were you to incorporate the number of outdoor users, then the number of maulings and fatalities by bears is minuscule.

The majority of bears avoid man and man's society. Therefore the likelihood of a man-bear encounter is relatively slight. Nevertheless there is a handful of bears that are unafraid of man, and little beyond extermination of this type of bear will deter it from a serious man-bear problem. When a bear attacks a man, quite frequently the bear wins.

Need for Education

The need to educate those entering bear country is great. Proper knowledge will save both man and bear. Ignorance will take its toll on both.

Two groups of people share bear habitat: The first group is the uneducated—those who have little knowledge of the nature and stamina of the bear. This majority sees bears only from the vantage point beyond the zoo cage or within the national parks. Their knowledge of bears is sadly lacking, or they have been brainwashed by Disney's anthropomorphic view of wild animals. The second group comprises the experienced and includes professional outdoorsmen. Perhaps the greatest danger among this group is the attitude of complacency. It is essential that outdoor users not become complacent and that their outdoor attitude reflect the desire to respect the outdoors and to be prepared for what it produces.

Bears run forty miles an hour. That equates to twenty yards a second or a hundred yards in five seconds. On flat ground and under ideal conditions, the world's fastest man can cover the same distance in ten seconds. I often hear people suggest they can outrun a bear. That will not happen unless they shoot their partner in the foot to deter the animal! More than one grizzly has mangled its victim before dying—after having traveled 200 yards with its heart shot out! A large grizzly bear can break the neck of a barnyard bull. Even the smallest adult black bear can kill a man with a swat. If a bear can kill a moose or another bear, what can it do to an unarmed man? We should respect these animals for the wild creatures they are.

It is important to understand bear behavior in order to anticipate their responses under various conditions. The following includes information about 1) bear nature— including speed, power, and tenacity; 2) bear behavior; and 3) bear deterrents.

Bear Nature

A bear's eyesight is equivalent to man's. His hearing is four to five times better. His sense of smell is even greater (unless he is upwind). Some bear experts feel that eastern black bears are less aggressive than their western and northern cousins, possibly due to their fat-producing diet (nuts and so on).

From cubhood, a bear competes for maternal support and food. Bears undergo a "pecking" order where the strong not only survive, but prevail. The dominant bear gets his choice of food and mate, thus dominating a territory. Given this background, it is no wonder a dominant bear is willing to defend its turf when man intrudes. (Not all bears are intensely defensive—it depends on the pecking order.) Though fewer people confront polar bears, these animals are cunning killers (for people residing in or visiting polar-bear country, I recommend reading *White Bear* by Charles Feazel, published by Henry Holt).

An attacking bear wants its victim on the ground where it can better deal with it. Often the bear will swat the person or bite into the upper torso in an attempt to maim or drop the victim. The bear's normal operation includes biting the head or neck as well as the legs. Bears bite in a similar manner to a dog, not a slow one-at-a-time bite but rather a rapid chomping, often going from head to foot with great speed.

It is difficult to conceive of the damage to human tissue that a bear's claws or teeth are capable of inflicting. Canine teeth reach an exposed length of 1½ inches and a bear's claws can attain over 6 inches in length (though 1 to 2½ inches is the norm). Besides the danger of the predator's fangs and claws, there is the accompanying danger of infection, which must be treated with strong antibiotics and drained in a fashion so that the wound can heal properly.

Although there is great concern with bear attacks, it should be noted that the common house or pet dog maims or kills far more people than bears—from 1985-1996 roughly twice as many people have been killed by dogs in Alaska as by bears. When a bear injures someone, too often innocent bears suffer the consequences of an incensed human population.

Bear Behavior

There are two kinds of bear attacks—defensive and predatory. Defensive attacks occur because bears want to eliminate the observed threat—they defend their territory, food, mate, cub, or self. Predatory attacks take place because the bear intends to eat its victim. Even though bears are unpredictable, certain behavior is indicative of a bear's intention, as the following chart shows:

Bear action	Meaning	People action
One or more signs within 75 yards		
1. Dropping head	You're a threat to the bear	Back off slowly. Do not make fast movements. Command the situation by speaking firmly and do not telegraph fear
2. Staring (directly) at	same as above	same as above
3. Turning sideways	same as above	same as above
4. Stomping or swatting ground with front paws	same as above	same as above
5. Making sounds— growling, huffing and/or popping teeth	same as above	same as above
6. Ears are up	same as above	same as above
7. Standing erect (nose may be skyward, head may sway from side to side)	bear ascertaining what you are	same as above
Within 30-50 yards		
Ears flat, pinned back Hackles up, Stiff legged Bouncing bear	You're too close	Back off slowly. Make no fast movements. Speak in a commanding voice and control the situation.
Predatory attack		
Bear follows then circles (closer); tries to get behind you; rush charge; knockdown; attempts to kill	He wants to eat you	Stand your ground. Maintain eye contact. Display your size (make your self bigger). Talk in a commanding voice. Fight the animal. If you have a weapon, use it!

Bear Deterrents

A number of deterrents exist. Before you purchase pepper spray, a flare gun, whistle, pistol, shotgun, or rifle, study the available research. Some pepper sprays are useless while some deterrents are better than others simply because they are more effective: a rifle works better than a whistle, for example.

In order to avoid bear attacks, the best advice you can receive is to get woods experience. The more you know about bears and their environment, the more adequately prepared you will be for an encounter. Before going into the woods, inform others of your planned activities and whereabouts—leave a map and specific information on your proposed itinerary, much like a pilot's flight plan. In way of preparation, you also should have a first-aid kit, the knowledge of its use, and a weapon that will repel a bear.

Practice common sense. Don't camp on a bear trail, or next to a salmon stream. Never go into the outdoors alone. And make sure your partner is reliable—that he won't run off and leave you to your own devices. If you are on a job site, practice spotting for bears then work closely with a partner using a buddy system to look out for each other.

When in bear country, you are well advised to sense for bear evidence. You may see, hear, smell or, in some cases, feel the presence of a bear. Bear evidence includes the animal; his tracks or feces; rub tree (with hair fibers) or "sign post" tree (where he stretches upward and bites or claws a mark for other bears); food signs such as a gut pile or mounded kill site; torn-up ground, logs turned over, or missing/eaten foliage; bear beds; bear trails or food corridors (like avalanche chutes) or streams (for fish); birds flying the area or making noise (around a kill); growling or roaring of adult bear(s); cub noises like whimpering or crying; strong odor of carrion or a bear "smell" (like elk and moose, bears emit a bear odor).

If you are in a park setting or on a float trip where others have preceded you (possibly leaving a messy camp), watch for or inquire whether there are problem animals in the area. In order to adequately protect yourself and others in bear country, you need to ask yourself if you are properly prepared to stop a bear. That applies equally to public lands and park lands (firearms are usually not allowed in parks).

A tent provides you some protection and may confuse the bear while providing you some time to react to a bear situation. Each person should have a light and access to a can of adequate pepper spray or some other bear stopper. Know your own safety-space zone. Do not allow a bear within that zone (probably no closer than twenty yards). If the bear charges, fire from thirty yards on—you'll likely get no more than one shot.

Understand that when you make noise by wearing bear bells, talking, or singing, you will alert a bear of your presence; however, this strategy sometimes has the opposite effect intended and will attract the animal to you. Keep your camp as free of food odors as possible. Do not keep food in your tent, and do not fry food in front of your tent. Attend to your children—whether in a campground, backyard, or hiking trail. Do not leave them unattended!

Women in bear country need to be extremely cautious. In studying polar bears and sensory attractants (involving seals and used tampons), it was concluded that polar bears reacted aggressively (maximum response) to these sensory attractants. I strongly recommend women not camp while menstruating.

Even though stalking bears make no noise, your good hearing in bear country could save your life. Get your hearing checked by a qualified person. Do not turn your back on a bear unless your safety is guaranteed. If you are in a group and a bear attack seems imminent, stand within a few yards of each other, make noise, stand your ground, try to look bigger (perhaps by raising your arms over your head or holding a jacket aloft) and "fight" the bear. This fight is a mental one where you telegraph confidence rather than fear. If a physical fight evolves, the group should attack the animal together—three to five people swinging sticks, yelling, and moving in unison, much as a pack of wolves surrounds a moose, which should confuse the bear.

If you are trailing a wounded bear, use extreme caution. Follow the spoor slowly, stopping often to sense for the injured animal (you may cover only five yards in five minutes). Your safety is enhanced by having a partner follow twenty to thirty yards away, whose sole job is to watch for the bear. After trailing for fifty to one hundred yards, switch positions—your partner follows the trail; you watch.

Both blacks and grizzlies can climb trees, depending on the tree and/or the bear's age. Therefore tree climbing to escape a bear does not always work, even if you have access to one. If you must react to a bear attack and do not have a weapon, jamming your fingers into a bear's nostrils may work, but it's not practical and should be used only as a last resort. Sometimes attacking the bear works (see story on Rade Peckovich and Bill Brody in *Alaska Bear Tales*). In the event of a mauling, utilize whatever is available (Stephen Routh used a branch and his arm). Playing dead is a strategy that only works in defensive attacks or when someone is nearby to shoot or deter the bear, and this action should be used as a last resort. First try talking down the bear or diverting it with something like a pack or stringer of fish. If you play dead, curl up in a fetal position and rest your elbows on your knees with your hands locked behind your neck and with your arms protecting your face. Move only after you think the bear has departed.

I highly recommend carrying an ELT (emergency locater transmitter) and/or a hand-held radio or cellular phone for an emergency. Protect yourself and others by reporting injured or problem bears to the authorities.

Sometimes, in spite of your best efforts to practice precaution and prevention, bear attacks occur.

Never trust a bear. People think that park bears are harmless, but remember that all bears are dangerous. Man in bear country is always in danger. When you enter bear country, I hope you incorporate the information in this book if you ever come face-to-face with a bad bear.

Appendix 10

Jerry Austin

During the 1996 Iditarod Sled Dog race some mushers saw polar bears along the race trail. One such musher was Jerry Austin. Since I've corresponded with Jerry in the past, I wrote for his experience, which he graciously supplied.

Wednesday 3 April 1996

When I reached Unalakleet, the town was abuzz with polar bear sightings by pilots and locals. I didn't think much about it since I see their tracks between St. Michael and Unalakleet fairly often, especially in years like this when all the ice in Norton Sound shifts around and mixes with pack ice from the Bering Strait. A couple of villagers told me they had seen tracks near their crab pots offshore.

I left Unalakleet at dark, traveled past Blueberry, and was about ½ mile from Egavik, which is right on the ocean, when my headlamp picked up some movement about three hundred yards ahead on the trail. I thought it was only some trail markers reflecting back, so I went on. A few seconds later I realized that among the reflectors was a pair of eyes staring at me. I stopped and set my hook and was trying to remove my .44 Magnum from a military-style holster when the eyes stood up, and I realized it was a bear I was dealing with, and probably a polar bear.

A number of grizzlies had also been seen, and in fact one of my neighbors had chased two off a dog trail just a week or so before the Iditarod began. I have a couple of lead dogs that bark a lot, Diamond and Rebar, so I spoke with them and got them barking, but the bear did not seem fazed by it, like most grizzlies are, so I concluded this must be a polar bear. It stood for several minutes and then moved off the trail several hundred feet and started sniffing around again. Several of the teams in front of me had females in heat, and I had one, so I thought this was probably why the bear was several hundred yards inland.

I didn't want to turn around, not just because I was racing but because I didn't want to show fear to the bear, so I pulled my hook and eased on by and down the trail with pistol drawn. The bear never paid any attention to me, and I'm glad it didn't since a dogsled is no place for accurate shooting. I've shot at a wolf before that was running right in the front of my team, and you don't get an accurate shot. At any rate, I took several deep breaths and was shaking pretty bad but continued to Egavik and then proceeded to the mouth of the river where the trail heads inland. I was now almost a mile from where I had left the bear.

I crossed the river, and just as the trail made a sharp 90-degree turn to the right, another set of eyes opened up about fifty feet from me on the left. Apparently this bear had been sleeping or waiting for me and stood up on all fours and immediately started padding toward me. The dogs didn't see it because they were completely into the turn. I drove the sled with my left hand and aimed at the bear with my right, but it pulled up and hunkered down at about thirty feet. I was a second or two away from firing and was greatly relieved that it had pulled back.

I never saw either bear again. They were about a mile apart and both of them were a stone's throw from the beach. The second one was larger than the first, which led me to believe I was dealing with a sow and a three-year-old cub, probably a male since it was a pretty good size.

I only saw one set of bear tracks in the area, which other mushers also saw. One of the teams a few hours behind me passed close to one of the bears but it did not move. Snowmobilers who were out looking for them did not find them in the dark. I was very shaken by the incident, and for several hours, until I reached Shaktoolik, I looked over my shoulder to be sure I wasn't being followed. I immediately told race officials who passed the word back to Unalakleet to warn my friends behind me.

Appendix 11

Darrell Thompson

In Search of a Record

In late March 1996 I went to Back Country Archery on Arctic Spur Road in Anchorage to talk with archer Bill Cypher about adjusting a compound bow a friend had loaned me. I noticed a photocopy of a hunter with a brown bear in an 8x10 frame on a coffee table. On closer inspection of the photo I was stunned to discover a bear the size of no bear I'd ever heard of. I was amazed when I read about this bear and its monstrous dimensions:

Darrell Thompson shot this bear near Port Heiden, Alaska, in the spring of 1954, with one shot in the chest from a .375 H & H. Thompson took the hide to biologists at the Fish & Game Department in King Salmon, Alaska, and they determined the following statistics from the nature of the hide:

> Estimated weight: 2,200 pounds
> Estimated age: 35 years
> Hide squared: nearly 14 feet
> Ear tip to ear tip: 25 inches
> Front paw: 13 inches across
> Skull scored at 34 ⁹/₁₆ inches—not entered into any record book

The official record for the largest brown-bear skull is under thirty-one inches.

I asked Bill if I could get a copy of the picture and use it in my upcoming book. He said he'd check with his friend Scott. A week later I stopped back and Scott Pierce had given Bill the okay to use the picture. Bill loaned me the photo; I took it to a print shop and got a hundred made before returning it to Bill with eighty extra copies.

The more I looked at that picture, the more curious I became. I wanted to learn about the hunt and was particularly interested in documenting these statistics. I decided to check with the Alaska Department of Fish and Game.

I drove to ADFG to see my friend Rod Perry, Wildlife Tech. I asked Rod if he knew if their records might list Thompson's bear. Rod said the department didn't start affixing official seals to legally shot bears until 1960, so there was probably no official record of its size. Rod knew Dean Thompson, the son of the man who shot it. I made a note of Rod's disclosure and decided to give Dean a call after I contacted ADFG's retired bear man Lee Miller.

Dean told me that Darrell Thompson lived in Anchorage, so I immediately called him. On 10 May 1996 I drove to this home near West Chester Lagoon. I spent a delightful afternoon with him. From the moment I met him I noticed his model airplanes. Hanging from his ceiling were two remote control planes he'd built, one a Norseman and the other a Piper 14. He said that the PA-14 had a 10-foot wingspan and a 6-foot fuselage, a 5-horsepower engine, and was modeled after his own N5184H. It cost around $5,000 to build, and it took over five years.

He told me that prior to his ferrying B-29s from Hoffitt Field to Eielson in 1942 he had hunted deer and elk extensively in the Flathead country of Kalispell, Montana.

Then he told the story of his 1954 bear hunt near Port Heiden. He took his client Hugh O'Dower, a millionaire building contractor from Kansas City, Missouri, to a favorite spot on the Uganik River at a Alaska Peninsula's Wide Bay.

They stalked within a hundred yards of the bear when the hunter dropped it. After congratulations and pictures Darrell enlisted the help of Johnny and Virgil Christiansen to move the hide to Darrell's bush plane. They estimated the hide weighed 300 pounds.

Darrell took the hide and skull to King Salmon. Since no records were kept of the bear's size, the only documentation is Darrell's picture and his testimony. Fish and

Game experts told me that shooting a 14-foot brown bear was equivalent to bagging a 100-inch bull moose or a double-curl Dall ram. Nevertheless, I wanted to pursue Darrell's record.

Since the remaining means of documentation lay in measuring the mount, I wondered what had become of it. Darrell told me that a taxidermist in Whitefish, Montana, mounted the bear life-size with the skull inside the mount. It was shipped to Hugh O'Dower's home in Kansas City, Missouri, where it had since been placed in the Museum of Natural History in Kansas City, Missouri.

I called the museum and spoke with Julie Matson on 24 May 1996, requesting her assistance in measuring the bear. I asked her to measure the front paw width, the length from nose to tail, and the width from the left paw over the shoulders to the right paw. I knew that if her measurements were near 13 inches on the front paw, it was likely Darrell's bear and would substantiate his claim. In the same manner a squared measurement of thirteen to fourteen feet would help verify Darrell's claim.

I called Julie again on 12 June 1997, and she told me that "a bear killed by a Kansas City man was moved to another institution." She said she would attempt the measurements on the bear in their museum and would call me with the results. As of 13 June 1997 I have been unable to verify the measurements of Darrell Thompson's record brown bear.

Bibliographies

Bibliography 1 Bob Nichols

"Bear attack probably unprovoked," *Anchorage Daily News*, Thursday 19 October 1995, pg. B2.

"Brown bear mauls hunter," *Anchorage Daily News*, 20 October 1995, pg. B4.

Information Bulletin, Province of British Columbia, 20 October 1995.

"Attacking grizzly killed by hunter," *Caledonia Courier*, 25 October 1995.

Phone interview with Robert Nichols, 29 October 1995 (by Cam Hill, Conservation Officer, Province of British Columbia, Ministry of Environment, Lands and Parks).

Leah Blain, "A happy ending," *Caledonia Courier*, Thursday 1 November 1995, pp. 1 & 3.

Robin Brunet, "Hand-to-claw combat," *British Columbia Report*, 6 November 1995, pp. 38-9.

Charles Powell, "Hunter fends off grizzly attack," *Safari Times*, December 1995, pg. 6.

James Shelton, "Grizzly bear tales can be grisly," *Safari Times*, December 1995, pg. 22.

Bibliography 2 Marcie Trent and Larry Waldron

S. J. Komarnitsky, "Bear kills runner, musician," *Anchorage Daily News,* Sunday 2 July 1995, pp. A1 & A10.

S. J. Komarnitsky, "Mauling deaths park 1st," *Anchorage Daily News,* 3 July 1995, pp. A1 & A8.

Mike Dunham, "Music community mourns loss of a local star," *Anchorage Daily News,* Monday 3 July 1995, pp. B1 & B2.

Danny Martin, "Marcie Trent an inspiration to local runners," *Anchorage Daily News,* Monday 3 July 1995, pp. B1 & B2.

Peter Blumberg, "Autopsies confirm bear killed hikers," *Anchorage Daily News,* Tuesday 4 July 1995, pp. A 1 & 8. *Anchorage Daily News,* 5 July 1995, pg. B4.

Natalie Phillips, "A simple service for mother and son," *Anchorage Daily News,* Friday 7 July 1995, pp. A1 & A10.

Natalie Phillips, *We Alaskans* (*Anchorage Daily News* Magazine), "The Mauling on McHugh Creek," Sunday 23 July 1995, pp. H6-H13. *Anchorage Daily News,* 25 July 1995, pg. B6. *Anchorage Daily News,* 11 August 1995, pg. B12.

Al Meiners, Superintendent, Chugach State Park. Interviewed by the author, 15 May 1996.

Bibliography 3 Darcy Staver

Department of Public Safety report, State of Alaska, case number 92-46183.

Bibliography 4 Antone Bear

Gail Randall, "Victim saw bear coming," *Anchorage Daily News,* 12 July 1992, pp. B1 & B2.

Bibliography 5 Eleonora Florance

Stan Jones, "Brown bear mauls woman at camp," *Anchorage Daily News*, Saturday 30 July 1994, pp. C1 & C3.

Hugh Curran, "I was like a little ball in her hands," *Anchorage Daily News*, 1 August 1994, pp. A1 & A8.

Office of International Geology, Mail Stop—917, 3 August 1994, Memorandum (To: Bonnie McGreggor, Jim Devine, Tom Ovenshine; From: Bruce F. Molnia).

Bibliography 6 Kathryn Warburton

S. J. Komarnitsky, "Zoo's polar bear mauls tourist who climbed over two fences," *Anchorage Daily News*, 30 July 1994, A1 and back page.

Marilee Enge, "Binky's victim blames herself," *Anchorage Daily News*, Tuesday 2 August 1994, A1 and back page.

T. A. Badger, "Binky bites off his 15 minutes of fame," *Anchorage Daily News*, Friday 30 September 1994.

"Polar bear attack costs zoo," *Anchorage Daily News*, Friday 2 December 1994.

Sheila Toomey, "That was the year that was," *Anchorage Daily News*, 1 January 1995.

"Body found in lion enclosure," *Anchorage Daily News*, 5 March 1995, pg. A6.

"Zoo death ruled suicide," *Anchorage Daily News*, 9 March 1995, pg. A6.

"Polar bear mauls jumper in zoo pit," *Anchorage Daily News*, 10 March 1995.

Personal visits and written input from Edythe McCuaig, April 1996.

Bibliography 7 Forrest Roberts

"Bear Kills Local Man in Valley," *Anchorage Times*, 9 September 1975.

"Bear kills local man in Valley," *Anchorage Daily News*, 9 September 1975.

"Killer Bear Is Reported Dead," The Blotter, *Anchorage Times*, 10 September 1975.

Official reports: (response of Jackie Allen, Matanuska-Susitna Borough, coroner to Dr. John Middaugh's query dated 25 October 1994).

Order of Autopsy, report, Certificate of Death, Department of Public Safety case report (27 pages.)

Bibliography 8 Henry Knackstedt

Jim Woodworth, *The Kodiak Bear*, The Stackpole Company, Harrisburg, PA, 1958.

Larry Kaniut, *Alaska Bear Tales*, Alaska Northwest Publishing Co., Seattle, WA, 1983.

Larry Kaniut, *More Alaska Bear Tales*, Alaska Northwest Publishing Co., Seattle, WA, 1989.

Bibliography 9 Mark Riccardi

Associated Press, "Soldier survives grizzly sow attack," *Anchorage Times.* Saturday 17 August 1991, pp. B1 & 3.

Jose Lambiet, "Soldier survives own bear tale," *Fairbanks Daily News-Miner* (reprinted in *Anchorage Daily News*), Saturday 17 August 1991, pp. B1 & B3.